W9-CDH-836

The Life and Legacy of Annie Oakley

THE OKLAHOMA WESTERN BIOGRAPHIES
RICHARD W. ETULAIN, GENERAL EDITOR

The Life and Legacy
of
Annie Oakley

By Glenda Riley

UNIVERSITY OF OKLAHOMA PRESS : NORMAN AND LONDON

92
O11r

Library of Congress Cataloging-in-Publication Data

Riley, Glenda, 1938–
 The life and legacy of Annie Oakley / Glenda Riley.
  p. cm. — (Oklahoma western biographies ; v. 7.)
 Includes bibliographical references (p.) and index.
 ISBN: 0–8061–2656–6
 1. Oakley, Annie, 1860–1926. 2. Shooters of firearms — United
States — Biography. 3. Frontier and pioneer life — West (U.S.)
I. Title. II. Series.
GV1157.03R55 1994
796.3′092 — dc20
[B]   94–10260
                      CIP

The Life and Legacy of Annie Oakley is Volume 7 in *The Oklahoma Western Biographies.*

The paper in this book meets the guidelines for permanence and durability of the Committee on Production Guidelines for Book Longevity of the Council on Library Resources, Inc. ∞

1 2 3 4 5 6 7 8 9 10

For Bess Edwards,

Annie's guardian angel,
who is generous of time and spirit

Contents

List of Illustrations   *page* ix
Series Editor's Preface   xi
Acknowledgments   xiii
Introduction: A Heroine for All Time   xv

1. "We managed to struggle along"   3
2. "The 'show' business"   27
3. "The birds were first class"   63
4. "To be considered a lady"   112
5. "Girl of the Western Plains"   145
6. "Why did I give up the arena?"   176
7. The Legend   206

Conclusion: Who Was Annie Oakley?   231
Note on Sources   237
Index   243

Illustrations

Annie Oakley, Frank Butler, and poodle George   *page* 95
Annie Oakley with shotgun, ca. mid-1880s   96
Annie Oakley with some of her early guns, medals,
    and a loving cup   97
Buffalo Bill Wild West lithograph advertising Annie
    Oakley   98
Annie in 1896 at age thirty-six in New York City   99
Annie and Frank's home in Nutley, New Jersey   100
Annie Oakley, ca. 1900   101
Annie's husband, Frank Butler, in New Jersey in
    1902   102
Annie as star of *The Western Girl* in 1902   103
Annie Oakley breaking five targets thrown in the
    air at one time   104
Annie with lariat   105
Dave holds an apple for Annie Oakley   106
Annie and friend Eddie Hoff, age seven, of New
    York, 1922   107
Annie shooting with her left hand, probably in 1926   108
Letter written by Annie Oakley in 1923   109
Annie's and Frank's graves near Brock, Ohio   110
Painting showing Annie Oakley shooting from a
    sidesaddle   111

Series Editor's Preface

GLENDA Riley's well-researched, smoothly written biography of Annie Oakley accomplishes three large goals. In addition to providing an illuminating story of an intriguing person, Riley uses Oakley to comment provocatively on gender roles of her times. The author also demonstrates how Annie became—and remains—a central figure in illustrating the Wild West.

More convincingly and more interpretively than any previous biographer, Glenda Riley details the mythos Annie Oakley created *of* herself *for* her audiences. Summarizing Annie's adroit uses of guns and horses, her avoidance of villainy and her assumption of heroism, her modesty and femininity, and her symbolic marriage to a lively and adventuresome West, Riley supplies a pioneering work of one individual's participatory role in molding and epitomizing the Old West. Dozens of earlier biographers achieved this goal in treating Buffalo Bill Cody, General George A. Custer, and Wild Bill Hickok, but Riley's work is the first scholarly biography to do so for a female figure.

Equally noteworthy is the author's use of Annie Oakley to clarify gender roles in the decades surrounding 1900. Annie opened the tightly shut door of respectability for women as users of guns. After her, the handling of weapons, hunting, and shooting became more acceptable activities for women. Indeed, over time Riley's Annie Oakley became an oxymoronic character: a feminine-gunman and lady-marksman, skilled at men's occupations without abandoning her Victorian gentility.

Obviously Annie greatly enlarged the meaning of Buffalo Bill's Wild West when she became a vivacious metaphor for a lively but nonetheless domesticated frontier. As Riley makes clear, Annie was no stereotyped "Wild Woman of the West," as were Calamity Jane and Belle Starr. Instead, the showman Buffalo Bill gradually relied on Annie to help draw crowds of women and families to his exhibitions, which otherwise displayed scene after scene of masculine violence. By midcareer Annie became for Buffalo Bill what such women as Eleanor Roosevelt, Babe Didrikson Zaharias, and Hillary Rodham Clinton, for example, have become for later times: authentic, skilled women who inspire men and women with their talents and thereby enlarge women's roles in American society and culture.

Like all of Glenda Riley's many essays and books, this appealing biography is impressively clear, thorough, and well organized. Her work palpably fulfills the goals of the Oklahoma Western Biographies series in supplying the life story of a captivating woman whose life and career illuminate American history and western mythmaking.

RICHARD W. ETULAIN

University of New Mexico

Acknowledgments

THIS study of Annie Oakley and the enduring West has benefited from the energy of many people. Historian Richard Etulain inspired it, Oakley's grandniece and president of the Annie Oakley Foundation, Bess Edwards, nurtured it, and archivist Jeanne Van Steen of the Nutley Historical Society enriched it.

At the Buffalo Bill Historical Center in Cody, Wyoming, numerous people pushed the project on its way. Special thanks go to curator Paul Fees, who opened his memory and his files to me, as well as applying his critical abilities to the manuscript; to Lillian Turner, who screened some rare movie footage for me; and to librarian-archivist Christina Stopka and librarian Joan Murra, who dutifully searched, retrieved, and photocopied.

At the Garst Museum in Oakley's hometown — Greenville, Ohio — director Toni Seiler supplied both information and copies of unusual photographs.

In Hollywood, producer William Self shared his own research and provocative ideas about Annie Oakley, and the staff and crew of the Time/Warner documentary "The Wild West" urged me to think, talk, and hypothesize about Annie Oakley and the meaning of the Wild West. Producers Jamie Smith and John Copeland especially asked questions and offered suggestions.

Here at Ball State University, Ray E. White lent his expertise on western movies and memorabilia. Research assistant N. Jill Howard worked hard and long to locate sources, make suggestions, and help fill gaps in the manuscript.

Along with many others, including William Edwards of the Annie Oakley Foundation, Larry Jones of the Winchester Club of America, and Christine Marín of Arizona State University Library, these people can take pride in the book's strengths. I take full credit for its weaknesses, with hopes that they are few. Among us, we have tried to follow the spirit of Annie Oakley's motto:

Aim at a high mark and you will hit it.

No, not the first time, nor the second and maybe not the third.

But keep on aiming and keep on shooting for only practice will make you perfect.

Finally, you will hit the bull's eye of success.

GLENDA RILEY

Muncie, Indiana

A Heroine for All Time

THE incredible woman who called herself Annie Oakley overcame poverty, prejudice, physical setbacks, and her own inner shyness to become a star shooter and a durable legend. Beginning in 1885, her shooting and riding skills helped draw standing-room-only crowds to open-air arenas, to Madison Square Garden, and to sites throughout Europe. Billed as "The Rifle Queen," "The Peerless Lady Wing-Shot," "Little Sure Shot," and "The Western Girl," she thrilled audiences at home and abroad. She also burned into the public mind a vision of the archetypal western woman—daring, beautiful, and skilled.

Was Annie Oakley really a press agent's dream or simply a press agent's creation? The answer is more the former than the latter, for Annie had the makings of a star even as a very young woman. She quickly learned how to combine talent, skill, beauty, femininity, and humility in one very appealing package. Throughout her career, critics rated her shooting ability as superb and her personality as sweet and unassuming. First the American public, then European audiences, idolized Annie Oakley; they admired her skill as a shooter and respected her attempts to remain a "lady." During an age of accelerating industrialization, war, divorce, and fear of moral decline, people evidently appreciated a shooting star who covered her ankles and calves with pearl-buttoned leggings, set riding and shooting records from a sidesaddle, and did fancy embroidery between shows.

But Annie Oakley was also a creation. Although she grew up on an Ohio farm long after the frontier had moved west of the Mississippi River, show-business hyperbole turned Annie into a gun-toting woman who hailed from the Old Wild West. Rifles, western-style dresses, boots, and saddles soon became her trademarks. Oakley's fans readily accepted this public persona; their fascination with the American West, their growing nostalgia for open spaces and simpler times, and their fear that the values Annie embodied were declining encouraged them to see her as a model western woman.

For at least forty of her sixty-six years, Oakley reigned as a major public figure. Then, in 1926, her death marked the beginning of her deification. Much as Buffalo Bill Cody came to represent the classic western man, Annie Oakley became the quintessential western woman. Today, many people still see the West of Buffalo Bill and Annie Oakley as the *true* West, a West not only of shooting, riding, and roping but also of honesty, hard work, generosity, individualism, cooperation, and success.

Granted, Cody and Oakley's West was dramatic, colorful, and exciting. Things happened: shooters hit their targets, riders stayed on bucking broncs, ropers lassoed steers, and heroes vanquished villains of all sorts. But Cody and Oakley's West was more than entertainment and Oakley more than a star. Annie's life provides a revealing study in values—both of her era and of ours. Because she represented a myriad of admirable qualities often associated with the American West, an analysis of her timeless appeal helps explain what the West symbolized to Americans in her age and still today.

As the twenty-first century approaches and changing views of our past force us to reassess the nation's western past, Annie Oakley retains her luster. Even as historians revise the customary saga of the American West by condemning its cruelties, documenting the wasteful exploitation of its resources, and adding such groups as African Americans and Hispanics to the picture, there is no need to revise Oakley. Although not born or raised in the American West, Annie represented a West of honesty, courage, hard work, and sensitivity toward others. Today, her life and legend makes an enduring West both attractive and possible.

But, because Annie Oakley is an integral part of the American public's continuing fascination with the Old West, she often seems more mythological than authentic. In addition, the genuine Annie is elusive because she was a private person who apparently did not keep diaries or preserve her correspondence. As a result, we can track Annie's career and whereabouts through newspaper clippings preserved by her husband, Frank Butler, but assessing the inner Annie is far more difficult.

Fortunately, the newspaper clippings serve as a kind of text, revealing how Annie Oakley embraced or resisted change over the years, how she chose to present herself to the public, and how she and Frank reacted to such crises external to their own lives as the Spanish-American War of 1898 and World War I. In addition, a myriad of anecdotal and incidental evidence fills in some of the gaps. Annie wrote several pamphlets and, shortly before her death, a brief and factually inaccurate autobiography. Frank left a few poems and letters; Annie's niece Fern wrote her own version of her aunt's life; and several octogenarians remember and are willing to talk about their memories of Annie. Also, several letters written by or to Annie have survived, as well as a sketch of Annie by her grandniece Bess Lindsey Walcholz. A discussion of these and other sources can be found in the "Note on Sources," which, rather than endnotes, is the standard format for volumes in the Oklahoma Western Biographies series.

Through such sources, we can reconstruct Annie's life story. We can also learn more than we might in a pure biography because the lack of personal sources forces us to place Annie Oakley in historical context. And we can read between the historical lines, hypothesizing regarding Annie's personal motivations and speculating about the underside of her personality. Yet it still remains easier to reconstruct what Oakley contributed to legends and myths than what she personally thought and felt during her lifetime. Ultimately, because her subterranean moods and feelings remain unrevealed by sources, the "real" Annie Oakley is impenetrable.

The Life and Legacy of Annie Oakley

CHAPTER I

"We managed to struggle along"

PHOEBE Ann Moses (or Mosey) was a late summer baby, born on August 13 in 1860. Even at the beginning she shook her tiny fists in the air and let the world know she intended to deal with life head on. As the fifth surviving child of a poor Ohio farm family, she could hardly expect ease and plenty, but the want, loss, and abuse that challenged her resourcefulness and forced her to become a survivor would have defeated most little girls. Annie, as her four older sisters dubbed her, seldom asked for trouble; it simply came to her unbidden.

Soon, for example, Annie began to notice the continuing strain on the family's limited resources. "When I was two," she later wrote, "there was a baby brother, worshipped by his five sisters," even though he represented another mouth to feed. When yet another child came along less than two years later, Annie felt torn between her love for the little girl and her own resentment of an increasingly difficult situation. The family home already bulged and the larder barely met the family's needs, although the children helped by feeding the stock, helping repair the fences, planting a garden, working in the fields, and gathering wild berries and nuts, including hickory, butternuts, and walnuts.

Of course, other Darke County children worked to help their families, but many of them, unlike Annie, also attended school. In addition, many other children knew what leisure time and entertainment meant. Hopscotch, jump rope, and "button, button, who's got the button?" were favorite games among the younger children. Older boys and girls attended singing school, learned to dance, and enjoyed sleigh rides, circuses, and county fairs. Annie experienced none of this. Instead, Annie stood on the cabin's plank floor, working alongside and watching her mother, whose back ached as she bent over a kettle of boiling laundry, whose face grew grimy as she cooked over the greasy smoke of the fireplace, and whose eyes squinted as she worked on the never-ending pile of mending. Sometimes, Annie must have wondered about the pretty pencil sketches and few paintings that her mother had stashed away until there was time to work on them once again.

Annie's parents, Jacob and Susan, recognized that their log-cabin farm, situated in the tract known as "fallen timbers" near Woodland township and eighteen miles from the county seat of Greenville, lacked the amenities and social graces. But it was far better than the inn that had once provided a meager living back in Pennsylvania before it burned down and left them homeless. Only four years before Annie's birth, they had picked up and followed the trail of the numerous Dunkards and Quakers who had begun to migrate to southwestern Ohio's fledgling Darke County earlier in the century.

Jacob and Susan soon discovered that Darke County, organized in 1817, had developed slowly. Although blessed with rich soil and plentiful trees, the area also suffered from drainage problems. As a result, throughout the 1840s, farming had struggled to survive. During the early 1850s, agriculture, based on the staple crop of corn, began to revive somewhat. Only in 1851 was the first flour mill erected. Then, in 1852, the Darke County Agricultural Society organized. But throughout the 1850s, the area still fought to establish itself. People worked their fields with the help of sickles, scythes, grain cradles, and oxen, lit their homes with candles or kerosene lamps, and cooked in fireplaces or on wood-burning stoves. Drainage continued to pose a problem, and primitive plank roads inhibited the transportation of goods to market. At the same time, the dissension leading to the Civil War tore at the young society's fragile roots. Some Darke County residents, notably Pennsylvania Quakers, assisted the Underground Railway; others, especially some of the numerous Southerners in the county, opposed it mightily.

Consequently, Susan and Jacob found that they could survive only by expending a huge amount of energy and ingenuity. They gleaned every resource possible from land and animals. Susan spent hours canning, drying, and packing fruits and vegetables in straw: apples, peaches, pears, cabbage, green beans, beets, turnips, parsnips, and potatoes. Jacob gathered, shocked, and cribbed corn for the stock; he butchered some of the stock, smoking the meat with hickory chips. When Jacob butchered a beef every fall, he tanned its hide for shoes. "The measurements were taken and the shoes made from daddy down," Annie explained. "The tops were stitched with heavy white floss for the younger children."

Annie was not yet six when a major tragedy struck the struggling family. Although a high proportion of Darke County men volunteered for the Civil War, at age sixty-two Jacob was too old and had too many dependents to serve at the front. He met disaster instead during the winter of 1865 when an early blizzard swirled about him and his horses as they tried to get grain to the mill and carry winter supplies home from the general store. Susan and her daughters awaited Jacob's return until midnight. When they heard the sound of horses' hooves muffled by the mounting snow, they rushed to the door. Jacob sat atop his horse, a frozen specter who had lost the use of both his hands and his voice. Susan and the oldest daughter, Mary Jane, dragged him inside and tried to restore him while the other children unloaded the horses and got them bedded down in the barn.

During the desperate winter that followed, Jacob remained an invalid. He never again rode the mail route that brought in the family's only cash income. Early in 1866, he succumbed to pneumonia and left Susan, at age thirty-three, with seven children under the age of fifteen. A year later, the eldest child, Mary Jane, also died, a victim of overexposure and tuberculosis. Susan sacrificed the farm as well as the pet cow, "Pink," to pay medical and funeral bills. "How we cried when she [Pink] left us!" Annie remembered. Susan then moved her dwindling family to a smaller farm she cash-leased from a sympathetic neighbor. Here Susan and the children did the housework, including processing food and making clothing, as well as tended the animals and farmed the land. "But every night," Annie remembered, "no matter how tired we all were, mother washed our hands and feet, brushed and plaited our hair into pigtails, took little John and Baby Huldie onto her lap, and sang hymns with us and prayed God to watch over us."

Annie, who was not yet seven, studied the situation to see what more she might be able to contribute. "I donned my homespun linsey dress . . . and started for the woods," she recalled. "There were plenty of quail, squirrel and rough grouse . . . I busied myself with traps made from the heaviest cornstalks, laid up like a loghouse and tied together by strings." Under these ingenious traps, Annie dug trenches and stocked them with grains of corn. Almost daily, several little birds fell victim to her cleverness.

Susan made the most of Annie's catches. She fried, broiled, and even fricasseed them. "Somehow we managed to struggle along for several years," Annie later wrote. But it wasn't enough for Annie. Sometime during this period, she climbed up above the fireplace and took down the old forty-inch cap-and-ball Kentucky rifle that had hung there since her father's death. She stuffed it with enough powder "to kill off a buffalo" and shot her first small game, perhaps a rabbit or a squirrel, through the head, just as her father had told her to so that the meat would remain unspoiled by shot.

Susan, who feared for Annie's safety and adhered to Quaker principles against firearms, forbade her daughter to use the rifle again for months. Within the year, however, Annie strode through nearby fields and woods, rifle in hand, confident of her ability to supplement the family's sparse diet with fresh meat. Still, the family's situation worsened. Susan, who earned only approximately $1.25 a week as a district health nurse, farmed out her children to helpful neighbors and friends who offered to relieve part of Susan's burden. At about age eight or nine, Annie reportedly moved in with Samuel C. and Nancy Ann Edington, superintendents of the Darke County Infirmary, or poor farm.

Coincidentally, the first inmate had arrived at the infirmary in 1856, the same year that Annie's parents had come to Darke County. By the time Annie got there, the infirmary housed an assortment of orphans, indigent Irish and African Americans, and people classified by the standards of the time as idiots. Certainly the infirmary was a sign of progress, for before its establishment, such people were "leased" to the lowest bidder, most of whom wanted to profit rather than provide quality care. Still, the three-story, brick infirmary that sat squarely on the Greenville and Eaton pikes just south of Greenville must have presented a dismal and frightening front to a young farm girl.

Under Nancy Ann Edington's direction, Annie claimed that she learned to knit and use a sewing machine. She earned a little money by sewing, darning, and patching inmates' clothing. In her spare time, she improved her skill at fancy embroidery. Within a few weeks, a better offer came along in the guise of a man Annie called a "wolf in sheep's clothing" and later identified only as the "he-wolf." He wanted a girl to watch a three-week-old baby boy while his wife cared for the house and older children. There would be plenty of opportunity to go to school, he promised, and to trap and shoot.

When Annie declared her desire to take the job, Nancy Ann, who Annie referred to as "Auntie," wrote to Susan, who gave her permission. "All went well for a month," Annie later remarked, "then the work began to stack up." She rose at four o'clock in the morning to get breakfast, milk the cows, wash dishes, skim milk, feed the calves and pigs, weed the garden, pick wild berries, get dinner, and care for the baby. In between, the "wolf" family, as she called them, expected her to trap and hunt.

"I was held a prisoner," she said. "They would not let me go." The "she-wolf" kept Annie out of school, fed her poorly, and one night, when Annie nodded over the stockings she was darning, struck her and threw her out into the snow. "I was slowly freezing to death," Annie remembered. "So I got down on my little knees, looked toward God's clear sky, and tried to pray. But my lips were frozen stiff and there was no sound." The return of the "he-wolf," generally believed to be a member of the Studabaker family, precipitated Annie's rescue. As he lumbered toward the house, his wife yanked Annie inside and tried to warm her by the fire. When he ducked through the door, his wife confessed her deed. They sent Annie to her loft bed in a feverish delirium and let her rest the next morning, although they brought her neither food nor drink.

In the meantime, the "wolves" regularly wrote to Susan, reporting that Annie was making progress in school and had made a good adjustment to their household. Believing she was helping her family and that her wage of fifty cents a week went to her mother in every letter, Annie hung on for almost two years. Then, "one fine spring day the family was gone." She wrote: "I was ironing a large basket of clothes. Suddenly I thought, why not run away?" Annie's loyalty to her mother and her family had gained the frail child scars and marks across her shoulders and back. She was no closer to knowing how to read and write than when she had arrived. And she had only a few sparse belongings to tie up into a bundle. Yet she locked the "wolves'" door and "put the key in a tin cup that set on a shelf in the spring house" before she started toward Woodland.

On that spring day, Annie made her way to the railroad station, where she boarded a crowded car and slid into a seat beside a kindly-looking gentleman who moved over to make room for her. When she told him she was running away and had forty-eight cents, he paid her fare and asked another passenger to put her off at the stop nearest Woodland. Annie later wrote that for the rest of her life, she regretted that she had neglected to ask her benefactor his name before he left the train. "But for years," she said, "I prayed to God each night to keep the good man who helped me get away from the wolves."

Annie walked the rest of the way home. During her absence, her mother's second husband, Daniel Brumbaugh, had died, leaving Susan with a baby girl named Emily. Susan had soon embarked on a third marriage with a widower named Joseph Shaw. Annie liked Shaw; she thought him a good man and a scholar who "was always reading one of his history books." Annie reveled in their warm welcome. But when she learned of her mother's bout with typhoid, her stepfather's bad knee and fading eyesight, and their loss of his land to a scoundrel, she said she returned to the Edingtons to earn her keep and contribute what she could to the family.

Here, according to Annie, one day the "he-wolf" burst into the schoolroom in search of her. She told Nancy Ann Edington of her troubles with the "wolves." "I could not sit down or sleep on my back for over three weeks. I had to milk the cows with my head braced against the cow's flank." When Nancy Ann saw Annie's shoulders, she cried out: "Your poor little shoulders and back are still green! How did you live through it?" She instructed her husband and son to throw the "he-wolf" out, with orders never to return. "That night," Annie wrote, "I slept untroubled for the first time in long months."

For the next few years, Annie lived first with the Edingtons, then with her own family. Legend says that because Annie had always disliked the name Moses and perhaps had even suffered the cruel taunts of other children regarding her name, she now called herself Annie Mozee. More likely, a long-standing variation in the spelling of the name underwrote Annie's choice. The 1860 census for Patterson Township, Darke County, for example, reported the family's name as "Mauzy"; a family Bible dated 1867 spelled the name "Mosey," and the headstone on Jacob's grave near Yorkshire, Ohio, says "Mosey." Annie, who lacked both a birth certificate to supply a spelling and the education to pursue the prevailing spelling in documents, probably heard it as "Mozee," but her brother John chose "Moses."

During her "Mozee" years, hard work and economic privation continued to dominate her life. Yet Annie later remembered these years as the "happy" part of her childhood. Because she had learned that death and cruelty abounded in the world, she cherished the security she found with the Edingtons and her own family. Also, she finally had an opportunity to learn to read and write, thus remedying a deficiency that bothered her greatly. Annie recalled that at the Edingtons, "there was a half-hour of reading aloud each night" and an occasional few hours in the schoolroom. Also, Nancy Ann Edington, who believed that Annie would be "a great woman if given the chance," encouraged Annie. Nancy Ann's son remembered that his mother moved Annie into the Edington family's living quarters rather than allow her to crowd together with the other children and the infirmary's collection of unfortunates.

For the most part, however, Annie had to sacrifice her thirst for knowledge to the need to earn money. She remembered that during her first week after returning to the infirmary, she "went to work on pinafores for the little school girls." She finished two for each child, six baby dresses, and six comforters. What Annie chose to remember from her first months of toil was not the hard work but rather her ability to buy Christmas presents for her brother and sisters. Instead of "the blows on her back given by a cruel Santa" on prior Christmases, she now received a skirt "finished in exquisite needlework" from her mother, hemstitched handkerchiefs from her older sisters, and a box of hazelnuts picked by her brother and two younger sisters.

After the holidays, Annie continued to work at the sewing machine and tackled other jobs as well. When the Edingtons asked her to take stock of the goods in the storeroom, she sat "by a kerosene lamp till midnight, listing the things we needed. It was a big job for so young a girl and my heart thumped for fear I could not do it." She concluded her inventory with a personal request. "And please may I have five yards of oil-boiled turkey red [fabric]?" She wanted to make bright cuffs and collars for the little girls' dark dresses; she thought the "little tots" should have "something pretty." Annie also oversaw the springhouse. With the help of Fannie, an inmate who "had lost her mind because her husband did not keep his marriage vows," Annie halted the perennial theft of butter and cream, produced "enough butter for everyone," and "saw that each tot had a glass of milk a day." Annie wrote with pride, "I got a raise that January."

Underneath Annie's cheerful exterior, her own personal needs and desires smoldered. She still feared the "he-wolf" and seemed afraid to return home, thinking that he might seize her there. Today, some of Annie's family members and several residents of Darke County believe that the "he-wolf," or perhaps a hired man named Wolf, had sexually abused Annie and that she suffered from the aftershocks of what some Greenville residents refer to as "molestation" and "rape." Even today, citizens of Greenville who know Annie's story remain divided on this point, some brushing off the charge as a fabrication of a young tomboy who failed to understand what she was implying and others claiming that Annie's employer most certainly sexually misused her. After investigating the matter during the early 1980s, novelist Marcie Heidish not only adopted the latter view but wrote an entire novel organized around the theme of sexual abuse in Annie's life. Heidish, however, has since revealed her own abusive childhood, an occurrence that may have disposed Heidish toward believing in the existence of sexual mistreatment in Annie's life. All that can be stated with certainty is that Annie had suffered and was now trying to make sense of her unhappy experience.

In addition to her fear of the "he-wolf," Annie missed her

family intensely. Yet Annie seemed to bear no animosity regarding her circumstances. In Annie's day, farm children all over the United States labored at home; their parents also frequently hired them out to other farm families or businesses. Also, family members and friends often offered assistance or sometimes a home to help out an overburdened family or a widow. Unfortunately for Annie, state legislatures had not begun to pass protective legislation for children, and Susan was in no position to provide her daughter with a modicum of school and leisure time, choose jobs carefully for her, or protect her in someone else's home. Consequently, Annie experienced, and learned to endure, hard work and privation.

While with the Edingtons, Annie longed for many other things as well: her home, the woods, the animals, and fresh air. "I was homesick for the fairy places," she wrote, "the green moss, the big toadstools, the wild flowers, the bees, the rough grouse, the baby rabbits, the squirrels and the quail." Finally, Annie decided to return home. She invested some of her savings in two linsey dresses with knickerbockers to match, a coat, heavy mittens, yarn stockings, copper-toed boots, traps, powder, and shot. While many of her contemporaries still played games and sat on school benches at least part of the year, Annie readied herself to work.

Once again, Annie labored alongside Susan in what she called the "struggle to build a little home." Watching her mother save every patch of material and every bit of food reinforced Annie's own growing sense of frugality. Then, when fall came, she disappeared into what she called "the deep, quiet woods." She studied animals' habits, then set and baited her traps. She not only supplied her family with game but sold the surplus to a Greenville shopkeeper named Katzenberger, or perhaps to the brothers George and Charles Katzenberger, for cash or ammunition. Katzenberger, in turn, shipped her produce to hotels in Cincinnati and other cities, which bought all that Annie could supply. According to legend, she was one of the few hunters who shot game through the head, thus supplying meat untainted by bits of lead shot.

If Annie experienced ecstasy, it was in the woods and fields. "Oh, how grand God's beautiful earth seemed to me as I glided swiftly through the woods." Annie claimed that she often "shot and wounded many a cottontail with the old single muzzle-loading shotgun, then dropped the gun and run the rabbit down, so that the rabbit might not suffer." Although she was a market-hunter, she maintained that she avoided being what she called a "game-hog." Certainly, in a day when plentiful game roamed the woods, including wild turkeys, geese, pigeons, deer, coons, minks, foxes, muskrats, rabbits, and squirrels, few people even thought about limits, yet Annie tried to exercise caution.

Years later, Annie remarked that she never had an aversion to handling a gun. On the contrary, shooting came easily to her. "I don't know how I acquired the skill, but I suppose I was born with it." As a result, her little business prospered. One Christmas, in gratitude, Katzenberger sent her two boxes of percussion caps, five pounds of shot, and one can of DuPont Eagle Ducking Black Powder. She was thrilled, never expecting to own another can of such fine powder.

Annie's small income proved the family's salvation. In Annie's eyes, her mother had put "two marriages of hardship and poverty behind her," then stepped into a third. Now Annie watched Susan and Joseph, who was going blind, worry as the due date for the mortgage drew closer. Annie laid by nickels and dimes from sales of game, and when the mortgage came due, she placed her savings in Susan's hands. "Oh, how my heart leaped with joy," she remembered, "as I handed the money to mother and told her that I had saved enough from my trapped game to pay it [the mortgage] off!"

Understandably, this high point in Annie's young life later became the stuff of legend and myth. Perhaps as a result of her own publicity, Annie too came to think of herself as a girlhood heroine. Also, time smoothed away the sharp edges of the pain she had suffered. In her autobiography, written shortly before her death in 1926, Annie looked back on her childhood as a "happy" period of her life; she now described her early life as "wonderful days of simplicity."

Had Annie possessed the ability to be more analytical, she might have written about the crucial lessons she had learned as a girl. Clearly, Annie had come to understand the basics of adapting, making do, and surviving. She adopted her mother's propensity to save and squeeze, even when unnecessary. Annie also responded to hardship by honing her skills and talents—ranging from sewing to shooting—for present and future use. Then, as she discovered that she could survive life's difficult situations, Annie proceeded to pursue her life with enormous self-confidence and pride in her work. When she began to prosper, Annie, recalling her own poverty, spent modestly, saved regularly, and shared her income with others in need, especially poor and orphaned children.

As a girl, Annie had also learned that meanness and anger kill the spirit; thus she looked for the positive or humorous side of every situation. For example, whenever Annie recalled the dangerous scrape that her brother, John, had with an infuriated wild boar, she added a touch of levity. Annie wrote that when the snorting, bristling animal, his mouth dripping white froth, pinned John under the house with no avenue of escape, she helped dig a hole and pull John through. "The angry brute charged," she remembered. "But too late. His nose came through the hole, but we hit it with a heavy spade, and in an hour he slipped out to the road, uttering threats as he went."

Moreover, young Annie absorbed traditional Quaker values. For the rest of her life, she put her family first. Also, she believed in honesty and hard work. She exhibited modesty and humility. And she shared the Quaker persuasion that women could make important contributions.

This last belief would have been reinforced by the fact that Annie grew up largely within a woman's culture. It was Annie's mother, her sisters, and Nancy Ann Edington who nurtured her and proved the stable, continuous figures in her life. As the men in Annie's life faltered, died, or even abused her, the women often stood ready to assist, comfort, or try to protect her. That women could and did indeed endure would have been firmly implanted in Annie's thinking.

In addition to these positive qualities, Annie also developed some negative traits. She tended, for example, to turn inward as a result of her girlhood experiences. Because of her childhood's chaotic nature, Annie not only learned to depend on herself but also developed a strong need to control the details of her daily life and environment. As an adult, Annie followed a strict regimen of practice, nutrition, rest, and public appearances. Although she needed to keep herself in shape, Annie carried her routine nearly to excess. As a case in point, every morning, reportedly without fail, she ate three dried prunes for breakfast and, whenever possible, poached an egg in milk, using a small, black, cast-iron frying pan she carried for that explicit purpose.

Annie also maintained her costumes, tent, and homes with such meticulousness that she frequently annoyed those around her. Even family members lamented Annie's tendency to act "particular," and her husband, Frank, deplored her ability to drive away cooks and other domestic helpers. She treated her own body with similar care, which suggests more than a trace of vanity in Annie's personality. Even when on the road, Annie followed an unvarying nightly routine to preserve her features, skin, and hair. Annie's niece Irene Patterson Black, who nursed Annie during the 1920s, recalled that as a result of Annie's daily care, her body was like a "chunk of marble," with no excess fat and free of marks even on an injured leg.

Annie sometimes responded in an irritable fashion to complaints regarding her near-obsessive behavior. That Annie was not above sharpness is revealed in her autobiography, which gives evidence of how her quick wit could turn into a caustic tongue. In addition, Annie's independent spirit led to her holding her inner self somewhat aloof from others, confiding little, except perhaps to Frank. Of course, Annie's life on the road militated against her making close female friends. Too, she saw family members only intermittently, and she lacked strong writing skills, but she seemed to make little effort to overcome these obstacles and to develop truly intimate relationships, even with her sisters or her niece Anna Fern Campbell Swartwout. During the 1910s and 1920s, for example, Annie took as her companion, confidant, and surrogate child an English setter named Dave. Nor did Annie confide her innermost feelings to a journal or diary or conduct extensive correspondence. Rather, she seemed content to live in the cocoon that she and Frank spun wherever they happened to live.

Annie's companion, partner, and husband, Frank Butler, came into her life sometime during the mid-1870s or early 1880s. The family's financial situation had eased even more because two of Annie's older sisters had married and left home. Now the oldest girl at home, Annie continued to help Susan and to hunt. When Jack Frost, the operator of a hotel that bought her game, suggested that Annie accept a shooting match, she followed his advice. Legend says that Annie was visiting at the home of her married sister Lydia (also called Lyda in some sources) in Fairmount, a suburb of Cincinnati, at the time. Lydia and her husband, Joe Stein, encouraged Annie and perhaps helped arrange a match on Thanksgiving Day, 1875, even though Annie had never been on a shooting range or shot at targets from a mechanical trap.

Annie's opponent, Frank Butler, later stated that the match took place in the spring of 1881 near the town of Greenville, Ohio, probably in the North Star–Woodland area. According to Butler's recollection, he walked approximately eighteen miles north of Greenville. When he arrived, he found "most of the county out" to support "their 'unknown.'" Annie, however, remembered that the match occurred "two miles out of Fairmount," where her eldest sister lived. According to her, it was the first time she saw a "real city." Certainly, Cincinnati would have provided the ideal setting for such a match. In that city, the Sportsmen's Club kept the first official shooting records in the United States, the American Sharpshooters Society operated, and the clay pigeon was reportedly invented.

The confusion over location is not easily explained, but the discrepancy in dates may have occurred because someone, perhaps the Wild West exposition's publicity agent, John Burke, later lopped six years from Annie's age to enhance her public appeal. If, according to publicity, Annie had been born in 1866 rather than 1860, she would have been only nine years old at the time of an 1875 match. Thus, six years had to be added, making the date of the match 1881. In newspaper interviews given in 1903 and 1924, Frank gave the date of the match as 1881, which was consistent with Annie's revised 1866 birth date, making her fifteen at the time.

Whatever the actual date of the match, Annie had no knowledge of her opponent's identity; she simply trusted in Frost's judgment and her own skill. Had Annie known that she would compete against Francis E. Butler, an accomplished shooter then appearing at a Cincinnati theater, the Coliseum on Vine Street in the Over-the-Rhine District, her audacity might have amused her.

As it turned out, Frank Butler was amused, at least initially. He frequently offered a challenge to local champions wherever he played and had bragged that he could outshoot "anything then living, save Carver or Bogardus," two of the era's shooting greats. In 1875, Captain Adam H. Bogardus earned a medal proclaiming him champion of the world; three years later, Dr. W. F. Carver declared himself "champion rifle shot of the world" after breaking 5,500 glass balls out of 6,208 in less than 500 minutes. When Butler saw Annie drive up to the grounds, he asked the identity of the pretty, slim country girl wearing a calf-length skirt. He reportedly laughed when he learned that she would be shooting against him.

Butler's smile soon faded. According to Annie, they used "two traps, gun below the elbow, one barrel to be used." Butler won the toss and took his position. He called "pull," which was quickly followed by the report of his gun and the referee announcing "dead." Then Annie, with her knees shaking, stepped up and yelled "pull." Again the call of "dead" followed. Their scores kept even until Frank missed his last shot; he had scored twenty-four out of twenty-five. Annie had to make her last shot to win the match. She exhibited the supreme self-confidence that would see her through thousands of future matches. "I stopped for an instant before I lined my gun. . . . I knew I would win!"

Annie scored twenty-five out of twenty-five. When she walked away with the fifty-dollar prize as well as the return from the side bet she and her brother had placed, Annie felt ecstatic. Gallantly, Frank Butler saw Annie and her family to their carriage. He handed them several passes to his show; someday such free passes would be called "Annie Oakleys." After attending the show, however, Annie seemed more impressed with Frank's poodle, "George," than with Frank. Annie never forgot that George, who reputedly disliked women, had brought her "a piece of apple that his master had shot from his head, and laid it before me." Later, she sent George her greetings, and George sent her a box of candy. The courtship had begun in earnest.

"Well, what fools we mortals be!" Annie later wrote. "If that poodle didn't lead me into signing some sort of alliance papers . . . that tied a knot so hard it has lasted some 50 years." Despite her youth and inexperience, however, Annie made an excellent choice. In Frank Butler, she found a husband, friend, shooting partner, teacher, business manager, agent, and father-figure. Ten years older than Annie, Frank contributed to their relationship a measure of stability and maturity that Annie had always lacked. With his shooting skills, Frank could always earn an income. And with his stage experience, Frank understood how to train and package the young, inexperienced shooter that he saw in Annie.

Annie and Frank even shared similar backgrounds. When Frank was eight years old, his impoverished parents had left him with an aunt in Ireland. Planning to send for him later, they sailed from Ireland for the United States. In the meantime, Frank objected to his aunt's treatment and in 1863, at age thirteen, worked his own way to America. Once in the United States, he largely educated himself and tried a variety of jobs, then turned to managing a dog-and-pony act that turned into a disaster in Philadelphia when one of his troupe, a former fire dog, deserted the stage for the fire station next door and was followed by the rest of Frank's canine performers. Probably during the early 1870s, Frank began shooting on stage, usually between acts while workers moved the heavy scenery. He developed both a true aim and a sound sense of the theatrical.

In addition, almost everyone liked Frank, for he was a genial, hearty man who refused to smoke, drink, or gamble. In an era when most men indulged in all of these pastimes, Frank Butler stuck to his own beliefs. As far as Annie's family were concerned, only two possible strikes stood against him: he was ten years older than she, and he had been married and fathered two children. The first issue dissipated when Annie's family saw how lovingly he treated her.

The second, however, lays shrouded by lack of information. Frank is usually described as a divorced man at the time he met

Annie, but whether he had already obtained a divorce or did so after meeting Annie is unclear. At the time, the divorce rate in Darke County numbered slightly more than sixty divorces to slightly more than three hundred marriages. Although Frank probably would not have divorced in Darke County, these figures suggest that divorce would not have been foreign to Annie and her family. But, like other Darke County residents of the time, they would have considered divorce dishonorable.

Typically, Annie never spoke of Frank's former wife or child. If she and Frank contributed financially to his earlier family, Annie never commented on it. And if the issue of his divorce troubled her, she never mentioned it. She, and her family, apparently accepted Frank without reservation or regret. In turn, Frank sometimes left Annie with Susan while he toured. Later, Frank and Annie regularly visited Annie's Ohio home and her mother, sisters, and neighbors.

The usual date given for Annie and Frank's marriage is 1876, but this cannot be verified. On the one hand, in Annie's autobiography, probably written during the mid-1920s, Annie gave her marriage date as August 23, 1876. She also claimed that she was fifteen at the time of the shooting match with Frank and that they had been married for nearly fifty years, both of which would support the 1876 marriage date.

Still, no marriage certificate or other documents exist to prove the 1876 date. Some family members speculate that Annie and Frank traveled together before they married and that Annie's niece Fern may have revised Annie's autobiography to disguise this indiscretion. If Fern indeed changed the wedding date to 1876 so that it would appear that Annie and Frank were married while they traveled together, her ruse succeeded; in spite of the lack of documentation, the 1876 date remains widely accepted.

On the other hand, sometime during the 1920s, Annie entrusted her niece Bonnie Patterson Blakeley with a marriage document issued to Frank and Annie on June 20, 1882. It is possible that once again Annie's revised birth date of 1866 demanded revision of other important dates in her life. If Annie had been born in 1866, as the Wild West promoters claimed, the wedding date of 1876 would have needed to be accordingly adjusted to 1882; otherwise, Annie would have been only ten years old at the time of her marriage. Thus, it is possible that Annie and Frank—who in the 1882 document, obtained in Windsor, Ontario, Canada, listed themselves as residents of Saginaw, Michigan—remarried to support the fiction of the 1866 birth date. The possibility also exists that they remarried because Frank's divorce had not been valid earlier.

At least one of her relatives by marriage, Rush Blakeley, and one of her biographers, Shirl Kasper, however, have assumed that the 1882 date was genuine and that Annie was twenty-two rather than sixteen at the time of her marriage. Certainly, the possibility that Annie and Frank met in 1881 is supportable. Newspaper accounts indicate that Frank Butler played in Cincinnati with a man named Baughman. Butler and Baughman earned brief mention in the *Cincinnati Enquirer* when they decided to join the Sells Brothers Circus. Shortly thereafter, circus posters advertised "Baughman and Butler . . . in a bullseye programme of startling, dexterous, critical hits." In 1882, similar advertisements indicated that Frank Butler had gained a new partner by the name of John Graham. Other evidence indicates that in 1882 Annie began appearing with Frank, in which case she would have joined him on the stage almost immediately after their marriage if it occurred in 1882.

Whether Annie married in 1876 or 1882, her life has a gap of six unexplained years. Did Annie, between the ages of fifteen and twenty-one, live at home with her family as a single woman? If so, did she allow neighborhood men to court her, or did she reject the idea of men and marriage until Frank appeared on her horizon? Or was she already a married woman who waited for her husband to return from his theater engagements?

In any case, Annie very likely became restive with the passive, waiting role assigned to women during the late nineteenth century. She probably also longed to escape a life of minimum comforts and little excitement. Certainly, her actions after 1882 suggest that both these suppositions are valid. Annie gradually adopted as a personal cause the need to revise prevailing ideas regarding women in shooting and in show business. She also worked hard to earn and save income that would provide more than a minimum standard of living. And, as often as she tried, she could never sacrifice the excitement of a life lived in many different locales.

Whatever the correct date of their shooting match and subsequent wedding, it is clear that Annie made a dramatic life choice when she agreed to marry Frank. Although men had not proved stable figures in her girlhood, she entrusted her future to a man. Perhaps Annie saw Frank as the reliable, long-lived father she had never experienced, or possibly Annie already recognized that she was capable and willing to carry a great deal of responsibility for her own livelihood. In addition, Annie separated herself from the women of her family, whom she could now visit only at intervals. Here her childhood experiences stood her in good stead; she had already learned how to succor herself from only intermittent times at home.

In marrying Frank, Annie also repressed her own fear of poverty. Clearly, Frank and Annie owned little when they married. According to one story, Frank brought fifteen hundred dollars in debts to the marriage. If true, neither Frank nor Annie mentioned the fact. To improve their financial situation, Frank continued to play on the stage while Annie reportedly stayed home with Susan or, according to another version, attended school in Pennsylvania, where she studied reading and writing to improve her still-inadequate skills, a lack that would bother her the rest of her life. In 1881, Frank joined the Sells Brothers Circus, where, according to a poster, he appeared along with "sixty tons of animal actors, a whole herd of learned elephants, and a caravan of educated camels." The following year he returned to the stage.

On May 1, 1882, Frank and his partner were scheduled to appear in the Crystal Hall in Springfield, Ohio. When Frank's partner fell ill before the performance, Frank, or perhaps Annie, suggested that she assist him during the act. "I went on," Annie explained, "with Mr. B. to hold the objects as he shot, [so] he thought. But I rebelled." She insisted on taking every other shot. That inaugural performance led to their touring the vaudeville circuit. In private life, Annie used the name Butler, but when she joined Frank on the stage, she chose Oakley as her professional name. She may have simply picked out a name with a firm ring. Like her choice of Frank as a husband, her choice of a name proved fortunate. "Annie Oakley" provided a solid base on which to build a career. And that is just what Phoebe Ann(ie) Mosey Moses Mozee Butler Oakley proceeded to do.

"Our first act," she recalled, "received a generous reception." Frank shot first, then Annie. To win over the audience, she often missed on her first try, then succeeded on the second shot. George worked with them; he jumped on a table and leaned his head against a target. After Frank placed an apple on George's head, either he or Annie split the apple with a bullet. George caught a piece of the apple in his mouth and walked toward the footlights, grabbing his share of the applause.

Annie soon began to design and sew her own costumes, a habit that continued throughout her career. She fashioned an ankle-length dress and leggings of durable cloth. She wore her chestnut hair loose, flowing down her back. Standing only five feet tall and weighing about 110 pounds, she must have created doubts in many people's minds. But when she hefted a rifle or a shotgun to her shoulder, she soon answered all questions regarding her competency. The shotgun itself may have been what Annie called her "first gun of quality," an 1878 Parker Brothers sixteen-gauge double-barrel, breech-loading hammer-mode shotgun. Weighing more than seven pounds, this gun featured a beautifully burled walnut stock, Damascus steel barrels, and delicate engravings, including several ducks and pheasants, on the lock plates.

Annie remembered those early days with fondness. She loved Frank, who, with great patience, helped her improve her reading and writing skills, develop new tricks, and refine her stage presence. She loved George, who traveled with them in railroad cars, bunked with them in theatrical boardinghouses, and walked at her side. And Annie loved the extra money that meant gloves, stockings, and pretty hair ribbons as well as savings in the bank. Even this early in her career, Annie showed how important money in the bank was to her.

In the background always stood Susan. Annie and Frank visited Susan between engagements. According to Annie's niece Fern, Annie seldom forgot Susan at paycheck time. And although Annie was now on the stage, she never surrendered the Quaker and family values of her mother. She refused to dress in a risque fashion, to wear makeup, or to use tricks to enhance her shooting. Frank always backed Annie in this area; he too believed in such traditional values as honesty and hard work. He frequently revealed his homespun philosophy in the sentimental poetry he wrote. In one poem, written on May 9, 1881, and bearing the notation "written . . . by her loving husband" (which also throws into question an 1882 marriage date), Frank called Annie a "charming little girl" with "rain drops in her eyes." Another poem, one of the most revealing of his inner self, Frank titled "What a Little Bird Said."

> Don't waste your brightest hours
> Pining for things beyond your reach;
> Live up to the golden rule
> And practice what you preach.
> Life is like a game of cards
> In which we pass our stand;
> Sometimes the stake is a true heart
> Oft time it's but a hand.
> Sometimes we take in the trick
> Which we should have past;
> But if you play your cards for all they're worth
> You're bound to win at last.

Given Annie's and Frank's homely values, the world of vaudeville and stock companies must have sorely tried their forbearance. After the Civil War ended in 1865, audiences increasingly called for more drama, more variety, and the exposure of more skin. As early as 1868, Lydia Thompson and the British Blondes thrilled Americans with their ample, tights-clad figures. Two years later, Mme. Rentz's Female Minstrels and numerous imitators presented the first widely viewed girlie shows in the United States. By the 1880s, female burlesque troupes toured regularly.

During the early 1880s, vaudeville star and producer Tony Pastor fought back. Intent on offering "clean" entertainment in "Tony Pastor's New Fourteenth Street Theater" in New York, he presented on October 24, 1881, the first variety show ever staged in the United States. He appealed to "high-brow" women by giving away dress patterns and sewing kits. Although Pastor's competition demeaned his bid for business, they underestimated the appeal of his show. A mixed audience of "ladies and gents" not only attended his offerings but provided him with steady patronage.

Butler and Oakley tried to avoid the seamier shows and to work for Tony Pastor when possible. Annie and Frank agreed that the world of "blue" vaudeville was not their world. They preferred something that appealed to family audiences and reinforced traditional values. Thus, a circus atmosphere must have seemed ideal. Certainly, Annie would have heard about circuses that criss-crossed Ohio during the 1860s and 1870s. Perhaps her brother, John, even joined the boys who rose at sunup to see the elephant herded into line for the circus parade and who then hurried back to the show ground to ride the horses to water, thereby earning their admission to the show.

Between the 1840s and the 1880s, circuses, thanks largely to railroads, provided a portable, affordable family show throughout the Midwest. These circuses also earned huge profits. For example, in 1881, Adam Forepaugh netted $240,000 and a year later $260,000. To keep ahead of the competition, Forepaugh's agents plastered his show's posters on everything from fences to public buildings to barns, often papering over a competitor's bill.

But competitors continued to challenge Forepaugh. In 1881, Phineas T. Barnum and James A. Bailey introduced the three-ring circus, soon forcing Forepaugh and others to follow suit. In 1883, Forepaugh tried to trump Barnum and Bailey by claiming that his elephant, Bolivar, outweighed Barnum's elephant, Jumbo, although Jumbo, who weighed six and one-half tons, held the title as the world's heaviest elephant. About the same time, the Sells Brothers introduced an "$18,000 Herd of Six Performing Colorado Cattle, the Only Ones Ever Educated and Exhibited in the Ring." Then, in 1884, Barnum and Bailey purchased a rare white elephant, which flopped with audiences because it was actually gray-white. Forepaugh, who despite his appeal to family audiences and family values was not above occasional chicanery to keep his show on the road, had one of his elephants secretly whitewashed. Forepaugh billed it as a genuine sacred white elephant "proved by the highest scientific authority" and called Barnum's elephant a fraud.

These circuses also routinely featured shooting acts. In a day when numerous people carried guns for protection or hunting or both, many wanted to see what the "experts" could do with weapons. In addition, theater audiences had long appreciated "western" plays about Daniel Boone and Davy Crockett, and vaudeville audiences expected every bill to include at least one trick shooter. Then, in September 1874, the newly formed National Rifle Association's Creedmoor range on Long Island provided the site for the American Rifle Team's upset victory over the world-renowned Irish shooters, further sharpening Americans' interest in shooting. The next few years witnessed a variety of shooters, ranging from John Ruth, who in 1879 broke nearly one thousand glass balls at a county fair in Oakland, California, to Captain Frank Howe, who in the early 1880s attired himself in boots, a leopard-skin jacket, and a sombrero and worked with a female partner, the beautiful Miss Russell, who dressed in tights but knew little about shooting. As a result, circus-goers presumed that shooters would occupy at least one of the rings during a circus performance.

In these halcyon days of the circus, Frank and Annie joined a circus company. In 1884, they signed a forty-week contract with the Sells Brothers Circus. Sometime after they reported to the home of the Sells Brothers in mid-April 1884, the idea seized Annie of simultaneously riding horseback and shooting. Although she had to keep the loads in her guns small and her shots low to avoid damaging the "big top," she delighted audiences and began earning a relatively large salary.

The four Sells brothers of Dublin, Ohio, just north of Columbus, had organized their first show in 1871. By 1884, they ran a successful and typical circus. Adam Forepaugh and Barnum and Bailey notwithstanding, the Sells Brothers advertised their troupe as "the greatest array of arenic talent." Their own railroad cars transported fifty cages of live animals, including a $57,000 pair of hippopotamuses, a $22,000 two-horned rhinoceros, a $50,000 aquarium of amphibious "monsters," a gigantic elephant named Emperor, and a huge giraffe. In addition, the company included the Chinese dwarf Chemah, the bicycling Stirk family, horseback rider James Robinson, equestrienne Adelaide Cordona, "lofty leaper" Frank Gardner, and "champion rifle shots" Butler and Oakley.

In 1884, the Sells Brothers Circus traveled eleven thousand miles to play in 187 cities in thirteen states, including Arkansas, Illinois, Kansas, Missouri, Ohio, and Texas. But, to Annie and Frank's chagrin, conditions with this popular show proved less than ideal. One-night stands demanded daily travel. Arrangements and paychecks frequently proved unreliable. Wet weather plagued the show and caused illness among members of its troupe. Both people and animals were poorly fed, and the care of stock was inadequate according to Annie and Frank's standards. During the course of the season, Annie protested an unsafe saddle and inferior housing for the troupe, among other issues.

Finally, when the weather turned cold, the Sells brothers' operation headed toward New Orleans to wrap up the season in conjunction with the World's Industrial and Cotton Exposition. Its managers hoped to take advantage of the twenty-five thousand visitors thronging the city, but persistent rain persuaded them to pack up and head home after only two weeks. Before closing, the show signed Butler and Oakley for the following season at increased pay.

In the meantime, Frank had been looking for work to fill in the coming winter months of 1884–85. He placed an advertisement in the trade paper, the *New York Clipper*, on November 29, 1884, stating that "Butler and Oakley, premium shots, will close a 40-week season with Sells Brothers' enormous shows in New Orleans, La., shortly, and will have a new and novel act, for Variety Theatres, Combinations or Skating Rinks, Never Before Introduced." A few days later, on December 4, Frank noticed an announcement in the *New Orleans Picayune*: Buffalo Bill Cody's Wild West Park (Buffalo Bill refused to call his Wild West a "show") would soon set up right off Canal Street, not far from the Sells brothers lot.

The Wild West, which had begun in Omaha, Nebraska, the previous year and now billed itself as "an original American amusement enterprise," opened in New Orleans on December 8, 1884. The Sells brothers planned to close their show on December 15. Between the eighth and the fifteenth, Cody may have attended the Sells Brothers Circus, but it is more likely that Frank and Annie visited the Wild West lot to see how Cody and his partner, Nate Salsbury, managed their operation. Within minutes, Annie and Frank evidently decided that Buffalo Bill, with his dedication to family entertainment, his emphasis on shooting and riding, and his excellent facilities for people and stock, was the ideal employer for them.

The year 1884 marked an important turning point in Annie Oakley's life and career. Until then she was little more than an embryonic phenomenon. She had learned how to survive, first at home in Ohio and then on the road with Frank. She knew the crucial importance of money. Most likely, she had also discovered that the role of passive woman waiting in the background did not suit her.

But in 1884, Annie began to think of herself as a potential star. She had already recognized that her show business activities would engage her in a continuing struggle to balance the three dominant elements of her life — entertainer, competitor, and lady. Now, in late 1884, Annie was considering adding another element to her life and her work — an association with the American West — even though she had been no farther west than Kansas.

Earlier that year, Annie and Frank had publicized Annie's friendship with Chief Sitting Bull, a realtionship begun in Minneapolis in March. By fall, it seemed that Annie was a natural for Buffalo Bill's Wild West. She embodied everything that he and his growing public held dear: humble beginnings, hard work, persistence, and lively personality. She had no apparent foibles or flaws. She was petite and pretty. She could shoot and ride. What more could the owners of the fledgling Wild West Exposition ask?

But, of course, neither Cody nor Salsbury had the gift of prophecy. They could not foresee what Annie Oakley would become. They knew only that they were already overloaded with shooting acts. Nor did Butler and Oakley recognize Annie's full potential as a Wild West star. Frank and Annie knew only that they needed good jobs, so they determined to catch the eye of the great scout and entertainer, Buffalo Bill Cody, or that of his shrewd partner, Nate Salsbury, and to persuade the pair to take an interest in what Butler and Oakley had to offer. Frank possessed unusual ideas and Annie unusual skill, but they would still need the intervention of fate to revolutionize their lives and inaugurate Annie's peak career years, 1885 to 1913.

CHAPTER 2

"The 'show' business"

ANNIE Oakley's initial encounter with William F. Cody and Nate Salsbury in 1884 resulted in disappointment; the two men refused to hire either Annie or Frank Butler. Discouraged and disheartened, Annie and Frank headed north to spend the winter playing variety theaters and living in theatrical boardinghouses. Their bid to join the Wild West seemed little more than an illusory dream.

What Annie called her "wounded vanity" got a lift, however, when she learned that Buffalo Bill's Wild West exposition already had a highly celebrated shooter on its bill. None other than Captain Adam H. Bogardus powered the shooting end of the Wild West program. Once a market-shooter in upstate New York, Bogardus had begun building his public reputation in 1869 when he accepted a challenge to kill five hundred pigeons in under eleven hours and won the bet with almost two hours to spare. In 1872, Bogardus defeated Abe Kleinman, the champion shooter in Bogardus's home state of Illinois, then wrested the U.S. championship from Ira Paine. Five years later, Bogardus shot his way to the world championship by defeating the English champion, Aubrey Coventry. Now, in 1884, Bogardus, along with his four sons—listed in the 1884 program as Eugene, age nineteen, Edward, thirteen, Peter, eleven, and Henry, nine—thrilled audiences by shooting up the Wild West arena.

William F. Cody had garnered enough show business experience to recognize the value of such a star act. A former western scout and hero of Prentiss Ingraham's dime novels, Buffalo Bill Cody went first on the stage and then into the arena and had turned into a savvy entertainer. He had no reason to add the unknown Annie Oakley to the bill when he already had Bogardus and his sons. Something would have to change before Annie got the opportunity to build her reputation as a well-known entertainer.

Long before Annie appeared on the scene, Buffalo Bill Cody had worked hard to establish his own reputation as an entertainer. After touring on the stage beginning in 1872, he had instigated the "Old Glory Blow Out" on July 4, 1882, in his hometown of North Platte, Nebraska. In preparation, he sent out five thousand handbills announcing shooting, riding, and roping competitions and listing the prizes offered. He had hoped to attract one hundred entrants; the event drew one thousand.

About the same time, Cody talked to Nate Salsbury regarding the possibility of mounting a full-fledged western show. Both entrepreneurs recognized the existence of a national, and perhaps even a worldwide, fascination with the American West. Stage plays, vaudeville, some fifty circuses, and a growing number of rodeos exploited this interest in the West. But when Cody broached his plan for an outdoor show depicting western life to Salsbury, the latter hesitated, so Cody turned instead to the well-known shooter W. F. Carver. During the spring of 1883, Cody and Carver assembled scouts, cowboys, Native Americans, Mexican-American *vaqueros*, bucking horses, emigrant wagons, a genuine Deadwood stagecoach, and, of course, the two most celebrated shooters in the United States, "Doc" Carver himself and Captain Bogardus.

The first, and last, season of the Hon. W. F. Cody and Dr. W. F. Carver's Rocky Mountain and Prairie Exhibition opened in Omaha on May 17, 1883. In his autobiography, Cody stated that he had taken "care to make it realistic in every detail." He added, "It was my effort, in depicting the West, to depict it as it was." He added, "The wigwam village, the Indian war-dance, the chant of the Great Spirit as it was sung on the Plains, the rise and fall of the famous tribes, were all pictured accurately." When the troupe reached Connecticut, the *Hartford Courant* judged it the "best open-air show ever seen. . . . [Cody] has, in this exhibition, out-Barnumed Barnum."

The show clearly stood to make big money if the partners could resolve the difficulties. Doc Carver, for example, created a number of problems. When he missed a shot in a Coney Island performance, he smashed his rifle down on his horse's head and socked his assistant, thus alienating both critics and the public. When Nate Salsbury attended a performance, he commented that the show needed stronger themes. Others believed that firmer management and tighter discipline would also help.

Yet, when Cody wrote home on August 16 from Coney Island, he boasted, "The papers say I am the coming Barnum." Then, in October, Cody turned up in Chicago, apparently fed up with Carver. Salsbury later recalled that Cody visited him at the Chicago theater where he and his troupe were playing and threatened that if Salsbury "did not take hold of the show he was going to quit the whole thing." According to Salsbury, Cody added that "he was through with Carver and that he would not go through such another summer for a hundred thousand dollars."

When Cody finally split with Carver later that fall, the two men divided their assets with a toss of a coin; Cody won the Deadwood stage. The aborted association dragged on, however. Carver charged Cody with being "dead drunk all summer," although, in reality, Cody had outshot the tippling Carver all season. Cody also took swipes at Carver and tangled with him in a series of court actions to stop Carver from using Cody's concepts and the name "Wild West."

After the split with Carver, Cody joined fortunes with Nate Salsbury by forming a company called "Buffalo Bill's Wild West — America's National Entertainment." Salsbury fell at the opposite end of the spectrum from Carver, who Cody once said "Went West on a piano stool" and whom Salsbury called "the fakir" of show business. Originally from Illinois, Salsbury had seen action during the Civil War, done a stint as a prisoner of war at Andersonville Prison, served a long stage apprenticeship, and then organized his own successful comedy troupe, the "Salsbury Troubadors." By the time the new, reorganized Wild West opened in St. Louis in the spring of 1884, Salsbury had demonstrated his sound management abilities. Salsbury also displayed disapproval of Cody's drinking on the job, his quarrels with his wife, Louisa, and his generosity to all supplicants, including old "pards."

Cody capitulated on the first point. Just before the opening performance, Cody pledged: "I solemnly promise you that after this you will never see me under the influence of liquor. I may have to take two or three drinks today to brace up on, that will be all as long as we are partners. I appreciate all you have done. . . . This drinking surely ends today and your pard will be himself, and on deck all the time." The making and breaking of such promises would prove a consistent theme in the relations between Cody and Salsbury over the coming years.

In most ways, however, the two men complemented each other. Cody provided showmanship and Salsbury business acumen. In Chicago, their show packed in 41,448 people for a single performance. As it toured toward New York, it left a trail of rave reviews behind. Then, during mid-summer, disasters began to plague the operation, and Cody repeatedly turned to Salsbury for support and advice. Bad weather, a horse-riding accident that hospitalized Frank North, and unexpected expenses all challenged Salsbury. Then the steamboat carrying the Wild West toward New Orleans to finish the 1884 season collided with another steamer and sank within an hour. Losses reached approximately twenty thousand-dollars, although the horses, the Deadwood stage, the band wagon, and the personnel survived. Cody telegraphed Salsbury, who, with his troubadors, was playing the Denver Opera House. "Outfit at bottom of river, what do you advise?" In a terse reply, Salsbury advised, "Go to New Orleans, reorganize, and open on your date."

In just eight days, Cody assembled herds of animals, wagons, and props. The show opened on time, only to experience forty-four days of nearly incessant rain. On one occasion, the troupe played to an audience of nine people. It was during this dismal period that Annie Oakley and Frank Butler approached Cody and Salsbury regarding employment. It is not difficult to understand why the partners said no. Receipts were down, and they did not need another shooting act, especially at the salary Annie expected.

Then in March 1885, Bogardus, now in his fifties, left the Wild West. He had never recovered his equipment—or his equilibrium—after the steamer crash. The rain-filled run on Balsam Street in New Orleans depressed him further. Annie and Frank seized the opportunity his departure provided; they again approached Cody, this time proposing that Annie give three performances free of charge. Cody and Salsbury could then decide if Annie was, in her words, "worth the price," or whether she should join another company. Although Cody feared that the diminutive

Annie would not be able to stand up to the recoil of Bogardus's ten-pound shotguns, he capitulated. The partners agreed that Annie and Frank would audition for the Wild West that spring in Louisville, Kentucky.

Annie remembered that she and Frank took "the first train out for Cincinnati," where she spent several weeks in April practicing on a local gun club's trap-shooting range. When they finally arrived at the Wild West grounds — the Louisville Baseball Park — on a Monday morning, the lot appeared deserted. "As we thought everyone was out in the parade, Mr. B. suggested we run through my act," Annie later wrote. "I noticed a man standing at a corner of the grandstand and thought it was someone who had just wandered into the grounds," she added. When Annie finished practicing, the man, who sported a cutaway coat, a derby hat, and a fancy cane, ran toward her crying: "Fine! wonderful! Have you got some photographs with your gun?" The man was none other than Nate Salsbury. He hired Annie Oakley on the spot.

Salsbury's offer must have been a tremendous relief to Annie and Frank, for they left behind them an Ohio river town where, according to Annie, "the best hotel was third-class and the theater impossible." Clearly, Oakley grasped the historic nature of the moment. "There was I facing the real Wild West, the first white woman to travel with what society might have considered an impossible outfit." As Buffalo Bill led her and Frank down the line of company officials, cowboys, Mexicans, and Indians waiting to meet them, Annie nodded and smiled at the bows, handshakes, and greetings they received. Among others Annie met that morning were "Major" or "Arizona John" Burke, the company's press agent; Jule Keen, treasurer; Buck Taylor, "King of the Cowboys"; Johnny Baker, the "Cowboy Kid"; numerous Sioux and Pawnee Indians; and every cowboy from Bronco Bill to Coyote Bill. Then a blaring cornet interrupted the touching scene, and everyone raced for the grub tent. "So began my life with the B.B.W.W.," Annie later mused.

The momentous and historic match that began that spring day in 1885 between Cody's rodeo-drama and the shooter Annie Oakley in what she called "the 'show' business" seems like a fairy tale.

During most of their association, Cody and Oakley respected and esteemed each other; he called her "Missie" and she called him "Colonel." He once inscribed her autograph book to "the loveliest and truest little woman, both in heart and aim in all the world." And she once described him as "one of the nicest men in the world."

Still, despite her assertion that "the whole time we were one great family loyal to a man," Oakley and Cody sometimes butted heads. True, their first season together spun by like a honeymoon. Buffalo Bill gave Annie, a virtual unknown, a solo spot midway through the program, after the Pony Express and his own shootout with Yellow Hand. Annie skipped into the arena, waving and blowing kisses. Dressed in leggings, knee-length skirt, loose blouse, and cowboy hat with a six-pointed star pinned to its turned-up brim, Annie presented a vision of Victorian sexuality; she was demure, feminine, and, with her hair hanging loose down her back, both girlish and erotic.

Moreover, Annie's skill stunned audience after audience. She swung a rifle or a shotgun to her shoulder while Frank, who now acted as her assistant and manager, loaded traps and released clay birds, which she downed singly at first, then finally four at a time. Then, with rifles and pistols, she smashed glass ball after glass ball. Next, she lay her gun down, threw balls into the air, retrieved her rifle, and broke the balls before they fell. She concluded her feats like the accomplished, yet unaffected, actress she was working to become; she charmed audiences with a bow, a kiss blown toward them, and a jaunty little kick that soon became one of her trademarks.

Annie remembered life on the road that first year as hard but satisfying. The company played one- and two-day stands throughout the eastern and central states, swung into Canada, and finished in Youngstown, Ohio. The troupe logged thousands of miles traveling in day coaches. When they had to travel at night, they used boards to extend their seats into beds and covered them with mattresses and blankets they carried with them.

"Five o'clock every morning we were all up," Annie wrote. When the train pulled into a camp, the roustabouts first bedded the horses in fresh rye straw and herded the buffaloes into a makeshift corral. Next, they set up one tent for Cody, another for Salsbury, and a smaller one for Oakley and Butler. Into Annie and Frank's tent, the crew rolled "two folding chairs, a steamer chair, a good rug and a chintz curtain," all packed in a tarpaulin. Annie and Frank later added two cots with thick blankets so they could sleep in the tent rather than at a hotel. In this temporary dwelling, Frank arranged Annie's guns around the walls while Annie sat in the middle, embroidery hoop in hand, between shows.

On the road, Annie often took a morning bath in a collapsible bathtub, then consumed a substantial breakfast. "Eat?" she later wrote. "Everything in sight! Good coffee, bread, butter, preserves, fine steaks broiled over wood coals, with fruits and berries in season." With such sustenance, Annie could, she boasted, "rope and hold the strongest horse . . . [and] smile at the torrents of rain." Oakley filled her afternoons with rehearsal, then "a rub of witch hazel and alcohol." Rolled in a blanket, she lay down in a hammock to nap. "Then a 5 o'clock dinner, an hour for writing . . . and I was ready for the night's performance."

Oakley repaid Cody and Salsbury's faith in her by practicing daily, performing hard, and drawing her share of fans to the arena. All this proved easy; Annie and Frank liked the show. Not only did the Wild West provide steady employment, but the company was well organized. As Annie related that first year in her autobiography, her and Frank's only real sorrow occurred when their dog, George, died in Toledo. The entire camp rallied behind them in their grief. "We buried him in a private lawn," Annie explained, with "his pretty table cover under him and his beautiful satin and velvet cover with his name embroidered upon it over him." As two cowboys lowered George's coffin into the hasty grave, several of the company's Indian women wove wreaths and chanted.

As the season progressed, the Wild West began to climb out of debt. The troupe performed in more than forty cities in the United States and Canada and achieved widespread artistic and financial success. Both William Cody and the press agent John Burke thought that Annie had brought good luck to the company, which wrapped up the season in Columbus, Ohio, with a profit reportedly approaching one hundred thousand-dollars.

But the last two weeks of performances played under the shadow of clouds and rain. "We were glad to hear the band play 'Should Auld Acquaintance Be Forgot,'" Annie said, "and part until the following spring."

Annie and Frank followed their established habit of spending part of the winter in Ohio with Susan and with Annie's sisters, who lived nearby. Annie, with Frank's help, continued to work on her reading and writing, and they both hunted. In addition, they practiced routines and devised new tricks for the coming season. In a way, Annie now engaged in remaking herself and her life, month by month, from a less than satisfactory beginning during her girlhood.

Then, during the spring of 1886, the Wild West began to prepare for a full summer's run at the new open-air arena and amphitheater built by the Staten Island Amusement Company at a resort called Erastina, where Oakley met the new members of the troupe. These included Civil War veteran Sergeant Gilbert H. Bates, riders Georgia Duffy of Wyoming and Della Farrel of Colorado, and a society woman who wanted to see the world from, according to Annie, "the back of a horse with the W.W. Co." After having difficulty locating a hot bath and having to pry herself loose from her parade mount after a long ride, the would-be star departed for home.

Much to Annie's dismay, another new addition, Lillian Frances Smith, a fifteen-year-old shooter from Coleville, California, stuck it out longer. Cody had recruited Smith the previous winter while his play *The Prairie Waif* appeared in Denver. He added Smith to the play's cast, billing her as "The Champion Rifle Shot of the World." When the show broke up, Cody brought Smith back to North Platte, where on April 20 she gave a shooting exhibition at Lloyd's Opera House. The editor of the local *Tribune* effused that Smith's shooting "bordered on the marvelous." Among other feats, she smashed twenty glass balls in twenty-four seconds with a Winchester rifle. When she reached the Wild West lot, Smith bragged that "Annie Oakley was done for" now that she had arrived.

In turn, Oakley looked askance at Smith's shoddy work, poor grammar, and what Oakley later called her "ample figure." Cody

had obviously failed to think through his handling of the intro-
duction of the stout and vocal Lillian Smith to the rest of the
company, especially to her direct competitor, Annie Oakley.
Perhaps the possibility of conflict between the two women never
occurred to Cody, since Oakley had splendid relations with the
Wild West's other star shooter, Johnny Baker. Annie tutored
Johnny, cheered him, and avoided duplicating elements of his act.
But Johnny was also younger, male, and far less aggressive than
Lillian Smith. Soon a volatile situation began to brew between
Oakley and Smith; a situation that would place Cody squarely in
the middle.

Perhaps partly because of her rivalry with Smith and a resulting
desire to impress her own name and presence on the public mind,
Oakley defied a raging infection and soaring temperature caused
by a bug flying into her right ear. For the opening parade in New
York City, Annie donned a new outfit, clearly marked with the
name "Oakley" on both sides, followed the seventeen-mile parade
route, then had to be lifted off her horse. Back in camp at
Erastina, Annie bled for five hours. The next morning a doctor
lanced her ear and diagnosed blood poisoning. Annie lost four
days of work. She later noted that it was the only time she missed a
performance "in over forty years." When she returned to the
arena, Annie leaned against a table while shooting.

After the grand opening, New Yorkers swarmed to the Wild
West; they boarded special ferries that docked at St. George, then
climbed aboard a train that ran directly to the Wild West portals.
They viewed either the 12:30 or the 7:00 performance, the latter
assisted by artificial lights. Within four weeks, the Wild West
drew approximately 14,000 visitors a day, a total of 360,000
people. When the entrance booth ran out of tickets and turned
potential customers away, the show's carpenters began building
additional grandstands.

Undoubtedly, Lillian Smith attracted her share of admirers.
Appearing in seventh position, only one act away from Annie
Oakley, who shot in fifth position, Smith broke twenty-five glass
balls per minute, shot glass balls revolving on a string around a
pole, hit a plate thirty times in fifteen seconds, and fired three
times toward a flying glass ball before hitting it with her fourth

shot. But Lillian also boasted of her skills, dressed in a less-than-modest fashion, and fraternized with the men in the Wild West troupe.

Whether Oakley ever complained to Cody about Smith's behavior is unknown, but relations between Cody and Oakley began to deteriorate. Biographers have assumed that Cody harbored jealous feelings when he heard the applause for Annie and read her reviews, but the applause and reviews themselves fail to support this theory. Buffalo Bill regularly received more applause than any other performer; he also dominated the headlines and opening paragraphs of most reviews, whereas Annie received mention farther down.

In addition, Cody's performing style differed from Annie's. The Wild West program explained that rather than a fancy-shot, Buffalo Bill was "what may be termed a 'practical marksman,' . . . a marvelous all-round shot." And, unlike Oakley, who reportedly refused to shoot from horseback to avoid competing with Buffalo Bill, Cody performed his most spectacular shooting tricks on horseback.

The ill feelings between Cody and Oakley simmered through the winter as a revamped Wild West, now a four-act review called the "Dawn of Civilization," played to capacity audiences in Madison Square Garden. The management of the Garden, which had opened in 1879 and covered three blocks north of Fifth Avenue and Broadway, must have been delighted, given their usual erratic and short-term bookings, to showcase the Wild West for six months. Indeed, the management literally raised the Garden's roof twenty-five feet to accommodate the performers, especially the shooters. Freshly painted backgrounds went into place, and a mammoth blower sat ready to power a cyclone.

Oakley performed many shooting and riding stunts in the Garden. She also introduced a new trick; she untied a handkerchief from the area just above her horse's hoof as she herself rode on, and dangled precariously from, a sidesaddle. In a similar manner, she picked her hat up from the ground. In appreciation of her efforts, the New York Ladies Riding Club rewarded Annie with a gold medal, the fourth in her growing collection.

Buffalo Bill's response to Annie's honor remains unclear. Nor did he take a stand regarding Annie's escapade with Jerry the moose. One snowy afternoon, Annie hitched Jerry to a sled for a joyride. They both enjoyed the outing until they turned a corner, and "Jerry's beadlike eyes espied a push cart laden with nice, juicy, red apples." Jerry headed straight for the cart and upset it with a nosedive. Annie said that the "vendor's hair stood straight on end" at the sight of the gigantic moose and apples careening all over the street. Jerry ate the apples, and Annie forked out a five-dollar bill to cover the damages.

Buffalo Bill must have been pleased, however, when Lillian Smith silenced Doc Carver, who continued to plague Cody. After Lillian's father challenged Carver to a match with his daughter in a St. Louis theater, Smith showed at the appointed time, but Carver failed to appear. Press agent John Burke immediately issued a statement. "The young lady has every right to say that she frightened off the Evil Spirit of the Plains," as Carver called himself.

Early that spring of 1887, Annie returned to Ohio to visit Susan and her now-blind stepfather, Joseph Shaw. Annie spent time practicing, but she also renewed herself by immersing herself in the female culture that had succored her through childhood. She spent hours with her mother and her sisters and visited neighbors.

In the meantime, Frank prepared for their impending departure to Europe. The Wild West would soon sail to London to help celebrate Queen Victoria's Golden Jubilee, the fiftieth anniversary of her coronation. In preparation, Cody and Salsbury had offered the Wild West as Nebraska's official representative at the queen's celebration. They also took the eventful step on February 26 of incorporating the Wild West and turning themselves into international entrepreneurs. Cody also sent press agent John Burke ahead to London. Burke carried letters from such reputed generals as William Tecumseh Sherman, Philip Henry Sheridan, George Crook, and Nelson Miles, who described Cody's military service, as well as a letter from Governor John M. Thayer of Nebraska, who stressed that Cody had been his "aide-de'camp . . . with the rank of colonel."

Whether or not he intended to, Cody, now known as "Colonel," prepared the way for his show, himself, and Annie Oakley to become living legends, symbols of an era passing rapidly into history. In particular, Cody became a master at attracting and pleasing audiences. He frequently promised to give his audiences "a visit West in three hours to see scenes that have cost thousands their lives to view." In an era when almost every American, as well as many Europeans, had a relative or friend living in the American West, this theme provided a sure-fire attraction. Because personal correspondence was slow and newspaper reports inflated, people wanted to know what really occurred in the nineteenth-century West, which many looked on as the greatest "frontier" in world history.

By the time cowboys and other personnel filed onto the steamship with the appropriate name *State of Nebraska* on March 31, 1887, a huge crowd, apparently oblivious to the chill in the air, jostled its way close to the ship for a view of the proceedings. The performers boarded hesitantly, especially the Native Americans, many of whom believed that a water venture spelled certain disaster and that they would never again see their homes. The stock followed; the animals loaded that day included 180 horses, 18 buffalo, 10 elk, 10 mules, 5 Texas steers, 4 donkeys, and 2 deer. Even the "Old Deadwood Stage," safely stowed in a nailed box, found its way into the ship's hold.

Despite the auspicious beginning, during the journey the ship experienced a violent storm, then a smashed rudder. Seasick Indians sang their death songs, but Annie seems to have ridden it out without incident. As the ship drifted rudderless for forty-eight hours, Annie spent ten hours "wrapped in an oilskin . . . strapped to the captain's deck." She remembered that the captain never left the deck during the troubled hours before he gained control of his craft and turned it toward England at last.

Unfortunately, little is known about the relations between Cody, Oakley, and Smith while on board, but these must have been stormy as well. Both women practiced from the deck of the ship, which would have brought them into contact and competition. Cody also would have taken the opportunity to shoot. Surely in such confined quarters, members of the troupe and the crew would have watched, and commented on, the relative merits of these performances.

Finally, at the end of April, the Wild West settled into its twenty-three-acre grounds near London. When the show opened on May 9, 1887, Londoners flocked to what they called "The Yankeeries." The Wild West drew half a million visitors during the first three weeks of May. According to newspaper reviews, Oakley grabbed most of the attention given to the women shooters, but at least one critic raved about Smith's shooting. In May, a typical review, which appeared in the *Metropolitan*, called Annie a "genius" and mentioned in passing that Lillian "also" exhibited skill. Then, on May 21, a reporter for the *Topical Times* committed the error of confusing the two women with each other. "As I pass her tent I see Miss Lilian [*sic*] Oakley, the 'shootist,' sitting composedly at the entrance of her canvas dwelling house, thinking probably of her Western home, and the folks she left behind her." Another described Oakley and Smith as "a couple of fine young Califorianesses."

By June, a number of newspapers had begun to concentrate on Annie more than on Lillian and to embroider Annie's emerging myth. A story in the *Dramatic Review*, for example, added a bit of drama to Oakley's life story: a trapped wolf had bit young Annie on the arm so badly that she fell in a swoon on her mother's doorstep; as a young woman, she had whipped a pistol out of her purse to dislodge a would-be robber from the Greenville mail train; and, as a performer, she had encountered notorious desperadoes during her early tours of Texas, a state she supposedly ranked as the "worst" of the "queer places" she had visited.

This and other romanticized publicity helped draw viewers to Wild West performances. From May through October, the troupe played to the thirty or forty thousand people who daily thronged to Earl's Court. The Wild West piqued the interest of VIP's as well. For instance, both William Gladstone, the former prime minister, and Edward, prince of Wales, commanded performances. Edward, a rather pompous-looking, chubby man, leaned out of the royal box to watch the show, especially Annie's stunts. "We all worked like little hound pups at a rabbit hole," Annie remembered. "As the last gun I had used lay smoking hot on the table, the Prince of Wales, who, with Alexandra, occupied the lower center box, asked if I might be presented." Annie remembered what she had heard about Edward's tendency to flirt, even as his attractive

and long-suffering wife, Alexandra, sat nearby, so she turned to
Alexandra, and then, instead of kissing the princess's hand, she
shook it. "What a wonderful little girl!" Alexandra responded.
Annie later claimed that she turned to Edward and said, "You'll
have to excuse me, please, because I am an American and in
America, ladies come first." Edward, who did not appear in the
least offended, replied, "What a pity there are not more women in
the world like that little one."

The *London News* of May 6 carried a favorable report of Annie's
actions. "Annie Oakley, the champion shot, put out her hand to
shake hand with the Princess, on the Republican principle of
ladies first." Unfortunately, the *London Daily Chronicle* inter-
preted Annie's actions as a gaffe that revealed "charming naivete."
Because Lillian Smith had also shaken hands, this remark must
have infuriated Annie. The *Chronicle* inadvertently aggravated
matters further by adding that Lillian Smith had also received a
summons to the royal box, where she "proceeded with perfect
self-possession to explain and show the working of the weapon in
her hand."

If Annie was disgruntled over this, she could console herself
with the numerous invitations she received to teas, receptions,
dinner parties, and balls, as well as an invitation from Prince
Edward to shoot a match against the Grand Duke Michael of
Russia. In addition, what Annie called "tons of beautiful flowers"
crammed her tent. Oakley's gifts, which Annie later described as
"books, dainty handkerchiefs, pretty lace, ties, gloves, fans, [and]
silk for a dress," also outnumbered Smith's. On Annie's birthday,
supposedly her twenty-first but actually her twenty-seventh,
more than sixty presents crowded her quarters, including a clock,
an English horse, a St. Bernard puppy, a carriage, and a photograph of Princess Alexandra from Alexandra herself.

Oakley also achieved more widespread public recognition than
Smith. People commented as Annie rode her horse in Hyde Park,
and a shoeblack who recognized her exclaimed, "There goes the
boss shooter." Perhaps most telling of all was the judgment of the
Sportsman and other papers that Annie Oakley of Ohio, rather
than Lillian Smith of California, was a charming "Western girl"
and a "frontier girl." Not one reviewer had negative comments to

offer regarding Annie. Codymania may have been sweeping England, but Oakleymania followed closely behind.

Still, Lillian Smith occasionally grabbed the spotlight from Annie Oakley. In June, sixty-seven-year-old Queen Victoria broke precedent by leaving Buckingham Palace and venturing to the Wild West arena, where she viewed a special performance from a box draped with crimson velvet. The queen called both Annie and Lillian to her. Lillian curtsied and showed Victoria her rifle. Annie remembered that Victoria turned to her and said, "You are a very clever little girl." According to the *London Daily Telegraph*, Annie "made the prettiest of curtseys before she scampered off." But the *Illustrated London News* ran a large, impressive drawing featuring Smith being introduced to the Queen.

Smith fared less well in London newspapers during a subsequent shooting match at Wimbledon, in which she and Oakley both participated. On July 19, the press reported in detail, Smith showed up wearing a bright yellow silk sash and plug hat and accompanied by a number of cowboys and celebrities. After shooting badly, Smith left the grounds in a huff. The following day Oakley appeared in her usual refined apparel and shot very well. According to the April 21 *London News*, "Annie Oakley appears to have been more successful at Wimbledon yesterday than her 'comrade in arms' was on the previous day." She did so well, in fact, that Prince Edward came forward to offer his congratulations to her.

About this time, a Wild West patron, James S. Carter, began to attend Wild West performances with a pair of field glasses and a stopwatch, determined to prove his suspicion that Smith cheated. On June 3, 1887, Carter revealed his findings in a letter to the *Shooting Times*. He claimed that the card she used to cover her rifle sight while shooting at swinging balls had a cutaway section that left the sights uncovered. He had also calculated that the swinging balls actually revolved 362 times a minute rather than 3,000 as she claimed. Meanwhile, back home, the *Sacramento Record Union* laughingly remarked that Smith was incapable of giving an interview in what the *London Topical Times* had referred to as "highly polished language."

The worst debacle in the escalating situation occurred in August, when the *Breeder and Sportsman* of San Francisco published an anonymous letter that attacked Oakley. Its author, who simply signed himself—or herself—"A California," asserted that Lillian Smith "was knocking the English shooters crazy" and left Annie Oakley "out in the cold." The writer also implied that Annie had forgotten her skills with a rifle and could handle only a shotgun and that Frank Butler posed as Annie's brother.

In his rebuttal, which appeared in the *Shooting Times* in late October, Frank Butler retorted that "any lady who distances all competitors and gets to the front, has her enemies." He added: "That letter was written in the camp of 'Wild West.' There was no need of the writer signing his name. All here knew who wrote it. His bad English was as good as his signature." Frank probably had in mind cowboy Joe Kid, whom Lillian Smith had just married. One cannot help wonder, however, if Lillian could have written the letter and referred to herself, as Cody did, as "a California." At any rate, Annie and Frank soon incorporated more rifles into her act and featured Frank more in newspaper publicity.

In the meantime, the American publication *American Field* reprinted London reporters' comments that Annie's marksmanship was "better than Buffalo Bill's" and that her shooting was "phenomenal." This report may or may not have exacerbated the growing breach between Cody and Oakley; after all, Cody had a vested interest in Oakley's success. Moreover, at the same time, another English reviewer had stroked Cody by commenting that if part of the exhibition fizzled, Cody could carry the entire show on his own capable shoulders.

Whatever his reactions to the press, Cody may have aggravated the situation further by continuing Smith's equal billing with Oakley. To Annie, this must have seemed highly unfair. Not only had Smith run off with Joe Kid, but some believed that she lied about her shooting records. Finally, on October 31, 1887, the *Evening News* carried a brief notice. Oakley and Butler would leave the Wild West that evening after its last performance of the season. They planned to rest, visit friends in Shropshire, and tour the Continent. The *News* felt certain that the Wild West would experience a serious loss, whereas Oakley's "personal urbanity" and "wonderful skill" would open many doors for her.

Neither Annie Oakley nor William Cody commented on the cause of their estrangement. Always a gentleman who refused to talk about private matters, especially those involving women, Cody was so tight-lipped that when in 1888 he published his updated autobiography, *Story of the Wild West and Camp-Fire Chats*, he omitted any mention of Oakley. He did remark that during Queen Victoria's visit to the Wild West, he had had "the pleasure of presenting Miss Lillian Smith, the mechanism of whose Winchester repeater was explained to her Majesty, who takes a remarkable interest in firearms." He added, "Young California spoke up gracefully and like a little woman." Neither do his personal correspondence or other papers comment on the matter.

Annie's and Frank's lips remained sealed as well. In her auto-biography, Annie simply wrote: "I had severed connections with the wild West at the close of the London season. The reasons for so doing take too long to tell." The newspaper accounts mentioned above indicate that Annie's rivalry with Lillian lay at the bottom of the schism, but other underlying reasons may have existed as well. Frank later threatened to expose the real reasons that Annie left the Wild West. This suggests that Cody and Oakley may have clashed over something in addition to Lillian Smith, something as serious as Annie's slot in the lineup or perhaps her open criticism of Cody's decision to forego an appearance at the Crystal Palace grounds in Sydenham.

At any rate, Annie and Frank left the Wild West at the end of its London run, just before it was to appear in Birmingham and Manchester. Less than two weeks later they staged an exhibition in Berlin at the Charlottenburg Race Course before Crown Prince Wilhelm and were scheduled to give another exhibition in Paris. Annie pleaded illness, however, and she and Frank skipped the Paris engagement, a decision that later caused a lawsuit and cost them fifteen hundred dollars.

The following year of 1888 proved strenuous for Annie and Frank. They had left the Wild West, sacrificing star billing, job security, fair wages, and good living to go on their own again. They soon settled into an apartment opposite Madison Square Garden, and

Annie began to demonstrate one of her great strengths — knowing how to survive the ups and downs of life. Frank too had learned early to expect adversity and change and knew how to adapt. Whatever depression, bitterness, or loss of hope they may have experienced, they kept it to themselves.

Frank placed an advertisement in the *New York Clipper* announcing that Annie would take a new melodrama called *Little Sure Shot, the Pony Express Rider* on the road and would welcome the assistance of a financial backer. Butler also organized shooting matches for Annie and negotiated a contract with Tony Pastor. On April 2, Annie opened with Tony Pastor's variety show at the South Broad Street Theater in Philadelphia, then traveled with the troupe to the Criterion in Brooklyn, the Howard Athenaeum in Boston, and Jacob & Proctor's in Hartford.

On the vaudeville circuit, Oakley helped draw capacity crowds and received good reviews but failed to overshadow the other performers, which included singers, dancers, comedians, vaulters, and Little Tich, who stood three feet tall and delighted audiences with his "big shoe dance." One critic called Annie a "modest, pleasant-looking young lady," and another noted that she was a "good" shooter. Annie appeared at the end of the program, perhaps because her guns fouled the air and created litter on the stage or perhaps because her name lacked clout in the world of vaudeville.

Annie and Frank's situation improved in mid-April when Annie presented a private shooting exhibition at the Boston Gun Club grounds. "There were a large number of spectators, fully one-half being ladies," the *Boston Daily Globe* reported on April 20. They flocked around Annie to see the elegant gold bracelets that the club secretary presented to her. In May, she played theaters from Toronto to New Jersey with Tony Pastor, giving shooting exhibitions along the way. Near the end of the month, one reviewer called her a "decided acquisition in the vaudevilles"; the *Syracuse Standard* referred to her as "a rattling shot" who gave "a spirited exhibition." Although reviewers then, as now, pounced on performers' flaws and lapses, not one critic panned her act.

Annie's stock was clearly on the rise. She and Frank knew how to whet appetites and garner publicity. By midsummer, Annie had even returned to the arena, but with Comanche Bill's Wild West rather than with Buffalo Bill's Wild West. The salary of three hundred dollars and hotel expenses for both Annie and Frank must have lured them, but when Butler discovered that the Comanche Bill Wild West, probably backed by empresario Charles M. Southwell, was a sloppy outfit and employed cowboys and Indians who originated no farther west than Philadelphia and had difficulty staying on horseback, he canceled the contract. "I can't afford to have you connected with a failure," he told Annie.

Butler then persuaded Comanche Bill's backer to merge with the Pawnee Bill (Gordon W. Lillie) Historical Wild West Exhibition and Indian Encampment, which sat broke and stranded in Pittsburgh. Annie recalled that with six days left before the opening performance, "rehearsals began in earnest." On parade day, July 2, 1888, spurs and the trim on saddles gleamed in the sun, and the show opened to a packed grandstand in Gloucester Beach, New Jersey.

Although Pawnee Bill's wife, May Manning Lillie, performed in the show and wore costumes remarkably like Annie's, the two women had no difficulties, perhaps because Pawnee Bill gave Annie top billing and otherwise treated Annie with the respect that she and Frank felt she deserved. Although Pawnee Bill called himself the "White Chief of the Pawnees—a young daredevil who performs miracles with a rope and six-shooter and rides like a fiend on a big black stallion" and referred to May as the "World's Champion Woman Rifle Shot," his posters proudly announced, "There is but one Annie Oakley—and she is with us . . . fresh from her London triumph with Buffalo Bill."

During July, Pawnee Bill also wagered two hundred dollars that Annie could kill forty of fifty pigeons with her light 20-bore guns. On July 31, before an audience of twelve thousand people, Annie eclipsed herself; she broke a record by downing forty-nine out of fifty live pigeons. Still, Annie found some of Pawnee Bill's other publicity stunts repugnant. When he made the wedding of a Kaw chieftain named Wah-Ki-Kaw and a white woman named Annie Harris into a public affair before eight thousand viewers, Annie turned disdainful.

In the meantime, Oakley's association with Pawnee Bill annoyed Cody and Salsbury. When Salsbury threatened to fight any company she joined, Frank Butler counterthreatened that he "might tell the reasons" that Annie had left the Wild West. As it turned out, Annie left Pawnee Bill of her own volition in early August. Pawnee Bill, after competing with Buffalo Bill's Wild West for the rest of the season, in October once again found himself broke and stranded, this time in Easton, Maryland.

Annie and Frank, however, had several of their own projects in mind. Annie continued to play with Tony Pastor while she made arrangements to take her own company on the road in a blood-and-guts western melodrama titled *Deadwood Dick, or the Sun-beam of the Sierras*. She also shot exhibitions and matches. While in Dayton, Ohio, she skirted a challenge from Lillian Smith, who had parted company with the Wild West and, according to the *Daily Herald*, now existed only on "what little reputation she can gain by matches with reputable persons."

Smith's departure from the Wild West may have opened the way for Oakley's return. Shortly, Frank Butler and Nate Salsbury resolved their contretemps and began to negotiate. On February 25, 1889, the *Baltimore Sun* announced that Annie would sail for Paris with the Wild West in time to help inaugurate the new Eiffel Tower and celebrate the Paris Universal Exposition in honor of the one hundredth anniversary of the French Revolution. The company left for the port of Le Havre in April, took a train to Paris, and played to an elegantly dressed but stony-faced audience of twenty thousand Parisians.

When Annie entered the arena and noticed "clackers"—men employed to start the applause—stationed around the arena, she asked Frank to shoo them away. "Mr. B.," as she called Frank, informed the men that she "wanted honest applause or none at all." Annie recalled, "As the first crack of the gun sent the stiff, flying targets to pieces, there came 'ahs,' then the shots came so fast that cries of 'bravo!' went up." The Parisians had a "show me" attitude, and Annie showed them. At the end of her act, Annie bowed to what she described as the "roaring, hat-battering, sun shade-and-handkerchief throwing, mad 20,000." The Parisians were icebergs no longer, Annie said; they were now to fight for her during her six-month run in Paris.

The rest of the season at the "Buffalodrum" passed in a blur of sold-out performances, dignitaries and royalty, parties, dinners, and balls. Annie received a number of accolades from her fans. For instance, President Sadi Carnot assured Annie that when she felt like changing her profession and nationality, a commission awaited her in the French army. The king of Senegal had a better idea. He offered Buffalo Bill one hundred thousand francs for Annie. "The lady is not for sale," Cody bellowed. Then he thought to ask, "What do you want her for?" To destroy the vicious tigers who devastate the country's villages was the king's reply. The monarch might also have added that Annie was pretty, sexually appealing, and wielded a certain amount of power. When Annie said she preferred to stay with the Wild West, the king dropped to his knees, kissed Annie's hand, and according to her, then "departed with the air of a soldier."

That fall, when the Universal Exposition closed, the Wild West left for a tour of other parts of Europe. In November, the troupe reached Marseilles. Here Annie took the opportunity to visit the Mediterranean island of Montecristo. Everywhere, she saw deceit and poverty. She claimed that the authorities freed a counterfeiter after he proved his money contained more silver than government issue and that beggars abounded.

In Italy, Annie and Frank visited Mt. Vesuvius, the ruined city of Pompeii, the Vatican, and the Coliseum. But Frank wrote that Naples ranked as "one of the dirtiest cities in the world" and that Italy itself was devoid of "good gun makers." Butler much preferred Florence, "a very pretty city, containing a great many Americans," and Milan, "the home of all that is artistic and beautiful."

But it was Barcelona that most deeply engraved itself in Annie's and Frank's memories. Here the company lost its beloved announcer, Frank Richmond, to Spanish flu. Several Native American members of the Wild West troupe also died, but Annie and Frank successfully battled the disease. Butler arranged the shipment of Richmond's body back to the States and then collapsed into bed while Annie "worked for an hour weakly trying to get into [her] costume, and took [her] place in the arena that afternoon." Annie then "had the flu in earnest." Most of the company spent the Christmas of 1890 in quarantine, then finally moved to winter quarters in Alsace-Lorraine.

Here Annie read a newspaper report that she had died in "a Far-Off Land" sometime early in December. Supposedly, she had fallen victim to pneumonia in Buenos Aires. Annie recoiled when she saw her picture draped in flags. Cody, back in the United States for the winter, wired Frank Butler in alarm. When Frank assured him that Annie had just finished a substantial meal, Cody wrote back, "I am so glad our Annie ain't dead, ain't you?"

Rather than complaining about the error, Frank placed a notice in the newspapers stating that Annie was "alive and enjoying splendid health," although "affected terribly" by the report of her death. Annie felt special concern for her mother, who reportedly cried for two days when she heard of Annie's death. Although mother and daughter had retained their affectional ties, regular communication proved difficult. Consequently, Susan had believed the newspaper reports and had begun to grieve the loss of her daughter.

Annie also wrote numerous letters to her family, friends, and concerned fans assuring them of her well-being and to reporters thanking them for their gracious obituaries. She marveled over "how many good traits" she had and must have felt especially gratified that the *Breeder and Sportsman*, which had previously run the scurrilous letter from "A California," had written that her death caused "the deepest sorrow throughout the entire sporting circle." It turned out that the death of Annie Oatley, an American singer, lay at the root of the confusion.

The following year of 1890 soon proved memorable not only for Annie Oakley and Frank Butler but for the United States as well. In retrospect, 1890 proved a turning point of sorts. During 1890 the U.S. Census Bureau announced the end of the American frontier by virtue of population density. In addition, a number of social commentators lamented that the age of the telephone, linotype, steam turbine, internal-combustion engine, electric elevator, and hand camera was corrupting the United States. Some observers even predicted the decline of American civilization.

To Cody and Salsbury, such news must have held a degree of promise. They had already made giant strides toward achieving acclaim and wealth before 1890 by immortalizing the rapidly disappearing western frontier, by playing long engagements rather than short stands, by producing a show in Madison Square Garden, and by taking the Wild West to Europe. Now, with the American frontier "officially" dead, the years ahead offered fertile ground to entertainers, impresarios, and media moguls who could breath life and vitality into the country's good old days. Fortunes could be made, publicity gained, reputations established, and legends generated in such a climate of opinion. A public that hungered for the Old Wild West and for the virtues, adventure, and drama associated with it would gladly pay to witness the spectacles Cody and Salsbury staged in arenas in both hemispheres.

Just as circuses replayed history in gaudy dramas ranging from Cleopatra to Columbus, so did Cody and Salsbury re-create an American past in increasingly larger and more dramatic versions of "The Attack on the Settlers' Cabin," "The Rescue of the Deadwood Stage," "The Pony Express," "The Buffalo Hunt," and "Custer's Last Fight." In addition, shooting, riding, conflict between heroes and villains, and an Old West theme provided a sure-fire formula for pleasing audiences and making them talk about the Wild West long after a performance.

In a letter written around 1890, General William Tecumseh Sherman congratulated Cody for illustrating "the history of civilization on this continent during the past century." He wrote, "You have caught one epoch of this country's history, and have illustrated it in the very heart of the modern world—London." Cody appreciated Sherman's remarks; Sherman's comments reinforced Cody's own beliefs about what held an audience's attention and made them come back for more.

In addition, in the same way that circuses relied on daredevils and death-defying stunts, Cody and Salsbury recognized the value of their shooters, cowboys, *vaqueros*, Indians, and other performers. The partners worked tirelessly to develop new stunts that would take both the performer and the viewer to the edge, then pull them back before disaster occurred. Then, after James A. Bailey of Barnum and Bailey Circus fame replaced ailing Nate Salsbury as manager in 1894, he and Cody began to change the show significantly by adding circus elements, including trained animal acts and sideshows.

Cody and Salsbury also took into account the women of the 1890s. For eight of Annie's sixteen seasons with the Wild West, management placed her in the number-two spot on the bill to reassure women in the audience and help them relax during the frequent bursts of gunfire. Annie began shooting with a pistol, then accelerated the noise and excitement until she shot with a full charge in her rifle and shotgun. In the words of John Burke, "Women and children see a harmless woman there, and they do not get worried." In the show itself, Cody and Salsbury presented women as something more than victims or assistants to the main performers. Certainly, in "The Attack on the Settlers' Cabin," women ran, screamed, and fell into rescuers' arms, but in other segments of the show, "cowgirls" guided horses through compli-cated drills, performed bareback tricks, and rode untamed bron-cos. Sometimes, women also shot; in fact, the star shooter, Annie Oakley, was a woman.

In addition, the Wild West exposition reflected racial and ethnic diversity, probably because Cody desired authenticity. Since diversity characterized the American West, the show had to include Native Americans, Mexican Americans, and, of course, Anglo Americans. African Americans and Asians appeared only infrequently, although Cody gradually added Arabs, Germans, Irish, Japanese, Cubans, Filipinos, and other groups, especially to the Congress of Rough Riders of the World.

Cody and Salsbury also continued to hone the Wild West into a remarkably efficient operation. When the company toured Ger-many in 1891, German troops studied its movements. "We never moved without at least forty officers of the Prussian guard standing all about with notebooks taking down every detail of the performance," Annie recalled. "They made minute notes on how we pitched camp—the exact number of men needed, every man's position, how long it took, how we boarded the trains, and packed the horses, and broke camp; every living rope and bundle and kit was inspected and mapped." They also took great interest in the camp kitchen, which served some 750 people tasty and hot meals every day.

The 1893 season proved the wisdom of expanding the Wild West exposition; despite worsening economic conditions in the United

States, the show cleared almost one million dollars in profit. Based on that circumstance, Cody continued to expand, even though profits declined. Within five years, the Wild West exposition's equipment included eight sleeping coaches, fifteen railroad cars for stock, sixteen flatcars for equipment ranging from electric-light plants to the celebrated Deadwood stage, and thirty-five baggage wagons for tents, tack, and other gear.

Evidently, Oakley and Butler understood Cody and Salsbury's strategy in attracting audiences, publicity, and profits; they appear to have supported it at nearly every turn. The time and effort they invested in Annie's performance also indicated that they realized that the right combination of shooting and personality would ensure them continued success but that real stardom required more. Annie and Frank obviously understood that everything from costumes, accessories, lighting, and music to the performer's social and technical skills during the act and his or her personal behavior in private life demanded careful orchestration.

In addition, Annie and Frank's European experience impressed on them the widespread appeal of the American Dream. They always remembered what they called the "scum" and beggars in Naples, as well as the filth and corruption that tarnished other areas of the Old World. Whether consciously or not, they understood that people who lived with such problems wanted to see, and believe in, the prosperous, clean, and uncorrupted American West. Although Annie and Frank may not have explicitly discussed the idea of wish fulfillment, they obviously comprehended its principle.

Annie and Frank also drew on their own moral beliefs in shaping and refining Annie's act and personal image. Although their show business acumen dictated the inclusion of drama, their own personalities demanded a "clean" aura based on solid family values. Consequently, Annie and Frank developed a routine and a persona for Annie that suited the times. Like the overall Wild West program, Oakley and Butler incorporated five basic elements into Annie's act and into her private life: guns, horses, heroes, villains, and the American West.

A crucial dimension of Annie's act and image was exceptional skill with that western symbol the gun. Employing guns as safe symbols of entertainment and sport, she performed a wide range of tricks, including shooting an apple off a dog's head, shooting the ash off a cigarette Frank held in his teeth and a dime out of his fingers, shooting holes in playing cards, and bounding over a table and then shooting two glass balls already in the air when she began to jump. She also pointed her rifle backward over her shoulder, sighted in a mirror, and hit targets behind her back.

In response, reviewers used such terms as "marvelous," "superb," "phenomenal," "extraordinary," "remarkably clever," "astonishing," and "intrepid." In 1896, a *New York Evening Telegram* reporter observed, "[Oakley] ruined more glass balls within a given time than I would like to pay for in a week." According to him, she "slammed" a rifle through the air in every conceivable direction, snapped the trigger, and yet another glass ball fell toward the ground.

Annie's skill with horses also assumed legendary proportions. She became a female cowboy who, being brave, strong, and clever, could easily handle the mainstay of western life, the horse. In 1887, for example, Annie trained a horse named Gipsy to follow her everywhere, including up flights of stairs and into a freight elevator. In 1898, one week after Annie bought a dark bay named Prince, she charmed female visitors to Stirrat's stables in New York City by giving Prince the word to kneel and bow to the ladies, shake hands, and perform other tricks. Another of the favorable reports that followed her every appearance said that Oakley, a "superb equestrienne," simply tightened the reins to persuade the fractious horse to draw up his left forefoot and drop to one knee in a salute.

The third element—heroes—is more complicated. In numerous ways, Annie herself played the hero on and off the stage. For instance, like a good westerner, she always acted in a clean-cut, outdoor, athletic way. Annie not only rode well but also performed cartwheels and sprinted near the end of her performance. Newspaper critics indicated that they and the public approved. In July 1891, the *Manchester Spy* noted that "athletes of the first water would hesitate to compete with her," for seldom could "a young lady, however muscular and fond of sports, sustain such a fast and smart sprint as Miss Oakley." And in 1893, the *Brooklyn Citizen* described Annie as "the wonderful woman" who could "leap like a gazelle, run like a deer."

Annie likewise proved reliable and tough. She frequently pushed herself to work under adverse conditions, including her own poor health, inclement weather, or accidents. When a portion of a grandstand collapsed in 1891 during a performance in Nottingham, England, five hundred people plunged to the ground during Annie's performance. Yet she continued her shooting and, according to one witness, "finished her work without a single miss, under the circumstances and excitement displaying remarkable nerve for a lady." Another witness declared that her coolness averted panic and that, as a result, only a few people suffered slight injuries.

Annie also maintained scrupulous honesty. Unlike other performers who relied on an accomplice to shatter targets by means of wires or other devices, Oakley never used tricks or illusion. Although temptations to employ artifice or cut corners must have existed, Annie and Frank strove to keep her act honest. On one occasion, a circus performer who fired a rifle while swinging from a trapeze and hit the bull's-eye every time attracted Annie's interest until she discovered that the woman fired blanks while a property man rang the bell behind the target. Another trick that interested Annie involved a rifle expert playing a piano by shooting discs that caused hammers to strike the piano wires. But during one performance, his gun jammed and the piano kept playing; a confederate backstage activated the mechanism. Shooters of the 1890s used other tricks as well. In one, an eight-inch-wide metal funnel painted to match the target surrounded the usual one-inch bull's-eyes; this device caught any bullet within reasonable range and funneled it to the bull's-eye. In the cigar-ash trick, a shooter need not come anywhere near the target; the smoker simply pulled a wire in the cigar's center and the ash dropped off at the appropriate moment. But Annie declined to use such artifice.

A related issue concerned whether Oakley broke glass balls with bullets or scatter shot because it seemed to the uninformed more difficult to hit a ball with a bullet. Frank Butler and others explained time and again that Cody, Baker, and Oakley had all used rifles that shot bullets into the air in the early days, but because the falling shells endangered members of the audience, tent roofs, and nearby buildings, especially greenhouses whose owners lost no time in submitting bills for damages, they had switched to shotguns that fired shotted shells, which typically held two hundred tiny pellets. Pellets did not go very far and fell harmlessly into the arena or a drop curtain. In 1894, Ralph Greenwood, who wrote for *Shooting and Fishing*, pointed out that neither Oakley nor any of the other shooters in the Wild West claimed to shoot bullets at glass balls but only fired bullets at stationary targets with backstops. Also, Johnny Baker frequently maintained that the difficulty remained the same whether using a rifle ball or shotted shell because, at the customary range of twenty feet, the pellets made a pattern only about the same size as the glass ball.

In addition to her heroic qualities, Annie also remained feminine yet sexual, both on stage and in private. Annie excelled in combining a proper Victorian image with a simple, innocent sexuality. For example, Annie never donned pants, always wore her hair long, and raised the ordinary act of riding sidesaddle to an art. When the bicycle craze for women erupted in the mid-1890s and such well-known figures as temperance reformer Frances Willard took it up, Annie learned to ride while wearing a modest skirted outfit. Without exposing her legs, she soon shot down live birds and glass balls while wheeling in a circle with her hands never touching the handlebars.

As a result, Annie became a symbol for women viewers, especially those who wanted to try their hands at some aspect of sports. One reviewer asserted that Oakley supplied "another living illustration of the fact that a woman, independent of her physique, can accomplish whatever she persistently and earnestly sets her mind to overtake." An even stronger recommendation came from a fan who wrote to Annie in April 1900, "For several years I have been trying to get my wife interested in guns and shooting, but until she witnessed your work with Buffalo Bill last season I had poor luck with it." He added that after seeing Annie, his wife became an enthusiastic shooter.

Furthermore, Oakley provided a way for women to identify

with the show and with the West. Instead of women watching men perform magic tricks with the assistance of a comely woman or throw knives at objects in a woman's hand or on her head, they could instead admire a woman, Annie Oakley, shoot things out of men's hands and utilize men in other ways as assistants in her act. In addition, Oakley's presence in the Wild West show reassured women viewers that women existed in the West and that they contributed a good deal to western development.

Annie also assured women that, although independent and perhaps employed, they could still show dependence on men. She always worked with male assistants; she even chose male dogs for her act. Of course, she depended primarily on Frank Butler, who supported and encouraged her. Frank frequently related his reaction to the first notice Annie ever received. "We were down in Jersey," he recalled, "and the Butler treasury was not in bond-buying condition." Yet he spent his last few dollars to purchase copies of the newspaper that had "treated her so kindly." When Frank finally had enough money to buy stamps, he "scattered those papers over the land." He quickly learned how to establish excellent relations with reporters and even made friends with writers for sporting journals. In 1897, a reporter for *Shooting and Fishing* stated that he knew of "no better advertising agent than Frank Butler."

Annie relied on Frank in numerous other ways. He arranged gun licenses, issued press notices and photos, penned articles under the pseudonym "A Wandering American," wrote letters under his own name, handled correspondence and contracts, arranged to get arms and ammunition through customs, and served as their financial manager. Butler also earned additional income by working as a representative for the Union Metallic Cartridge Company and the Remington Arms Company. In 1902, Annie told an interviewer that the financial part was always in her husband's hands. She stated: "I owe whatever I have to his careful management. . . . I am not accustomed to looking after money matters, and am not a very good manager in that regard."

Annie also leaned on Frank's splendid sense of humor and stock of funny stories. For instance, when in 1893 Annie and Frank visited an English lord's hunting park, the servants treated Annie like royalty but scorned Frank. When Annie and Frank discovered that the servants thought Frank Butler was Annie's butler, he burst into laughter.

In addition to admitting her dependence on Frank, Annie projected a family image in her act and her life. Shortly before proclaiming the "closing" of the frontier, the U.S. Census Bureau had announced that somewhere between one out of every four-teen to sixteen marriages in the United States ended in divorce, the highest divorce rate in the world. Of the regions of the United States, the West had the highest divorce rate, a finding that horrified numerous Americans. Annie assuaged fears concerning the changing American family and underwrote traditional values by regularly including Frank and their current dog in her act. As her family, Frank and the dog helped establish a domestic aura and sent a message of family unity. When Annie shot a coin out of Frank's fingers or an apple off a dog's head, she demonstrated the trust that should exist between family members.

Annie and Frank also emphasized their close ties with her family in Ohio. The 1892 notice that she was to "pay a somewhat extended visit to her mother in Darke County" was typical. Then, Annie's mother visited the Wild West for the first time on July 4, 1895, when it played in Piqua, Ohio, and again in Greenville in 1900. On both occasions, Susan appeared with her three daugh-ters, all in Quaker dress. Unintentionally, they emphasized An-nie's highly moral and domestic background.

Audiences showed their appreciation for Annie and her clean-cut image in several ways. In July 1893, for example, when the Ohio building at the World's Fair in Chicago sponsored Annie Oakley Day, one visitor expressed his pleasure by noting, "This honest and simple little woman is a favorite all over the shooting world." In July 1900, a huge crowd turned out for the Wild West's performance in Greenville; afterward the Honorable C. M. An-derson and Will F. Baker of Greenville gave Annie a silver loving cup inscribed "From Old Friends in Greenville, O." Anderson praised Annie for the accuracy of her shooting as well as for her "unsullied life."

Annie herself regularly acted in a sensible and kind way. Over the years, she befriended almost everyone in the troupe, including the numerous Native Americans who lived in their own separate camp. Annie also treated people outside the troupe well. When an African-American man informed her that he had named his new twin daughters after her, Annie I and Annie II, she responded by sending birthday presents to the two Annies for years afterward.

But Annie and Frank also realized that a truly laudable hero also had a foible or two. To increase her appeal, they allowed her to reveal the odd traits and eccentricities of any good hero. When Annie missed a shot, she stamped her foot on the ground and pouted in full view of the audience. When she hit, she gave a satisfied little kick. At the end of her act, Annie blew kisses to the crowd and gave a distinctive jump-kick as she exited.

Apparently the strategy worked; viewers flocked to Annie's performances, cheered her, and shouted her name. Critics too seemed universally enthralled. One reviewer stated that Oakley was the "crowning charm of the whole show," as was "nightly testified by the ringing cheers" that greeted her appearance. Another called Annie a "magnetic lady" and maintained that such human touches constituted "half her performance."

Unlike Oakley's heroism, the fourth component of her act—the presence of villainy—lay latent and implied. For instance, although Annie did not use her guns as instruments of violence, except perhaps when shooting live pigeons, an element of potential violence always existed. She could easily shoot anyone who threatened her family, her friends, or herself. In addition, Annie obviously possessed power. Frequent explosions of gunfire, smoke and fire, and glass shards drifting from above convinced audiences that she, the hero, could defeat any villain who challenged her.

The fifth factor—the West—was especially important because it united the other four into a coherent package. Guns, horses, heroes, and villains appeared in everything from circuses to melodramas, but in the arena the West unified them and gave them a twist that other shows and exhibitions lacked. Annie incorporated the western motif by wearing a cowboy-style hat and dresses that, as one viewer observed, "reminded one very forcibly of the wild West," by using western tack and western-style guns, often ornamented with tooled silver, and by allowing publicity that identified her with the American West.

The total of these five factors—guns, horses, heroes, villains, and the West—in Oakley's act and in her life effectively imparted larger messages to her audiences, fans, and the public in general. In an era of economic depression, labor strikes, and war, Oakley presented positive American characteristics. She seemed to stand for the virtue of western expansionism, the possibility of family stability, and the triumph of good over evil.

During the 1890s, Annie and Frank's success and popularity soared. Yet, sometime late in the decade, they began to reassess their priorities and goals. Life on the road and in the camps, regular appearances before audiences filled with high expectations of her, and never-ending interviews, receptions, and photograph sessions were beginning to take their toll on Annie. In addition, she was now a mature woman who had both experienced the thrill of success and recognized its costs. Annie had fought to overcome what she termed "prejudice" against women in show business and in sports. Her own breakthrough and stardom had opened the way for other women performers in the arena as well as women contestants in rodeo. Still, although nineteenth-century restraints on women in general, and on showwomen in particular, often challenged and motivated Annie, they wore on her as well.

By the mid-1890s, Annie began to reveal signs of her changing perspective. In 1896, she observed that her work often proved less than fascinating. "It is hard work like everything else." About a year later, Annie's friend, reporter Amy Leslie remarked that Annie was tiring of the rigors of the business and had said, "It used to be fun, but I don't believe I care so much for it nowadays." Then, in 1899, Annie told a Tennessee reporter, "I have thought several times I would not go with the show another year, but I always do."

Oakley's statements may have also reflected some disgruntlement with developments within the Wild West company. In 1894, when Nate Salsbury fell ill and James A. Bailey replaced him as manager, Bailey brought in trick animal acts and sideshows. With profits down that year, Bailey also reinstituted one- and two-day stands to avoid playing against other shows and increase quick gate receipts. At the same time, both Cody's drinking and his domestic turmoil increased, and he began talking about retirement. In June 1897, Cody mentioned 1900 as a possible retirement date. When the date arrived, the aging showman remained in place but acted increasingly cranky. He snapped at a reporter and even said he hated his long hair and retained it only to please the public. "Long hair is business and not art with me." The next year found Cody deep in debt because of his various projects, including the town he named after himself in Wyoming, and full of talk about divorcing his wife, Louisa.

Given such internal upheaval in the Wild West, Annie and Frank had to think of their own futures. As astute as they were, they must have also realized that new trends in the world of entertainment and leisure would soon bring to an end the heyday of big arena shows. For instance, Thomas Edison's experiments with the phonograph, and later the radio and motion pictures, offered tremendous possibilities for changing the nature of entertainment. More specifically, the year 1892 marked the invention of basketball and the building of the first Ferris wheel for the Chicago World's Fair. In 1893, Florenz Ziegfeld entered show business. In 1895, Nate Salsbury staged *Black America*, the epitome of the black minstrel show, on Staten Island, and David Belasco's *Heart of Maryland*, a Civil War melodrama, opened. The following year, William Gillette starred in the Civil War melodrama *Secret Service*. By then, New York City alone had seven vaudeville theaters; to one, Ziegfeld brought the steamy European singer Anna Held. Then, in 1898, the first musical written, produced, and performed by African Americans, and a black revue written by Will Marion Cook, opened on Broadway.

At the same time, events of the 1890s made many Americans desperate for an avenue of escape, however temporary, from their many problems. Beginning with one of the worst depressions in history in 1893, Americans suffered through widespread labor strikes and violent repression in 1894, the Spanish-American War in 1898, and the assassination of President William McKinley in 1901.

During the Wild West's 1901 season, Cody depended on Oakley, now a well-established old-timer, to draw crowds. He issued a splendid poster featuring "The Peerless Wing and Rifle Shot" wearing some of her medals, surrounded by vignettes of her Ohio loving cup and such moments in her personal history as her shooting from a bicycle and hunting with her dogs. Unfortunately, accidents bedeviled the company all season. One Bear's tepee burned down, an artilleryman lost his right hand when a cannon discharged prematurely, the wagon carrying the electric-light plant crashed after its brakes failed, and one section of the show train ran into another in a heavy fog. Even dexterous Annie slipped in the arena during one of her performances.

Then, on October 28, 1901, after the troupe had boarded its three-unit train in Charlotte, North Carolina, to head for their last performance of the season in Virginia, came the final accident. The engineer of a southbound freight moved to a siding as the first unit of the Wild West passed and then, assuming it was a one-unit train, returned to the main track. At 3:20 A.M., he and his crew saw the lights of the second unit approaching. Both crews jumped to safety.

Annie and Frank slept in that second section in their private compartment. The crash threw Annie out of her bed and slammed her back against a trunk. At first, newspapers reported only slight injuries to her hand and back, but further examination showed damage to her spine. Doctors at St. Michael's Hospital in Newark, New Jersey, who performed five operations on Oakley's spine, said they had "never seen such fortitude displayed by any previous patient."

Soon after the accident, Frank Butler announced his and Annie's departure from the Wild West exposition. Although most biographers have assumed that they left because of the accident, Frank's letter of resignation, which is unfortunately undated but mounted with other items from 1901 in Oakley's scrapbook, suggests the existence of long-standing plans, perhaps even known to Cody before the accident. Its text omitted any mention of the accident. Instead, Frank wrote, "It is like giving up a big fortune to leave the dear old wild west, but a better position influences us and we must go." Butler planned to replace Jack Hollowell as northeastern representative for the Union Metallic Cartridge Company of Bridgeport, Connecticut, and give Annie a chance to try her hand at enterprises other than those in the arena.

If Frank and Annie exaggerated her injuries from the train crash, as biographer Shirl Kasper has argued, they may have done so to ease their departure from the Wild West. Using her injuries as an unstated but widely understood excuse for resigning would suggest that Annie left the Wild West out of necessity rather than a desire to desert a troubled ship. The couple also attributed Annie's startling white hair to the accident, but other possible explanations exist as well. Annie's friend Amy Leslie claimed that the change occurred when a careless attendant left Annie for forty minutes in a scalding bath at a celebrated health resort. And one family story suggests that, much like her sisters and brother, Annie was already turning gray-haired before the accident, which simply provided a good reason for her to stop disguising the truth.

Still, when Annie Oakley resumed shooting, she wore a curly brown wig to cover her white hair. Although several observers remarked that she looked young, blithe, and gay, times had definitely changed. On December 24, 1902, Nate Salsbury died at his home near Long Branch, New Jersey, and Cody took Bailey as his new partner. Cody's 1901 poster now seemed like a valedictory to Annie and a return to the Wild West less attractive to her than ever.

Beginning in late 1901 Annie gave exhibitions and shot in matches, starred in several plays, and reportedly rejected an offer from Cody to return to the Wild West. Several years later in 1909, Frank resigned his position with the Union Metallic Cartridge Company, and Annie agreed to make her arena comeback by appearing in Vernon Seavers's Young Buffalo Show between 1911 and 1913. Just as she had with Cody's Wild West, Annie shot, rode, and acted her way into the hearts of several generations of Americans.

During these years Annie and Frank followed their long-established and effective formula. Annie performed, still wearing long-skirted, fringed outfits and still stunning audiences of old and new fans by shooting down glass balls and smashing clay pigeons. Annie also mentored younger shooters; her protégé was Vernon Seavers, Jr., the eight-year-old son of her employer and billed as the "youngest cowboy in the world." And Annie continued her benevolence, including inviting orphans to attend performances as her guests.

At the same time, Frank Butler managed Annie's act and wrote articles and press releases, which promoted the "real" wild West and its star, Annie Oakley. One perceptible difference was that Frank now allowed publicity agents and reporters to call Annie the "world champion" and "one of the highest salaried arenic attractions in the world." Another was that Frank permitted photographs of the young Annie Oakley of the 1880s and 1890s to appear beside the older, plumper Annie, accompanied by somewhat exaggerated tales of Annie's triumphs in the "old days."

Always the consummate showpeople, Annie and Frank claimed that they were having an "enjoyable" time with the Young Buffalo Show and thought it a splendid representation of the Old West. They smiled their way through the 1911 season, traveling 8,226 miles. They rejoined the Young Buffalo Show again in 1912, despite its merger with the Colonel Fred Cummins Wild West and Indian Congress, which introduced fire-eaters, snake-tamers, and elephants into the arena. In addition to her other feats, Annie now twirled a lariat.

In 1913, Annie received the ultimate praise when the *Greenville Courier* urged every Darke County resident to attend the Young Buffalo Show to display "love" for Annie, one of "Our Own." In a gesture that in a sense brought her own life full circle Annie gave free tickets to occupants of the Darke County Children's Home. In the troupe's final performance on October 4, 1913, in Marion, Illinois, Annie Oakley made her last appearance in the arena. She and Frank intended to build a retirement home in Cambridge, Maryland, and enjoy their hard-won leisure.

It was in 1913, then, that Annie ended her career as a Wild West star and began to take her place in the chronicles of American show business. Between 1885 and 1913 she had carved herself a reputation as a superb performer and a distinguished personality. It was Annie's work in the arena, from Cody's Wild West to the Young Buffalo Show, that brought Annie more exposure and fame than she would gain from any of her other activities. Still, Annie Oakley's activities in the "show" business provide only a partial glimpse into those richly textured years; far more remains of her story than is usually told.

CHAPTER 3

"The birds were first class"

"I was justly proud of my shooting," Annie Oakley wrote in her autobiography during the mid-1920s. Other comments such as "the birds were first class" and "I thought I should win on the morrow" also pepper her memoir and reveal her obvious relish for competition and sports. Whereas Oakley looked on her activities in the Wild West arena as a job, she viewed match and exhibition shooting with enthusiasm and hunting with passion.

The newspaper clippings she included in her autobiography further indicate her competitive nature. Of the hundreds of clippings in her extensive scrapbooks, she chose to reproduce only three. Each described a match, and each reported that Annie "broke all records." Still other clippings indicate that Oakley triumphed in hundreds of matches during her lifetime. One 1900 report of a Brooklyn match proclaimed that even though the shooters had trouble seeing the white birds against ground blanketed with snow, "Annie Oakley Scored No Misses in Seven-Bird Shoot."

Annie took justifiable pride in such top scores, but in her peak performing years between 1885 and 1913 she also appreciated the additional income from matches and exhibitions. Because she wanted to avoid the poverty she had experienced as a child, she budgeted carefully. Some of her colleagues, annoyed by Annie's frugality, even accused her of drinking Cody's lemonade rather than buying her own. Although the charge remains unproven, it is true that Annie seized opportunities to earn extra money and to supplement her salary from the Wild West. In 1893, for instance, Oakley earned $100 per week with the Wild West, a salary five times that of the cowboys and the highest pay in the troupe; by 1900 the figure had jumped to $150 a week.

Annie declared that the sum "was not as big as most folks think." Of course, Annie received this pay only during the show's season. Also, her appearances with the Wild West entailed numerous expenses, which she and Frank tried to meet in a timely fashion with something left over for their savings. Sometimes they provided their own housing and food, sometimes not. Also, when arranging shooting matches, they had to put up guarantees, often of $100 or more, which they sometimes forfeited if Annie lost a match. And, even when Annie failed to win, the expenses entailed remained the same, including costumes, guns, ammunition, publicity, transportation, charities, and gifts to relatives and friends.

Annie admitted that compared with the average worker, who earned less than $500 a year during the 1890s, she had made "a good deal of money" in her time. In addition, Frank contributed financially by participating in shooting matches and working as a sales representative for Union Metallic Cartridge Company between 1901 and 1909. According to Annie, she and Frank did not squander their income in "selfish, extravagant living." Instead, they believed in "simple living," supporting charities, and sharing their wealth with family members and friends. Retirement also had a central place in their budget. Because Annie and Frank had no pension plan, they had to provide for themselves.

Thus, Annie Oakley and Frank Butler turned to matches and exhibitions to supplement their other earnings. With glee, Annie recalled an 1889 match. "I won two fine prizes here and a full purse of money was sent to my New York bank." Besides winning purses, Annie also frequently reaped return from the side bets Frank placed on her.

Still, money was not the Butlers' driving force. Around 1889, during a match Annie shot on a guarantee basis with shooter Fred Kell, Annie and Frank revealed that they also had empathy for other people's problems. When Frank discovered that the match was draining the last resources of Kell's backer, he called it off. Annie said that later, when Frank asked her if he "had done right," she reached out her hand in "warm approval."

Legend has it that Annie participated in her first shooting matches as a girl living in Ohio and that because she shot so well and won so often, local competitions increasingly barred her participation. Then, Annie's win over Frank Butler must have convinced her of the benefits of competitive shooting; she won the purse and a husband as well.

Once Oakley gained prominence on the vaudeville stage and with the Wild West, invitations poured in. No matter whom Annie worked for, from Tony Pastor to Buffalo Bill Cody, she secured permission to shoot matches in between shows or during her time off. For instance, when the Wild West played in London in 1887, the elite Notting Hill Gun Club issued her an invitation. Also that summer, Edward, prince of Wales, invited her to shoot against the grand duke of Russia. The following year, a club in Newton, New Jersey, offered her 75 percent of the gate receipt to compete against English shooter William Graham. In 1889, when the Wild West played Paris, the Circle des Pitineau often invited her to shoot with its members, as did the Marseille Gun Club.

During the London summer of 1887, Oakley beat some of the top shooters in the world and proved herself in a society where shooting was the country's dominant sport. In June, for example, she defeated Michael, grand duke of Russia, after Edward, prince of Wales, wrote to Colonel William F. Cody: "Will the little girl, Annie Oakley, who shoots so cleverly in your show, object to shooting a friendly match with the Grand Duke Michael of Russia? We will arrive at Earl's Court at 10:30 this morning." He signed it simply "Edward."

Annie recalled that "on the minute," four carriages rolled in through the Wild West's private gate. Edward's entourage included sixteen members of the royal family and, of course, the grand duke himself, accompanied by his retinue. According to Annie, she and Michael shot at fifty targets; she scored forty-seven against his thirty-six. Many people expressed their delight because Michael reportedly sought Princess Victoria as his royal wife, a match most English citizens disapproved. As a consequence, Annie received what she called "the most amazing and unexpected publicity" she ever experienced, whereas the grand duke returned home defeated by Annie and rebuffed by Victoria.

By July 4, 1887, Annie had competed in a total of thirty-one matches and won twenty-five prizes. She also displayed her shooting ability later that month in the infamous meet involving

Lillian Smith at Wimbledon. On this occasion, Prince Edward pushed his way through the crowd of excited onlookers to congratulate Oakley.

The following year, back in the United States, Annie kept up the hectic pace. She defeated top shooter Phil Daly, Jr., at a tournament he organized in Long Branch, New Jersey, and state champion Miles Johnson on his own Jersey soil. When, in that match, Oakley missed her forty-seventh bird, "a blue twister," she asked Johnson if he had brought the bird from England, where the pigeons flew, she thought, like "greased lightning." He smiled. "No, I trained that fellow in order to get in one miss on you."

Beside her regular wins, Annie also took great satisfaction in providing a role model for women shooters. As she matured, Annie increasingly realized the barriers confronting women, especially those who wished to participate in shooting sports. She would never have described herself as a political person, but in a modern sense she was indeed political: Annie Oakley consciously worked to open competitive shooting matches to other women.

Oakley especially tried to set a good example in both her conduct and her performance. In 1893, *American Field* paid her the ultimate compliment: she could "successfully compete with any man." The article continued, "Many of her sex are experts when firing at hearts, but I question if there is another woman in this fair land who can pierce the heart aimed at four times out of five, especially if they will keep twelve paces away from the object of their aim."

In time, more women shooters joined Oakley on the circuit. In 1899, a Mrs. M. F. Lindsley, who shot under the name of Wanda, competed with Annie in a match in White Plains, New York. Lindsley fell behind Annie, who tied one of the male shooters for first place. In 1901, four women competed in a New York match. The newspaper account of the match, titled "Ladies at the Traps," referred to all four women by their married names. The only one mentioned by both her own and her husband's name was Annie Oakley, or Mrs. Frank Butler.

In subsequent years, women continued to join the ranks of gun clubs and to enter matches. In 1902, even Anna Held, a popular actress and the wife of Florenz Ziegfeld, revealed her shooting abilities in a New York match. The following year, Mrs. S. S. Johnston of Minneapolis was only one of the lady contestants in the annual Grand American Handicap.

Oakley also encountered Lillian Smith on the match circuit. At the tenth annual Grand American Handicap, held in Kansas City in 1902, three women shooters took part: Oakley; Johnston, who described herself as strictly a sport shooter; and Lillian F. Smith, who claimed she had been shooting for only two years. Actually, Smith had been appearing on vaudeville stages under the name of Winona, an Indian princess, show-business-style. Annie outshot both Johnston and Smith, although her shooting captured no prizes. If Oakley faced Smith in other matches, both she and the newspapers failed to mention it.

With the exception of Smith, Annie maintained friendly relations with many of the women shooters who regularly appeared on the circuit. Frank once stated that "some of the best lady shots in the country" were counted among Annie's dearest friends. He continued, "As she was the pioneer in that line she is always proud when they score well, for what better monument can she leave behind than lady shots and lady gun clubs."

Women showed their appreciation for Oakley's efforts by flocking to see her shoot. For instance, a match in 1899 attracted what one viewer described as "a large number of lady marksmen." Women shooters also formed clubs in Annie's honor. One of the earliest, the Annie Oakley Rifle Club of Newark, invited her to their first annual ball on February 19, 1889. Dressed in a fitted lavender silk dress and buff-colored felt hat, Annie took part in the grand march. For the rest of the evening, colored gas jet glittered and music wafted through the pavilion. In the course of the festivities, the club presented her with a special horseshoe and a bouquet of flowers.

Public enthusiasm and interest also mounted as Annie won match after match. In 1887, a congregational minister in Jersey City even preached a sermon based on Oakley's shooting, which he declared a form of healthy recreation. He concluded by enjoining his congregation, "If you will all aim as straight for Heaven as Annie Oakley does at the objects she shoots at, you can all be 'Little sure-shots' and will be sure to get to Heaven."

Others praised her in more prosaic ways. In 1887, a reporter termed her "queen of the female wing-shots." Later, in an 1891 letter, a shooting expert labeled her "Queen of Lady Shooters." Within the year, another commentator emphasized her patriotic value: "she keeps up the credit of the stars and stripes in a foreign land."

Consequently, huge numbers of people thronged to Oakley's matches. In 1888, one observer remarked that at a Philadelphia match, "thirty-one thousand people saw, or tried to see, this match." He continued, "The traps had to be moved farther out three times as the vast overflow from the large grandstand closed in."

Because Annie achieved such success in match shooting, other shooters and the public took great interest in the guns she used. During her lifetime, Oakley owned hundreds of firearms and once estimated that they would line her tent "on all four sides" if the guns were stacked close together. But she favored several over the rest, including plain Stevens pistols with walnut grips. Also, Annie often used a Stevens spur-guard Gould model single-shot .22-caliber pistol with a ten-inch, gold-plated barrel. She later bought to match a gold-plated, pearl-handled Smith & Wesson American model #3, a .44-caliber pistol.

Regarding rifles, Oakley once wrote that she used the caliber best suited for her work, often a .32. She also owned three Stevens .22-caliber sporting rifles, all produced between 1872 and 1875. Each had a wooden forestock and tip-down-style barrel. In 1895 she obtained one of her favorite rifles, a .32/20 Model 1892 lever-action repeater, specially made for her. In many of her tricks she featured this light rifle with a gold-plate receiver, half-round barrel, and fancy wood in the stock. Frequently, she also used this gun in her mirror trick when she shot over her shoulder at targets behind her. Annie also used a Marlin .22 repeating rifle. Marlin rim-fire repeaters first appeared in 1891 and gained great popularity with arena and other shooters who liked the Marlin's versatility in accepting the .22 short, long, and new long rifle cartridges. Oakley frequently split an ace of hearts with a Marlin Model '91, .22 caliber.

Among shotguns, early in her career Oakley favored a 16-gauge, hammer-type, especially the Parker Brothers models, but she often recommended the lighter 20-gauge, which eliminated some of the recoil and forced a shooter to make up for the gun's light weight with his or her own skill. London gunmaker Charles Lancaster made four or more shotguns for Annie during 1887, at least two of them 20-bores weighing only five pounds each. Annie also favored a Spencer repeating pump shotgun, which held six shells. With it, she set a new record by hitting six balls thrown into the air at once. Sometime around 1900, Annie stated that she preferred hammerless shotguns weighing about six pounds and that she often used 12-gauge shotguns because of the availability of ammunition.

Gun companies occasionally produced distinctive shotguns for Oakley. Grateful that her appearances publicized sport shooting for women, they built special editions as gifts for her or as advertising promotions. In 1889, the Hunter Arms Company of Fulton, New York, made for her an L. C. Smith 16-gauge, hammerless, double-shotgun; on the lock-plates were gold engravings, one of her as a girl, the other as a woman. The Hunter Company asked the celebrated New York jeweler Tiffany and Company to engrave the gold plates, which a Mr. Hartigan then mounted. One of Hartigan's colleagues, Charles Rogers, remembered that after Hartigan perfectly mounted the lock plates on the gun, his supervisors gave him a bottle of Napoleon brandy and the rest of the day off.

After the special Annie Oakley shotgun passed all inspections and tests, a company official laid it on a piece of black velvet for all the workers to take pride in and admire. According to Rogers, the gun gleamed like a jewel and, when presented to Annie, made her "a friend and booster for the L. C. Smith gun for the rest of her shooting career and life."

Still, Oakley resisted the temptation to give endorsements for specific types of guns and tried to maintain impartiality toward munitions companies. Early in the 1890s, she told a *Shooting and Fishing* correspondent: "There is Purdey; there is Grant; there is Lancaster; there is Francotte. Each makes a good enough weapon for anybody." She added that she used a Lancaster and a Francotte almost continually but could not say that one was "better than the other." She noted that she also owned a Premier Scott, which she thought "a good deal of."

During the mid-1890s, Annie explained further that she cared only that a gun be "of fine quality." She usually preferred plain guns with good wood in the stocks and open sights. Often she used guns produced by Parker Brothers of Meriden, Connecticut, those the Remington Company made after taking over Parker, and those of the Winchester Repeating Arms Company. In her view, guns, rifles, and pistols came in many styles; saying that any one make was "superior to all others would show a very narrow mind and limited knowledge of firearms." She believed that the shooter's physique, type of game, and "fancy" should govern his or her choice of gun. "'The best gun' is the gun that best fits the shooter."

Oakley did speak, however, without equivocation on the issue of inexpensive guns. "I do not believe in using cheap guns." Shooting an inexpensive gun seemed to her "like driving Star Pointer with a clothes line—you never know when the line is going to give way." She explained that she did not mean a gun should be expensive in its engraving and ornamentation. Rather, she meant a gun should have the qualities of "strength, safety, balance, fit and ease of manipulation." If, after finding these qualities in a firearm, purchasers had "that love for firearms such as the art-lover has for paintings," they might add "such orna-mentation."

Oakley also favored specific types of ammunition. Throughout her career, she preferred Schultze powder. While in London in 1887, she mentioned her preference for Schultze powder. An official of another London powder company protested and re-minded her—and the public—that she also used an equal quantity of his company's powder. He must have been further annoyed in October, when an official of Schultze Gunpowder Company, also of London, presented her with a gold medal bearing the Schultze trademark and her initials, commemorative of her stay in Eng-land.

Annie continued to maintain her allegiance to Schultze pow-der. In 1889, she smuggled some of her favorite Schultze powder into France, which forbade the importation of foreign powders.

When her supply ran out, she turned to French powder, which exploded one of her guns and gave her a serious bruise. Frank concluded the French powder had a lot in common with the French match—"both go off when good and ready." He maintained that no matter how carefully one loaded French powder into cartridges, no two ever fired alike. A friend saved the situation by sending her a dozen eggs packed in Schultze powder. "The duty on the eggs was about 40 cents, which I gladly paid," Annie remembered.

Because Oakley used such great quantities of ammunition, her reactions meant a good deal to the companies that produced it. In 1899, Frank estimated that Annie had fired forty-eight thousand shots during the past season at a cost of three hundred dollars a week. In a pamphlet issued around 1899, titled *Annie Oakley: A Brief Sketch of Her Career and Notes on Shooting*, Annie estimated that "the various shells, primers, wads and metallic cartridges" she had used would supply an army. She feared that the amount of ammunition she had consumed during her career would "appall most persons."

In this small pamphlet, available simply by sending in a two-cent stamp to cover return postage, Oakley came as close to a product endorsement as she ever would. She stated, "After what seems to me to be exhaustless experiments, I have selected Union Metallic Cartridge Co. ammunition as the most satisfactory to me." She explained that she used "UMC Smokeless Shells loaded with 39 grains of Schultze Smokeless Powder and an ounce of shot." In her rifles and revolvers, Annie used "UMC Metallic Cartridges," which she said were not "the only load" but "good enough" for her.

No doubt, Frank influenced Annie's preferences. In fact, the writing style and content of the *Annie Oakley* pamphlet sound more like Frank Butler, who worked as a sales representative for UMC between 1901 and 1909. Undoubtedly, Frank's association with UMC also accounted for the picture of Annie that appeared on UMC cartridges.

Oakley gained fame as a match shooter, but she had to tolerate hazards as well. For one, Annie did not always win. In 1888, she lost one match to shooter Al Bandle of Cincinnati and another to Phil Daly, Jr., of Long Branch, New Jersey. A decade later, although she had more experience, she still lost occasionally. In an 1898 match, for example, she only tied for third place in a strong field of shooters.

Another danger of match shooting was the ever-present possibility of injury. In 1886, while practicing the day before a match against well-known shooter William Graham, Annie injured her left hand. As she put a target into a trap, the spiral spring flew out and cut her hand between the first and second fingers. According to her, the doctor "used a 14-inch catgut for five stitches." He also suspended her arm in a sling and ordered her to avoid using her hand for two weeks. The next day, Graham took one look at her and agreed to call off the match, but his backer claimed they had won by default and demanded the purse. Although Frank preferred to take the loss, Annie picked up a gun with her right hand and began to shoot.

"The birds were fast," she remembered, "but ran pretty even." Annie shot well, and she and Graham each brought down ten birds. On the eleventh, Oakley drew, in her words, "a streak of greased lightning." With her first shot, she cut the tail feathers off, then she whipped her left hand out of the sling onto the barrel so that she could fire a second shot. She ripped three of her stitches open, and blood began to flow. Frank dashed forward, called a halt to the proceedings, and told the audience they could have Annie's percentage of the gate. Annie remembered that she retired from the field "amid cheers."

Inclement weather also created its share of difficulties. On January 16, 1888, in Merchantville, New Jersey, Annie Oakley again faced William Graham. Within minutes of her arrival at the shooting club, the temperature dropped to zero, and sleet shrouded the grounds. Frank rubbed brandy on her arms and hands and gave Annie one of her favorite Lancaster 20-bore guns. Approximately one thousand people watched as the fierce wind repeatedly carried her birds out of bounds. Once again, Oakley lost to Graham. "I went down in defeat with a score of 33–36," she recalled. Still, despite the storm, the gate receipts covered the two hundred dollars she lost.

A week later in Easton, Pennsylvania, Oakley met Graham for a second round. Annie's fans also showed up; according to her, they still felt "optimistic for the second shoot." Because Easton lay buried in snow, optimism was probably difficult to muster. Then an outcry erupted when Annie's fans learned that she was staying in Room 13 at an Easton hotel. "You should have heard the howl," she wrote. "The old hands at the traps threw up their hands and said it was all off, unless I moved at once." She refused to move. After all, she pointed out, her birthday fell on the thirteenth, and she had joined the Wild West on the thirteenth. When Annie finally arrived at the grounds, she saw horses with scoops and men with shovels clearing paths and areas around the score and traps. Although Graham wanted to postpone the match, Annie felt "ready and anxious to shoot." She defeated Graham handily, twenty-four to nineteen, even though her fans retained their superstitions.

Weather bedeviled Annie on numerous other occasions. In 1893, she shot an entire match in a gale-force wind that carried many birds out of bounds. Despite the storm, Oakley won the match by downing fifty out of seventy birds while her closest competitor killed forty-five and missed twenty-five.

Controversy sometimes assailed her as well. During the mid-1880s, for example, a dispute erupted about the cruelty and inhumanity of killing live birds. After a match, gun clubs sometimes gave the dead pigeons to hospitals and orphanages; other times, they allowed dealers to gather up pigeon carcasses and sell them to hotels and to merchants who packed them in brine and sold them again. In an era increasingly attuned to conservation issues, these actions seemed insufficient to many people. In 1902, the organizers of the annual Grand American Handicap, held that year in Kansas City, announced that they would not use live birds in future meets. Other organizers followed their lead haltingly. Yet match reports from 1903, as well as subsequent years, indicate that live birds continued to serve as targets. In 1907, Oakley, who disliked controversy, agreed to shoot in a match using live birds, the Fourteenth Annual Target and Live Bird Tournament in Betteron, Maryland. Either Annie felt the conflict had not yet created insurmountable problems or, more likely, she felt the need to prove herself against men by shooting the most difficult targets of all—live birds.

Annie relied heavily on Frank to help her face such difficulties. But Frank had his special concerns as well. He seemed almost possessed by a fear that the numerous impostors who claimed to be Annie would undercut her reputation with their flawed performances. As early as 1887, when Annie and Frank left for Europe, Frank tried to foil impostors by running an advertisement in the April 2 edition of the *New York Clipper*: "Don't Forget This. There is only one ANNIE OAKLEY. And she leaves for Europe with the Wild West."

Then, while in England, Frank developed an intense dislike of music-hall shooters. Frank thought England "over-flowed" with these "humbugs." He sneered, "Bells are rung, balls are broken, [all with] blank cartridges." Of course, in a country where gunowners had to pay license fees and hire game preserves for shooting, music-hall audiences, composed largely of non–gun owners, could be easily fooled. "There are," Frank snapped, "a great many so-called champions tolerated in England that would not last long in America."

Frank tried to retain his composure regarding phonies, but in September 1891, after hearing of a match-shooter in Connecticut who traded on Annie's reputation by calling herself "Little Sure Shot," he lashed out "I hope the sportsmen of Wilmantic or any place else where this bogus party may appear, will not think they have seen Annie Oakley." Frank noted that he usually paid little attention to such people, but this case seemed to push his forbearance to its limits. This usually gentle man—who one observer in 1895 described as "an athletic, good-natured man" and to whom others extended the courtesy titles "Colonel," "Sir," and even "Dr."—felt compelled to condemn such impostors.

Obviously, phonies continued to pose a problem for Frank Butler, if not for Annie Oakley, who seldom mentioned the matter. During the late 1890s, Frank condemned a dime-museum impersonator. He had come across a man and woman, who would "never starve for the want of a hard cheek," posing in a dime museum, the man as a long-haired cowboy and western bad man, the woman as "Little Sure Shot." Frank explained that museums

were "full of long-haired humbugs," but he did not want anyone
to think that Annie Oakley had to stand posing eleven hours a day
in a cheap museum.

To avoid contact with such impostors and humbugs, Frank
refused to apply the term "champion" to Annie. In an 1898 letter,
Frank explained that using the title "champion" drew challenges
from hundreds of shooters, many of them little more than "dime
museum freaks." He added, "Since Annie Oakley first went
before the public I think she has received at least one hundred so-
called challenges; I say so-called because not one of them ever had
a dollar back of it." One female challenger, Frank maintained, had
a soiled personal reputation and three living husbands, whereas
another had killed her partner while shooting an apple off her
head and, after being acquitted because it was an accident, billed
herself as "The Woman Killer."

In 1890, Frank declared that Annie shot "to please the public
and the company" she worked for. Despite her numerous wins in
private matches and tournaments, she never claimed any championship. If Annie had used the title "champion," Frank continued,
she would have had to shoot against every so-called champion in
the world. "There are several she would not care to have her name
used in connection with."

Frank Butler also worked diligently to protect Annie's reputation as a lady. "No women with a shady past or doubtful reputation," he asserted, "can ever enter into a personal contest with
Annie Oakley while I am managing her, as she values her personal
reputation far more than her shooting one." In this regard, in 1891
he accused some of Annie's challengers of wanting free advertising. He added that Annie already had more engagements than she
could fill in the next three years.

The matter of impostors had obviously become a sore spot with
Frank over the years. As Annie's manager and press agent, he had
worked to maintain her shining reputation and image; thus
imitators clearly exasperated him. Annie, however, appeared more
concerned about false press reports. In 1894, she admitted that
the press helped make her famous, but she also accused reporters
of dreaming up some ridiculous stories. One was the report of her
supposed engagement to an English noble. "Think of the feelings

of my husband," she said. Another time, the press announced that she had been arrested for carrying deadly weapons in Queenstown, although she was in New York City at the time.

Oakley's biggest run-in with the press, and one of the most traumatic events of her adult life, began on August 11, 1903, when the *Chicago American* and the *Chicago Examiner*, both William Randolph Hearst newspapers, ran unverified headlines in the best yellow journalism tradition: "Annie Oakley Asks Court for Mercy—Famous Woman Crack Shot . . . Steals to Secure Cocaine." The report claimed that Annie lay in a cell at the Harrison Street prison as a result of stealing a pair of trousers from an African-American man, Charles Curtis, to pay for her drug supply. Supposedly, police officers had taken Annie to Justice Caverly's Harrison Street police court, where she plead guilty and received a fine of forty-five dollars and costs. The judge sentenced her to twenty-five days for care and treatment.

Ernest Stout, the reporter who wrote the story, said that police officers had sworn that they had arrested the real Annie Oakley. They had also described her "shattered condition" as "pitiful" and had deplored her "destitute" state. Stout apparently further embroidered the story. He wrote that Oakley's "striking beauty" was now gone. "Although she is but twenty-eight years old," he continued, "she looks almost forty."

When Stout's shocking story went out on the Publishers Press telegraph wire, other newspapers picked it up without checking its accuracy. The *Rochester Times* ran the headline "Annie Oakley, Famous Rifle Shot Is Destitute," and a New Jersey paper informed its readers that Annie Oakley was a cocaine victim. Annie wrote to many of the papers with an angry denial. On August 12, 1903, she informed the *Brooklyn Union Standard* that the woman posing as Annie Oakley was a "fraud" and that she, the genuine Annie Oakley, had not been in Chicago since last winter. Annie demanded that the newspaper contradict the story. Then, on August 13, Oakley ordered the *Philadelphia Press*: "Contradict at once. Some one will pay for this dreadful mistake."

Publishers Press immediately sent out a retraction, and newspapers apologized in print and sometimes in letters to Annie. One

editor assured Oakley, "As the *Daily News* was the least in offence,
I mean to make it the greatest in atonement, so far as correct
publicity is concerned." Several newspapers also initiated investi-
gations as to the root of the story. Some claimed that the arrested
woman had given the name Elizabeth Cody, posing as Buffalo
Bill's daughter-in-law. Somehow this Cody connection turned
into Annie Oakley, although Oakley was not related to Cody.
Another group believed that the imposter was a vaudeville performer, Maude Fontenella, who had once appeared in a burlesque
Wild West show as "Any Oakley."

None of this appeased Annie, who said that the "terrible piece"
nearly "killed" her. "The only thing that kept me alive," she
recalled, "was the desire to purge my character." Those who
accused her of overreacting or wanting to garner huge monetary
settlements failed to understand her long climb from the back-
woods of Ohio; she was not about to let some careless error
destroy her image and perhaps even her employability. Even if the
story was an error and not malicious libel, she knew that people
believed what they read. Retractions and apologies would go
largely unnoticed. Annie believed that she had to create an issue
to make the truth of the matter stick in the public record and the
public mind. Unlike P. T. Barnum, who reportedly said he preferred press abuse rather than silence, Annie wanted the truth or
nothing.

Still, it is difficult to explain Annie's single-mindedness in
pursuing legal action against the offending newspapers, most of
whom apologized and retracted the story. For nearly six years,
Annie set aside her own career and personal life, traveled widely at
her own expense, and appeared in courtrooms under great duress.
Since she was never an opportunist, it seems unlikely that Annie
expected to garner great financial rewards from her quest. A more
likely explanation is that she felt she had lost control of her life and
career. For a woman who maintained equanimity by controlling
her immediate environment, this loss would have represented a
disaster. The only way to bring her life and career back into
balance would have been to regain control, through legal action if
necessary.

Clearly, Frank encouraged Annie in the belief that her integrity had received one too many challenges. Given his near-preoccupation with denouncing all impostors and maintaining the purity of Annie's reputation, Frank understandably supported, or perhaps even goaded, her. From impostors and fakes to false press stories, he had fought, almost compulsively, to maintain her unblemished reputation. After all his efforts, the taint of a drug charge would destroy Annie's clean-cut image for all time.

Oakley's friends also rallied, many sending letters and telegrams urging her to sue. One wrote to her in 1903 saying that he would take great satisfaction in seeing "the guilty parties punished" and would regard victorious lawsuits as another trophy in the enormous collection she already had "in the eyes of the American Sportsmen." That same year, reporter Amy Leslie, Annie's old friend, advised her, "Make those people pay you big money." Leslie thought fifty thousand dollars "a small enough sum to demand." She noted, "They have heaped every disgrace on you." Leslie added, "Every decent paper will applaud you."

Furthermore, Oakley was far from alone in her complaints about the sensationalized journalism of the time. During late November of the same year, President Theodore Roosevelt lashed out at the *Boston Herald* after it reported that the Roosevelt children had chased a terrified Thanksgiving turkey around the White House grounds, plucking at it and yelling while their father laughed at their antics. Roosevelt reacted with outrage, especially because the story was one in a long series of "malicious falsehoods"; he cut *Herald* reporters off from "all facilities of information."

Oakley had no similar recourse available to her. Instead, she decided to sue the newspapers involved in maligning her. Annie lodged twenty-five libel suits for twenty five thousand dollars each, then gradually initiated more for a total of fifty-five suits. Since each libel case was fought as a separate action, Oakley's suits took her all over the United States between 1904, when the first trial began, and 1910, when the bulk of them ended. In the largest libel episode to that date, Oakley sued such newspapers as the *Chicago American* and the *Chicago Examiner*, the *St. Louis Star*, the *Brooklyn Citizen*, and the *New Orleans Time-Democrat* for the publication of several false, scandalous, and malicious libels injurious to the good name, fame, credit, and reputation of Oakley.

In 1904, the year the trials began, Annie said that she had no choice. "The only thing left for a person who is slandered in the press in the north is to sue for money." She added that in the South, "They do things differently and simply kill the man who slanders the good name of a woman." Annie also emphasized the importance of Frank's encouragement in her decision. According to her, he had said, "Well, I am able to earn our living if necessary and we will spend what we have to get you justice."

Throughout the trials, an overwhelming number of Annie's fans, friends, sporting journal writers, shooters, and other supporters sent her clippings and wrote letters of support. According to one 1904 observer, Annie had borne up like a "little heroine," with the knowledge that she had the "heartfelt sympathy and confidence of her hundreds of friends in all parts of the country." He added a widely felt sentiment: "Were Miss Oakley to receive a million dollars from her traducers, it would not repay her for the torture and anguish of mind and body she has suffered."

Some of Annie's supporters even took the witness stand on her behalf. Annie too testified, and given her penchant for honesty, she must have regretted changing her age, a deception that required a minor perjury on the witness stand. In 1904, Annie testified that she was thirty-eight, although she was actually forty-four.

In every other way, Oakley proved herself a highly creditable witness. As in the arena, she carefully orchestrated her appearance and impact. She wore small diamond earrings and her hair tinted gray. On one occasion, Annie appeared in a black dress with white cuffs and a bit of red velvet around the collar. Another morning Annie appeared in court in a dark suit, a black hat, and a long black veil that she drew back when she took the witness stand. Most observers remarked favorably on Oakley's courtroom appearances, admiring her "well modulated and low" voice. Jurors seemed charmed as well, leaning forward to hear her describe her life and career in a manner that one observe described as "polished courtesy."

Some defense attorneys also treated Oakley with respect, but others stooped to any ploy to discredit her. Some accused Annie of wanting notoriety, others of seeking money. A few tried to make her past sound as seamy as possible. Court records reveal that a lawyer in Scranton, Pennsylvania, told a twelve-man jury that Annie not only had traveled with the notorious Buffalo Bill but also had been "the companion of red men for seventeen years" and turned handsprings as she finished "her stunt before the people."

In the face of such attacks, Oakley demonstrated aplomb. When the Scranton lawyer stated, "You're the woman who used to shoot out here and run along and turn head over heels, allowing your skirts to fall, and you wore buckskin leggings," she shot back, "I beg your pardon, you're wrong." She explained that she had never worn buckskin leggings, or allowed her "skirts to fall," or showed immodesty in any way. Another day she reportedly subdued a lawyer who asked her to define education. "It is," Annie said, "a very good thing when backed by common sense, and a very bad thing in the head of a cheap lawyer."

During a trial in Charleston, South Carolina, probably in 1906, Oakley finally became provoked by such statements. She attacked the defense attorneys in a statement to the jury. "If the gentlemen who fought for South Carolina during the Civil War conducted their defense with as much cowardice as the defense has been conducted against one little woman in this suit, I don't wonder that they received such a sound thrashing." She then announced her decision to turn around and walk out of the courtroom immediately. "[This will] give one or all of you gentlemen who are such gallant defenders of woman's honor a chance to further your cowardice by shooting me in the back if you so chose."

Oakley's niece Anna Fern Campbell Swartwout, who traveled with Annie during many of the trials, remembered the agony Annie suffered. According to Fern, before a trial date, Annie would "often fast and pray for days" because she believed "her mind was clearer when she got on the witness stand." Annie herself said, "[I] prayed to God every day to only spare my reason so as to let me clear myself of this." Although Annie was despondent because she felt that the affair both aged her and incurred expenses beyond her means, she swore she would keep on until the end.

As it turned out, the end was a long time in coming. Sometimes, court actions dragged on because Oakley's attorneys asked a court to set aside, on the basis of technicalities, verdicts that involved especially small amounts of money. A new trial would follow, so that some of the suits were heard two or even three times. An example occurred in the cases of *Butler v. Evening Post Publishing Company* and *Butler v. News & Courier Company*, heard in the Circuit Court of Appeals, Eighth District, in November 1906. In this instance, the court combined the two cases to "avoid waste of time and unnecessary expense." The plaintiff asked the court to set aside, on the basis of technicalities, the original judgments for the defendants. To Annie's satisfaction, the court honored her request and remanded both cases for new hearings.

In other cases, defendants caused delays by resisting the settlements that juries awarded. In November 1905, the jury that heard *Butler v. Every Evening Printing Company* in the Delaware Circuit Court awarded Oakley thirty-six hundred dollars and court costs. The defendant asked the court to set the verdict aside, partially because of the "excessive" sum involved. After additional hearings, the court upheld the original judgment on the basis of other similar cases in which juries decreed larger awards even though "the libel was not more gross or injurious than that in question." In May of the following year, when the Every Evening Printing Company also asked for a revised decision on the basis of technicalities, once again the court upheld the original judgment.

Newspaper magnate William Randolph Hearst carried his defense one step further. In 1906, he sent a detective to Greenville to investigate Oakley's background and find some tidbit that Hearst could use to quiet her in the courtroom. Overall, the detective succeeded in doing little except annoying the citizens of Greenville. An outraged Greenville editor called the possibility that Annie had any dirt in her history "absurd" and labeled Hearst's investigation "a base libel" against the county's favorite daughter.

After the bulk of the trials ended in 1910, Annie had little more to say publicly about her ordeal. She was presumably exhausted, wrung out from warm support on the one hand and bitter attacks on the other. Frank, however, in a short article titled "Annie Oakley's Vindication" and released from their home base at a New York City hotel, breathed an almost palpable sigh of relief. Annie,

he wrote, had appeared in courts in nearly every state in the
Union. She had sued fifty-five papers and either won or settled
with fifty-four of them. Most verdicts favored her, although
courts sometimes reduced the amount decreed by the jury in the
original verdict. Some of these cases Annie had fought up to the
Supreme Court. "The general impression is that she made a lot of
money out of these suits," Butler remarked. He added that if
Annie had indeed made "a bundle," they would have contributed
every dollar above her expenses and lost earnings to charity.
Annie, he insisted, did not seek money. She wanted vindication.

Still, people generally believed that Annie had profited. An
opposing lawyer estimated that Oakley received a quarter of a
million dollars; Annie's niece Fern put it closer to $800,000. But
no one seemed to take into account the costs involved. When the
hurtful article appeared in 1903, Annie had been about to open in
Langdon McCormick's new play *Out of the Fold*. She forfeited that
income as well as money from the matches she could have shot had
she not been in court. In addition, Frank Butler and his brother
Will spent a good deal of time investigating details and collecting
documentation.

Also, the amounts awarded Annie were seldom large. Her
largest award, $27,500, came from William Randolph Hearst.
Another sizable one, $20,000, came from the *St. Louis Star*.
Others typically fell under $5,000. In Oakley's suit against a
Topeka newspaper, the court awarded damages of only $1,000,
although the jury had ruled for a much larger amount.

Rather than a large monetary return, Annie seems to have
garnered a psychological reward. She was back in control, even
though she had gambled her entire life and career. Had Annie
failed in her quest for what she regarded as justice, she might have
never worked again. Her place in history might have been that of a
money-hungry, vindictive ex-star. The newspaper reporters who
had helped build Oakley's career and had contributed plaudit
after plaudit might have consigned her to infamy or have forgotten her entirely.

As it was, Annie not only won most of the cases but also won
back the favor of most newspaper reporters. Fortunately for her,
even those affected by court judgments upheld her cause. Some

went so far as to suggest that reporter Ernest Stout had been taking dope when he wrote the original story. When the trials dragged to an end, most reporters resumed attending Annie's matches and exhibitions and reviewing them with the usual enthusiasm. A few years after the *Hoboken Observer* paid out $3,000 to Oakley, one of its reporters sent her a favorable clipping accompanied by a note. "Although you dug into us for three thousand 'Iron Men' at a time when three thousand was a large sum with us—you see we still love you."

The home folks in Greenville also continued to praise their favorite daughter. In a county history published shortly after the trials ended, one of them called Annie the "frail little woman" who expended $90,000 and a lot of grit to fight some of the most prominent newspapers and "brainy men" in the country. Oakley won, he concluded, an almost unanimous verdict in justification of her outstanding and unblemished character. Family members also sided with her; according to Annie's descendant Beatrice Blakely Hunt, they believed that Annie sued not to make money but to protect her good name.

During the prime trial years, 1904 to 1909, Frank continued to work for the Union Metallic Cartridge Company to support himself and Annie and pay for the cost of litigation. Butler spent most of his time on the road for UMC, taking part in matches and setting up a canvas tent and a table with UMC advertising and gifts, such as Annie Oakley pins and UMC flags. Although early in his time with Annie, Frank had admitted that he would never outshoot Annie—or many others either—he now proved himself a competent shooter. When Frank first joined UMC in 1901, he shot so well in a match that one observer quipped, "He [Frank] must be working for a promotion from the way he is pulverizing his targets lately." Then in May 1903, Frank shot in a match at the West Branch Road and Gun Club in Pennsylvania and tied for second place with the state champion.

Frank also served in other capacities at matches. In a 1903 match at Wilkes-Barre, Frank, representing UMC, acted as squad judge in the live bird events. One source reported, "[Butler's] reputation is so wide that it would be needless to say more than he pleased every man who went to the trap for the fairness he displayed." Clearly, people loved Frank. Sometimes his reputation even overshadowed that of Annie during these years. A 1903 announcement stated that Frank Butler had arrived in town to participate in a match and that his wife, "who was Annie Oakley, formerly with the 'Buffalo Bill' show," might shoot as well. The following year, a similar notice reported, "[The] only Frank Butler is with us." In 1906 alone, Frank shot a remarkable total of two hundred matches.

While on the road, Frank made a number of new friends. Sometime during the trial years, Butler met comedian Fred Stone, who had also traveled with a circus at one time and then in 1895 had gone on the stage with his partner, Dave Montgomery. Later, Stone would play the scarecrow and Montgomery the tinman in *The Wizard of Oz*. In 1907, Stone hunted with Butler, who turned him into a trap-shooter. Fred soon built three traps on his Long Island farm and invited Frank and Annie to visit, and to tutor, him. A lifelong friendship developed among Fred Stone, his actress wife, Allene Crater Stone, Frank, and Annie, a friendship that proved to be an unexpected benefit the Butlers accrued from Frank's time as a traveling representative for UMC.

Over the years, match shooting provided both benefits and difficulties for Annie Oakley and Frank Butler. Still, they maintained the energy and enthusiasm to stage in addition a large number of exhibitions, especially during the 1890s and early 1900s. Like match shooting, exhibition shooting required agility and coordination, but it tended to be a more individual matter that called for great endurance. Rather than shooting in selected events, competing against other shooters or sometimes with other shooters, Annie alone carried an exhibition. Her typical program, which demanded both concentration and speed, included shooting coins tossed in the air, firing in rapid succession at small bull's-eyes, splitting a playing card held edgewise, sighting in a table knife to shoot objects behind her, hitting five targets thrown up at one time, clipping off with a repeating rifle piece after piece from a potato held on a stick, snuffing out cigars held in an assistant's fingers, and smashing marbles so small that only puffs of white dust gave evidence of their destruction.

Annie once explained that she had refrained from giving exhibitions until one occasion when her "love of shooting" finally influenced her to accept an invitation. Afterward, she came to recognize exhibitions as opportunities to "show the world that shooting was a healthful exercise and pastime that might be followed with benefit to health." Of course, exhibitions also brought in extra money, as well as advertising Annie Oakley. Only when working for the Wild West did Annie agree to neither advertise nor charge an entrance fee for her exhibitions. Presumably, Cody and Salsbury viewed Oakley's exhibitions as in direct competition with their show and feared that such exhibitions might siphon away viewers. Probably an opposite principle operated: the more people who read about or watched Annie, the more who also developed an interest in attending a performance of the Wild West.

But Oakley's agreement with Cody caused no major difficulties for her because newspapers gave her enough free advertising in notices and reviews, and the organizers of exhibitions often sent Frank a handsome monetary "gift" the following day. Annie remembered that while in London, she shot many exhibitions at "London fetes," and no one ever mentioned compensation. "The following day my husband and manager, Mr. Butler, always received a check for 50 pounds, $250." According to Annie, she earned $750 extra in a single week. In other cases, however, Annie shot exhibitions absolutely without charge. In Vienna in 1891, for example, she returned the gift of a purse of gold. She requested that its owner give it instead to the orphans' home that had been the beneficiary of her exhibition.

As with match shooting, Oakley used exhibitions to interest women in shooting. As early as 1888, when the Boston Gun Club issued an invitation to members for a "private exhibition shoot" to be held on April 19, featuring Annie, the invitations explicitly included members' "lady friends." Then the invitations added, perhaps at Oakley's instigation, that "ladies" were "specially invited to participate" and would receive a "cordial welcome."

As the years passed, Annie increasingly extended special invitations to women viewers and expressed her hope that her feats would encourage other women to take up shooting. But Annie, always tactful and never strident, appealed to women in a way that would not offend men. As a result, Annie drew large numbers of both female and male fans to her exhibitions, which usually combined skill with her own humorous touches. In other cases, her skill created humor unintentionally, as at the Boston Gun Club in 1888, when two viewers tossed half-dollars in the air for her to mark as souvenirs. The force of her bullets carried the coins into oblivion, and "roars of laughter greeted the disappointed souvenir hunters."

Despite huge crowds and attendant confusion, Annie's good nature usually triumphed. When, in 1896, Oakley shot an exhibition in Greenville, Ohio, one observer noted that the surging crowd strained the resources of the police but contained "over four hundred ladies" who lent calm and charm to the occasion. While Annie shot, a mass of friends and well-wishers jostled her, yet she continued to smile and perform.

Soon, medals and gifts began pouring in. In February 1887, a gun club in Pine Brook, New Jersey, presented Oakley with another handsome gold medal inscribed from "her many friends and admirers." Then, during the summer of 1887 the Notting Hill Gun Club in London gave her a gold medal, the first it ever presented, with an engraving of the Notting Hill grounds on its face and with an inscription on its clasps, "Presented to Miss Annie Oakley by the members of the London Gun Club, June 11, 1887." When Annie later shot in Marseilles, France, she received three medals in three weeks.

Over time, Annie also received a sterling silver tea service, silver loving cups, a set of Limoges china, other Limoges pieces including an umbrella stand, a set of crystal glassware, a dagger in a gold-leaf scabbard, and jewelry, including pins, brooches, bracelets, necklaces, and rings. During the mid-1890s, a countess in Paris unclasped her bracelet, which contained seven handsome Roman mosaics, and gave it to Oakley in recognition of her skill. When Annie gave an exhibition to benefit the orphans' home in Vienna, Baroness Rothschild gave her a heavy link pin, each link encrusted with diamonds.

In response, Annie always gave short but gracious thank-you speeches. At Notting Hill, she proclaimed her enthusiasm for

England and promised to wear the club's medal with pleasure. Usually, however, Annie donned only a few of her medals for publicity photographs and special appearances. True to her word, she always wore her favorite, the Notting Hill medal, with obvious pleasure. But Annie never wore any of the jewelry she received or, for that matter, much of any kind of jewelry. When her fans asked to see Annie's collection of medals and jewelry, Frank began shipping it around the United States and Europe and displaying it. As early as June 1891, he laid out in Belgium a magnificent assortment of gold and silver medals as well as gold brooches, bracelets, and rings, some with diamonds or other stones.

Clearly, exhibition shooting often proved more materially rewarding than match shooting, for a shooter could not lose in an exhibition. Still, exhibitions posed their own difficulties. Among these were the frequent presence of scoffers and doubters. At one Tennessee exhibition, a group of skeptics put their heads together and grumbled that Annie Oakley used artifice to achieve her tricks. They even talked of wagering fifty dollars to prove it. Then they witnessed Annie shoot a meadowlark on the wing, smash a brick tossed in the air, and with her second barrel, shatter a piece of the brick as it fell toward the ground. The knot of critics dispersed, forgot their talk of a fifty-dollar wager, and joined the growing ranks of Annie Oakley fans.

Advice-seekers also hounded Annie and sapped her energy. People who wanted to shoot as well as she did asked her again and again for her opinion. In 1891, she responded: "[Shooting] is just like pointing your finger at the object. . . . Do not look at your gun, but simply follow the object with the end of it."

Around 1900, Oakley admitted that she had often taken lightly inquiries regarding her shooting; she had believed they came from curious people. When she finally realized that such people "really wished to be enlightened," Annie issued a more comprehensive statement. "You must shoot until you overcome confusion at quickly sighting on a moving object," she advised. In other words, a would-be shooter had to practice. Annie continued, "When the game is flushed you naturally bring the gun to the shoulder, glance along the barrel, aim directly at the game, or make the proper allowance ahead, above, or below, according to the direction the game is going, press the trigger and feel that you have finished your effort, regardless of the result." She further advised a slow, deliberate shot but explained that she did not mean a "slow, pottering shot," which was little more than a "bad habit." Oakley concluded by reemphasizing the necessity of practice, which would, she argued, "usually make steadiness."

In addition to pressure from advice-seekers, an occasional conflict, such as the one-eye, two-eye debate, engulfed Annie. Although such controversies may now seem petty, they absorbed a good deal of time, energy, and newsprint. They also provide examples of the type of flare-ups that impinged on Annie's personal life and made her long for privacy. The one-eye, two-eye discussion, for example, began innocently enough in 1887 when an ardent shooter raised the question of which was better, sighting with one eye or two. Annie replied, "I will say that I always shoot with both eyes open . . . but I don't mean to say that there are no good shots who shut one eye." Another shooting fan responded that he had tested shooters who claimed they kept both eyes open, only to discover that they actually squinted one eye at the moment of sighting.

At this point, English gunmaker Charles Lancaster stepped in on Annie's behalf. During the summer of 1887, Lancaster had helped Annie overcome her difficulty with the English pigeons called blue rocks, which, according to Frank, flew like "lightning." In Annie's view, Lancaster proved himself "a wide-awake gun maker," for after noticing that she used an American-made gun weighing seven and one-half pounds and measuring a three-inch drop in the stock, Lancaster made her a lighter gun with less drop. Of Lancaster's gun, with its twenty-eight-inch barrel, six-pound weight, light trigger pull, and short stock, Annie said, "The fit is perfection." Lancaster and Oakley became friends, and Annie improved her blue rock scores. Now Lancaster declared that whether a shooter used one eye or two depended on the drop in a gun's stock. He noted that Americans tended to use stocks with a lot of drop, which allowed the gun to come well under the right eye.

Out of this debate came a related dispute, one that must have tried Annie's patience because she finally withdrew from it. The

20-bore dispute erupted from Lancaster's mention of the 20-bore guns he was making for Annie. A London hunter replied that 20-bores were far too light for use in the field. From Berlin, Oakley responded that Lancaster's 20-bores suited her fine and had less recoil than heavier guns. She concluded that she had nothing further to say. "I do not wish to be mixed up in any controversy."

Several of Annie's fans seemed displeased at her defection. As illustrated here, the public's incessant demands on Annie's time and energy may partly explain her occasional retreats from public exposure and her almost obsessive need to keep her life tidy. This dispute also reveals just how much Annie lived in the public eye and how tiring it must have been for her. In this instance, one fan accused her of failing to understand 12-bores and 20-bores. Others spoke out for small bores, whereas still others supported large bores.

Still, Annie held herself aloof. The debate ground to a halt when Annie began to grass—or bring down—most of her birds at a distance of twenty-three yards using her new 20-bore guns from Lancaster. After she defeated the birds she described as "little blue streaks of birds that made for the high stone wall like greased lightning," there seemed little left to say against 20-bores.

In spite of such controversies and other drawbacks to exhibition shooting, Annie regularly accepted invitations to demonstrate her skills. Also, sometime during the early 1900s, she joined a rifle squad sponsored by UMC and the Remington Arms Company, firms that eventually merged in 1912. Annie traveled with the UMC squad for a number of years. Probably organized by Frank Butler, the squad consisted of Annie, Frank, and several other men. In 1909, the squad, which then included Annie, Frank, Captain Tom Marshall, who had twice won the Grand American Handicap, William Heer, who held the world's target-shooting records, and George W. Maxwell, who with one arm had won several state championships and the western handicap, drew fifteen hundred people to an exhibition in Bradford, Pennsylvania.

Obviously, Frank shared Annie's love of sport shooting and was widely known among sport shooters. Butler traveled extensively, shot all over Europe and the United States, and twice held the championship of New Jersey. He was one of the first to use his own shooting as advertising for his company. When Frank resigned from UMC in 1909, the year before Annie went with Vernon Seavers's Young Buffalo Show, *Forest and Stream* stated, "No one's retirement from the professional ranks is more heartily regretted."

After the Butlers joined Vernon Seavers's Young Buffalo Show in 1911, however, Annie gave more exhibitions than Frank, who now returned to his post as her manager. During shows, Annie shot in the company of seventy-eight-year-old Captain Adam Bogardus, who had also returned to the "show" business, but between shows, she gave exhibitions. On March 2, 1912, for example, Oakley shot at the annual Sportsman Show in Madison Square Garden.

Years later, Annie wrote that she had given exhibitions in fourteen different countries. "I have met the enthusiastic shooters of different lands, from the titled nobleman to the person occupying the humblest station in life, and, too, from the lady of royal blood to the rancher's daughter." She was pleased that all "were infatuated with that love of shooting which makes an equality among the shooting fraternity far and near."

Between matches and exhibitions, Annie loved to hunt. As early as 1893, at the height of her fame, Annie admitted, "Truly I long for the day when my work with the rifle and gun will be over with, and when I can take to the field and stream as often as true inclination may lead me there." A few years later she exclaimed, "I have a preference for game shooting, a sport that seems to increase as I grow older."

Perhaps Oakley loved hunting because she began her shooting career as a game hunter or perhaps because hunting allowed her more freedom than did commercial shooting. Or maybe commercial shooting was finally beginning to wear her down. Annie often said that she did fancy shooting only "for the money" there was "in the practice." Then, in 1900 she stated, "I care very little for exhibition shooting, and only do it as a matter of business." She added, "I love to shoot in the field."

Oddly enough, hunting was the only shooting endeavor that

brought Annie satisfaction but no income, an interesting turn-about, since hunting had brought in her first wages. She no longer went into the field as a game hunter, as she had when young; now she sought relaxation and sport there.

Of course, Annie had never given up her first love, hunting. Every time Annie and Frank visited Ohio, they hunted. Irene Patterson Black, the daughter of Annie's half-sister, Emily Brum-baugh Patterson, and thus a niece of Annie's, remembered that during Annie's visits, the family could be assured of a tasty evening meal. When the women brought up the subject of supper, Annie went to the woods and brought down a quail or other small game. She then returned to the kitchen, laid out some news-papers, and plucked the birds, without leaving a feather behind her to litter the table or floor. In addition, Annie cleared her mother's farm of snakes. According to the nearest neighbor, Lela Border Hollinger, Annie hit blue racers and blacksnakes as they sunned themselves on the old wooden fence.

Frank and Annie also hunted in between Wild West perfor-mances. On one occasion, she, Frank, and Johnny Baker went hunting and bagged, in Annie's words, "a large hare brought down by Johnny Baker, and a small roebuck brought in by a briar-scratched Annie Oakley." Other times, they downed prairie chick-ens, rabbits, ducks, and grouse.

Annie and Frank also accepted numerous invitations to hunt. In 1887, for example, they gratefully accepted Englishman R. Edward Clark's invitation to hunt with him. Annie and Frank subsequently spent twelve days roaming over Clark's five thou-sand acres, "shooting partridges, pheasants and black cock," despite "the latter being scarce and the mountain climbing hard." Rising at dawn to follow the pointers for twelve to fifteen hours and returning to "a hot bath, a delicious dinner," and "gathering around to open fire in easy chairs to talk over the day's sport and bygone days," all followed by a 9:30 bedtime, was Annie's kind of life.

Then, in 1888, Annie and Frank hunted in Virginia. "We both enjoyed the quail shoot in the Shenandoah valley," Annie recalled. "The shooting was hard enough to bring the blood to our cheeks." She brought down three birds before her guest got off a shot and, during the course of the hunt, killed twice as many birds as he and three times as many as Frank.

When, in 1896, Annie and Frank hunted near Hot Springs, Arkansas, a member of the party wrote that Oakley killed quail while others hoisted their guns to their shoulders. He joked that because she shot so rapidly, he twice shot at one of her birds after she had already killed it. In that hunt, Annie killed sixteen more birds than any other hunter.

The following fall, the Butlers hunted in Crowson, Tennessee, where one observer remarked that Annie's shooting in the field "excited a great deal of admiration from all who were fortunate enough to see" this "clever hunter." Tennessee hunter Joe Eakin, who held a record of six dozen quail in one day, said of her, "Miss Annie's so quick with her gun that if you want to get a shot at a bird you must shoot mighty quick or wait till she misses, and that may keep you waiting some time."

Despite her love of hunting and her accuracy, Annie sometimes demonstrated sympathy for her quarries. She recalled that while in Germany, she spent a day hunting on a private preserve where she hoped to "shoot a roebuck." When she entered a five-acre tract of buckwheat, Annie spotted three roebuck just as "they filled their little mouths with the green sweet." Her guide instructed her to bring down the male. But because she always preferred to give the game a fair chance by shooting them on the move, Annie replied, "Not for a million marks." She later remembered, "Just then I gave a low whistle and three little heads went up like lightning, and three pairs of clean little heels were about all we could see as they entered the thick clover."

Another time, Annie did shoot at a roebuck but failed to make a clean kill. Because she had no more cartridges, she crept into the thicket to help the wounded deer. She grabbed one of its hind legs, then whistled for Frank's assistance. But Frank mistakenly seized her heels, so both Annie and the deer rapidly emerged from the thicket backward.

Like Annie, Frank also loved to hunt and sometimes proved his own brand of cleverness. In 1903, when a band of hunters near Atlantic City, New Jersey, chased down a UMC banner "rising, falling and waving over the reeds," they discovered Frank Butler using it to flush out mud hens. Butler immediately supplied them with similar banners and gave out UMC advertising packets to more than twenty hunters in boats.

Of course, hunting also had its dangers. Both Annie and Frank recognized the perils involved in hunting, especially after a stray bullet hit the field clubhouse in Nutley, New Jersey, and another came close to hitting Frank while he hunted in a field nearby. A few years later, Annie, or perhaps Frank if he was indeed its author, included a safety statement in the pamphlet titled *Annie Oakley*. It concluded that anyone handling a firearm carelessly or aiming at a person he or she "did not intend to shoot" deserved to be forever shunned.

To both Annie and Frank, a careful and dedicated hunter was the ultimate sportsperson. Annie liked to relate an incident that occurred when she played in Milan. A telegram to a gun club member on a hunt in Africa advised him, "Your manager has robbed you and skipped." The intense hunter replied: "Cannot leave. Am on the track of a lion."

As a match and exhibition shooter, as well as a hunter, between 1885 and 1913 Annie Oakley established herself in the annals of American sports. The guns, medals, and other memorabilia she and Frank Butler collected at first filled trunks, then entire rooms. Many who viewed Annie and Frank's collection of guns, medals, and gifts ranked it as the finest in the United States and Europe.

As an entertainer, Annie's reputation would have persisted to some degree, but Oakley extended herself beyond the Wild West arena. Thus, she gained widespread respect as a competitor who was also obviously a skilled athlete. These qualities gave her reputation incredible longevity. Since Annie's death, more articles about her have appeared in sports and hunting magazines than in any other type of publication. The premier edition of the *Winchester Repeater*, published in 1986 by the Winchester Club of America, carried just one story about a shooter. That shooter was Annie Oakley.

Moreoever, Annie Oakley, sport shooter and hunter, bridged the world of women and men. With what was then regarded as feminine dignity and decorum, Annie operated in a male culture based on guns, shooting, and killing. At the same time, Annie proved herself as competition-minded as any man; she was pleased that she beat Frank Butler in their initial match and delighted that she later bested male competitors or outshot other hunters. Because Annie found it possible to combine sweetness with toughness, and recognized the benefits of doing so, she not only opened the world of sport shooting for herself but worked to slash a wide enough path for other women to follow.

Annie Oakley, Frank Butler, and poodle George, 1884. Courtesy of the Annie Oakley Foundation, Greenville, Ohio.

Annie Oakley with shotgun, ca. mid-1880s. No medals as yet adorn her chest.
Courtesy of the Buffalo Bill Historical Center, Cody, Wyoming.

Annie Oakley with some of her early guns, medals, and a loving cup, ca. mid to late 1880s. Courtesy of the Buffalo Bill Historical Center, Cody, Wyoming.

A Buffalo Bill Wild West lithograph advertising Annie Oakley, "The Peerless Lady Wing-Shot," ca. 1890. Courtesy of the Buffalo Bill Historical Center, Cody, Wyoming.

Annie in 1896 at age thirty-six in New York City. Courtesy of the Annie
Oakley Foundation, Greenville, Ohio.

Annie and Frank's home in Nutley, New Jersey. Courtesy of the Nutley Historical Society, Nutley, New Jersey.

Annie Oakley, ca. 1900. Courtesy of the Buffalo Bill Historical Center, Cody, Wyoming.

Annie's husband, Frank Butler, in New Jersey in 1902. Courtesy of the
Annie Oakley Foundation, Greenville, Ohio.

Annie as star of *The Western Girl* in 1902. Courtesy of the Annie Oakley Foundation, Greenville, Ohio.

Annie Oakley breaking five targets thrown in the air at one time, place and date unknown. Courtesy of the Nutley Historical Society, Nutley, New Jersey.

Annie with lariat, undated (probably ca. 1913). Courtesy of the Annie Oakley Foundation, Greenville, Ohio.

Dave holds an apple for Annie Oakley, place and date unknown. Courtesy of the Nutley Historical Society, Nutley, New Jersey.

Annie and friend Eddie Hoff, age seven, of New York, 1922. Courtesy of the Annie Oakley Foundation, Greenville, Ohio.

Annie shooting with her left hand (she was ambidextrous), probably in 1926.
Courtesy of the Annie Oakley Foundation, Greenville, Ohio.

One of the few surviving letters written by Annie Oakley. Written in 1923, three years before her death. Courtesy of the Nutley Historical Society, Nutley, New Jersey.

Annie's and Frank's graves near Brock, Ohio. Courtesy of the Annie Oakley Foundation, Greenville, Ohio.

Painting done for the New Jersey Bell Telephone Company for a September 1964 Tel-News program. The drawing shows Annie Oakley shooting from a sidesaddle. Courtesy of the Nutley Historical Society, Nutley, New Jersey.

CHAPTER 4

"To be considered a lady"

DO Annie Oakley's efforts to open arenic and shooting sports to women between 1885 and 1913 mean she was a feminist? Oakley herself would have rejected such a designation and claimed instead that she was a model Victorian lady. Closest to the truth is that Annie defied convention on one level but embraced it on another. On the one hand, like any avowed feminist, Annie tested and broadened the limits of women's sphere. On the other hand, however, she clung to the concept of ladyhood, thus wrapping the cloak of respectability around her efforts to stretch the acceptable boundaries of women's activities.

This duality often resulted in a seemingly contradictory Annie Oakley. One September day in 1891, for example, Annie buckled her skirt around her ankles, stood on her head, seized a gun, and turned it upside down. From this unladylike position, she yelled "Pull," then smashed a clay pigeon into smithereens. But when the London gunmaker who witnessed the feat reported it to the public, Frank Butler felt compelled to justify Annie's behavior. Frank assured the public that Annie could hit both clay and live pigeons while standing on her head but that she did so only in private or in the presence of "a few intimate friends." In the arena, he explained, Annie left the trick to the Cowboy Kid, Johnny Baker, for she considered "it not proper for a lady to do."

For years, Annie had ranked ladylike conduct high on her list of priorities. Both her Quaker background and her midwestern values encouraged her to accept many of the era's prescriptions regarding true womanhood. But acting like a lady also offered Annie definite advantages. Victorian ladyhood carried with it an extensive body of rules, rules that would allow Annie to keep her life and environment under strict control. Acting like a lady also protected Annie from the slurs and slights cast at show, vaudeville, and Wild West women during her day. No one could, or did, put Annie into the stereotypical category of fast-living, low-acting, and hard "show women." In addition, because a lady usually originated from the middle or upper classes rather than from rural poverty, ladyhood meant social mobility—a step upward—for Annie. She associated with the best people, received respectful treatment, and established residences wherever she chose.

Understandably, then, even more than favorable press reviews, Oakley thrived on compliments regarding her ladylike behavior. While in London in 1887, for example, she received what she regarded as the highest compliment of her life. As she tried to grass—or bring down—the notoriously fast English blue rock pigeons, J. J. Walsh, editor of London's *Field*, watched quietly. Annie hit only five birds out of twenty and, in her words, "could have been led home easily by a lingerie ribbon." When Walsh approached her after the match, he proffered an accolade she always cherished: "Miss Oakley, I certainly expected to find you a better shot than you are, but not to find you so much of a lady."

The following year in Paris in 1888, Annie publicly revealed that her "highest ambition" had always been "to be considered a lady." Although she excelled in a predominantly male profession—the Wild West arena—and bested men at their own sport—shooting and hunting—she had no desire to wear trousers, gamble with the fellows, or swagger and swear. Nor did Oakley seek independence, power, or such political prerogatives as suffrage or the right to hold office.

Instead, Annie fully intended to maintain the numerous qualities that society of the time associated with a real lady. Like the majority of Americans of her day, Annie believed that a quintessential Victorian woman must embody five major qualities. A genuine lady should be modest, married, domestic, benevolent, and a civilizing force.

According to prevailing social standards of the late nineteenth and early twentieth centuries, a lady always demonstrated modesty, whatever the circumstances. For one thing, a true lady always maintained an attractive yet demure appearance. Because Annie adhered to these standards throughout her life, she often startled people. In 1888, for example, a reporter went to an interview with her fully expecting to meet a "strong, virile, masculine-like woman, of loud voice, tall of stature and of massive proportions." On the contrary, Annie stood five feet tall and weighed a little more than one hundred pounds. Despite the strong hands and taut muscles Annie developed first from farmwork as a girl then from working with six-pound and heavier guns, people invariably described her as little, tiny, dainty, and girlish.

Oakley fostered this image by wearing her hair long and loose. She also avoided wearing makeup, jewelry, or her medals, for she feared she would look "a vain, foolish girl." The overall effect enhanced her best features—her blue-gray eyes and her smile—so that most people judged her good-looking and even sexually appealing. In 1894, the *Brooklyn Citizen* described her as "the wonderful woman" who could "leap like a gazelle, run like a deer, shoot faster and straighter than any cowboy in the troupe" and who was "pretty to boot."

Annie also favored feminine, modest apparel, innocent of what one fan called "man-slaying artifices." Oakley always wore plain but elegantly cut dresses or skirts and blouses—as a woman of the middle or upper classes should. Even when performing in the arena, shooting in matches, giving exhibitions, or hunting, Annie refused to wear trousers or other masculine attire. Instead, she donned skirted outfits of fine broadcloth or tan gabardine materials that resembled buckskin but were lighter and easier to maintain. During the summer, she switched to costumes of washable material, usually in blues or tans.

When Annie first traveled abroad in 1887, her simple style of dress aroused a great deal of interest among English women. One wrote to *Society Times* praising Oakley's riding costume, which she thought "cool, comfortable, and handsome." According to Annie, this letter resulted in so many requests for dress patterns that she could have started a "business as a lady's tailor."

When Annie returned to England during the early 1890s, many people asked what English women should wear while shooting. In 1892, Annie responded that they would have to reform their usual costumes, for it was "impossible to shoot brilliantly in a tight-fitting bodice—absolutely impossible." Moreover, ladies who walked through "fields of wet roots . . . wearing skirts down to the ground" would get soaked and muddy. Their pleasure would soon "give way to misery." Annie recommended instead a loose-fitting bodice of some soft material, preferably tweed, and a skirt falling halfway between the knee and the ankle, a costume that would be both becoming and practical.

The following year, however, she drew back a bit by saying she would not advocate any one costume. "For I have been in the habit of clothing myself to suit each climate, always taking good care to keep my feet dry and warm." Perhaps women had complained that such outfits elicited strange reactions, especially from men. Certainly, Annie received her share of shocked looks. That very year, Bergen County farmers had plainly showed their discomfort when they encountered Annie, out hunting in a ladylike but utilitarian outfit, including calf-length skirts and stout leggings.

Clearly, Annie was determined to retain the public's high opinion of her, and ensure her entrance into high society, by looking as much like a lady as possible, although pursuing what were then regarded as men's sports. Even when clothing styles relaxed among some women, especially arena "cowgirls," Annie maintained her formal ladylike look. While other women adopted bloomer outfits, split skirts, and trousers, Annie wore skirts. As a result, these women often elicited such terms as hard, sexy, and loose, whereas Annie remained soft, sexual, and chaste.

In 1899, for example, while sport shooting, Oakley wore a tailor-made suit of dove-colored cloth, an ankle-length skirt, a military-style jacket with rolling collar and loose sleeves, and a loose-fitting waist of red checked silk set off by a high white collar with a silk tie matching the waist. On her feet she wore heavy-soled, tan shoes that laced to the ankle. According to one observer, Annie's hat was "a feature in itself." It had a brim of stiff felt that extended four inches in width around her head and refused to flap in the strongest wind, a crown of soft felt, and a wide silk band with a few feathers in it.

When Annie shot in the 1902 Grand American Handicap, she wore a similar outfit, but designed for summer wear. Annie appeared in a loose-fitting bodice, an ankle-length full skirt, sturdy flat-heeled shoes, and a female version of a bowler hat. At the reception following the match, she posed for a photograph with the other shooters—all men attired in dark suits and gleaming starched collars. In her long-sleeved, high-collared, long-skirted dress of light color, perhaps gray or lavender, Oakley stood out, yet still looked modest and demure.

In private life, Annie followed a similar style but allowed herself a few more furbelows, including plain but elegant gowns, elaborate hats, fur collars, and fur muffs. For instance, in 1892, she attended a reception dressed in a pearl-gray silk dress with salmon trim, high sleeves, and a large white hat featuring Brussels lace and white ostrich feathers. Gone forever was the gingham that Annie reportedly wore in that first, significant match against Frank Butler back in Ohio. Annie's appearance was no longer that of a poor farm girl; she now looked the part of a Victorian lady.

Besides her dress, Oakley demonstrated her modesty in other ways. She adhered to prevailing standards of female decorum by refusing to ride a horse astride. In keeping with her beliefs, Annie declared riding astride a "horrid idea." Instead, she performed horseback tricks from a sidesaddle, a contraption with a flat seat, on which the rider sat sideways, and a thick, leather-covered hook, which the rider used to anchor herself by her leg to the horse's back. In exhibitions, using this device and wearing full, ankle-length skirts, Annie Oakley lay back against her horse while traveling at a gallop. With her skirt draped gracefully over her legs, she pointed her rifle in the air and almost always hit her target. Or Annie might sit upright, shooting while her mount jumped a fence.

In the arena, Oakley refrained from shooting while riding, perhaps to avoid competing with Cody, but she would retrieve a handkerchief or her hat from the ground by dangling off the side of her horse from the sidesaddle or by draping herself across the horse's back and reaching down the other side. Using the sidesaddle to her advantage, Annie created the illusion, whatever her mount's speed and gait, that she floated on the horse's back.

Reporters must have been tempted to spice up Oakley's restrained image and present her to the public in a more dramatic guise, yet newspaper publicity was amazingly accurate most of the time, perhaps because of Frank Butler's diligence in supplying editors and reporters with information and photographs. Only occasionally did publicity appear that must have rankled both Frank and Annie. In June 1892, one London newspaper raved about Annie's sweet personality, saying she was "one of the most unaffected, good natured girls conceivable." But next to this item appeared a sketch of a woman, presumably Annie Oakley, with unkempt, curly hair and bedroom eyes. She wore a sexy blouse, a very short skirt that barely covered her hips, tight-fitting boots, and held a smoking gun. One can only wonder whether Annie's ladylike demeanor remained in place when she saw this picture.

Other descriptions that may have irritated Annie appeared at home rather than abroad. In 1893, one reporter claimed that Annie favored "a saucy dress of scarlet plush and embroidered buckskins," which she wore as she "dance[d] herself over the vast lawn where the soldiers prance[d]." In 1898, Amy Leslie similarly misrepresented Annie's arena costume as a "jaunty doll-skirt habit of military blue, trimmed with silver braid and lined with white pique, from under which flutters the most fascinating assortment of lingerie, which might fill with envy the top tray of a ballet girl."

An especially annoying report appeared in *Field and Stream* just after Annie returned from her second trip to Europe during the early 1890s. Although her frequent walking and riding kept her trim and attractive, the magazine reported with little tact that Annie had returned from Europe a bit chubbier than when she left. "'Little Sure Shot' has not grown any 'littler' since her extended vacation, but has increased in avoirdupois."

These and other similar comments indicate that Annie, like it or not, lived most of her life in the public eye. Moreover, both the public and the media were ready to pounce on any indiscretion, unusual item of clothing, or even a slight weight gain. Why Annie's own friend, Amy Leslie, would publicly describe Annie as a woman who favored frilly lingerie is difficult to explain, unless Leslie hoped to soften Annie's often austere image. Or Leslie may have simply wanted to increase her own readership. In either case, Leslie's misrepresentation must have given Annie pause, making her more cautious than ever regarding both female friends and the press.

In Annie's day, a second component of true ladyhood was marriage. Annie Oakley not only married as a young girl but stayed married until her death in 1926. In 1902, she remarked that she "was rather an oddity among professional women," for in twenty years, she had had only one husband. The following year, reporter Amy Leslie described Annie, the woman and wife, as "plain, kindly, homelike and genuine." According to Leslie, the Butlers' married life was quiet and domestic; they lived "one of the most retired, modest, commonplace sorts of life" when not on the road.

Annie and Frank had what reformers of the era termed a companionate marriage. Respect, reciprocity, and romance characterized their personal relationship, which was based on companionship rather than a male-dominant, female-subordinate model. Equality and versatile roles defined their public relationship, which was a business partnership rather than a male-breadwinner type.

In addition, over the years Annie's and Frank's economic contributions shifted back and forth, but neither saw the other as a lesser partner. At first, Frank earned most of their income. Then Annie joined him on the stage. When Frank realized her superior skills, he retired from the act and became her manager. In 1901, Annie left Buffalo Bill's Wild West, and Frank resumed the major responsibility for supporting them. Both, however, toured with the Union Metallic Cartridge Company's exhibition team. In 1911, Annie joined the Young Buffalo Show, and Frank resumed his position as manager until she retired in 1913.

Frank played a critical role in both their marriage and their business partnership. Perhaps, like Annie, his early life convinced him that a good income was far more important than who earned it. Or possibly he appreciated the rewards in being the behind-the-scenes person. Therefore, in an era when most men not only expected to be the primary earner in a family but also sought public recognition for their achievements, Frank Butler fulfilled himself by looking after Annie and working at jobs that suited him, including doing publicity for the Wild West and representing the Union Metallic Cartridge Company.

Besides facilitating Annie's career, Frank played a crucial role in both Annie's successful career and her maintenance of true womanhood. It was Frank, after all, who allowed Annie to act sedate and restrained, for he usually dealt with the complexities and aggravations of publicity, contracts, travel, equipment, and finances. While traveling, for example, Frank always carried a hidden one-hundred-dollar bill to tide Annie and him over should they be robbed or run out of money. In addition, Frank bragged about Annie's exploits. While she sat quietly and presented the image of what one reporter called "a modest, retiring, lovable little woman," Frank effectively promoted her.

Frank's many contributions were not lost on Annie, who often said, "Frank's job is taking care of me." According to her niece and namesake Anna Fern Campbell Swartwout, Annie also knew when to let Frank boast about himself. Whenever Frank said that he let her win that first match in Ohio, Annie would flutter her eyelashes and smile. Or he might say that he wished he had let one of her swains have her, and rather than getting provoked, Annie would simply reply, "I wish you had too."

Throughout their marriage, the Butlers seemed to be a happy, outgoing couple who enjoyed the spotlight. Still, because they used different names, many people thought Annie was unmarried. Also, Annie appeared girlish, sexy, and appealing well into the early 1900s. Male fans often desired her, perhaps as much for her power and wealth as for her appearance. Thus, among Annie's fan letters, she frequently found offers of marriage, which she sometimes handled with tact and delicacy. Annie treated gently the twenty-one-year-old lad who claimed he had not missed a day's performance since the Wild West opened and declared that she "was the one little girl" he could ever love. When Annie informed him that she already had a husband, he left for South America.

But on other occasions, Annie revealed her tough, sarcastic, and even disrespectful side. When a French count wrote to her in London in 1887 saying he dreamed of the day he could take her home to France and his mother, Annie acted in a most unladylike way. Judging him "the ugliest monkey you ever saw," Annie shot a bullet through the photograph at "the place where the brains should have been." She wrote "Respectfully declined" across the chest and returned his photograph to him. Annie proudly repeated this story throughout her life, which suggests that she failed to see the discrepancy between her own ladylike aspirations and her sometimes cranky behavior.

Of course, most people did understand that Annie Oakley and Frank Butler were husband and wife, a fact newspapers frequently mentioned. Also, the Butlers often entertained and appeared in public together. Their rich social life included everything from informal receptions in her tent to opening nights at the opera. In 1895, while playing in Massachusetts, they held an informal reception for a group of their friends, nearly all members of the Worcester Sportsmen's Club and their "ladies." The Butlers held the party in Annie and Frank's tent right after the show, gave their guests a tour behind the show's scenes, and concluded the festivities by presenting each woman with an autographed photograph of Annie as a memento of the evening.

Annie and Frank also accepted many of the invitations that poured in on them. In 1892, they attended a reception in New York with what one observer called "celebrated people, good music, and gay dresses." In 1898, a New York newspaper reported that "Dr. Butler and wife (Annie Oakley)" had attended the performance at the Opera House the previous evening. Also among their invitations were wedding invitations, including a 1907 announcement from the New York Rockefellers. In that same year, a Pinehurst, North Carolina, society reporter described the Butlers as "social lions" of the Carolina Hotel's season.

Annie and Frank's only sorrow may have been their lack of children. Neither of them ever mentioned the subject; it was not a subject discussed publicly, especially by a Victorian lady. Because family, friends, and curious reporters apparently avoided the issue, their feelings about childbearing remain unknown.

Annie and Frank's lack of children may very well have been a matter of choice, for birth control was available, if somewhat difficult to obtain. Just before Annie and Frank married, preventing conception became more difficult because of an act of the U.S. Congress. This act of 1873 was known as the Comstock Law after the YMCA's leader of its "Suppression of Vice" campaign, Anthony Comstock, who recommended the legislation to Congress. The law reflected a widespread reaction against the growing use of contraceptives in the United States and accompanying fears that birth control would destroy the American family. In 1873, then, Congress passed a law banning "any article or thing designed or intended for the prevention of conception or procuring of abortion" as well as the advertisement of such contraband. There is evidence, however, that birth control information and such devices as the forerunner to the diaphragm, the pessary, continued to circulate, especially in urban areas.

Perhaps Annie chose not to have children because she had helped her mother through so many travails, or maybe Frank wanted no more children because through divorce he had lost his children by a previous marriage. Possibly they both agreed that it would be extremely difficult to raise children on the road, or perhaps Annie feared the chaos that children would introduce into her orderly life. Or maybe they had no choice in the matter because conception simply never occurred. Recent medical studies indicate that women who follow an intense athletic regimen often stop menstruating; perhaps Annie never conceived because of her level of physical activity.

One last potential explanation of Annie and Frank's childless state exists. If Annie was sexually abused as a girl, she may have sustained injury that prevented conception or may even have turned away from sex for the rest of her life. It is conceivable, even though unlikely, that she and Frank had a nonsexual marriage, that he played the role of father to her role as daughter, and that children were never a possibility.

Certainly, Annie demonstrated her love of children on many occasions. During her first tour of England, she held monthly teas for London children. She recalled that her six months in London "were made happier" by her "children friends." Apparently, Annie later continued to include children among her guests, for in 1892 a reporter described the warm way in which Annie welcomed children into her tent. "She is as fond of children as they are devoted to her." In 1899, Annie commented that she enjoyed the letters she received from children more than those from adult fans.

Annie also lavished love and attention on Johnny Baker's two daughters. She sent them money for clothes and toys and had their likenesses painted on a gold-encircled brooch, which she frequently wore. After Baker's wife died, Annie and Frank invited the girls for frequent visits and said more than once that they were "the smartest children you ever saw." In 1899, a poem by an anonymous poet recognized the tie between the Butlers and the Baker children. Called "We've No Mama," it concluded with the following lines:

Now I hear her, Annie Oakley
Whispers "Babies, don't forget!
Yes, I know you have no Mama
And you are your papa's pets
Yes, I love you as a mother; And your Frank, he loves you too.
Don't forget us, dearest babies; For our love is pure and true.

Annie also paid a great deal of attention to her sisters' children. In later years, Hulda's girl, Anna Fern, born in 1888, complimented Annie, as well as Frank, for noticing everything Annie's nieces and nephews did and said even though they were "only little bits of humanity" at the time. Fern remembered that Annie made the children laugh with funny pranks, like sticking bits of paper to her face, and that Frank wrote poems for them. After Fern visited the Wild West with her family in Piqua, Ohio, in 1895, Buffalo Bill sent her a .44-caliber Winchester, and Frank taught her how to shoot. When Annie learned that Fern also liked to sew, she sent her dress material and patterns. Annie often asked Fern to accompany her to some of the libel trials between 1904 and 1910, and in 1911, when Annie joined the Young Buffalo Show, she took Fern touring with her. Understandably, Fern developed absolute devotion to Annie and Frank and sometimes acted like the daughter they never had.

Emily Brumbaugh Patterson's daughter, Irene, was another niece whom Annie favored. Irene remarked that every month of her young life, she received a package from her Aunt Ann and Uncle Frank. In it were items of clothing, underwear, bits of lace, or money. At one time, Annie had small gold pins shaped like guns made for each of her nieces, then destroyed the mold. Irene claimed that she was the only niece who still had her pin and that she wore it every time she left the house.

Even neighbors' boys and girls benefited from Annie's love of children. Lela Border Hollinger recalls that whenever Annie came to Greenville, she visited the Hollingers, who occupied the farm next to Susan's home. Annie usually shot holes in dimes to amuse Lela and gave her dollar bills, which Lela now wishes she had saved rather than immediately spending.

Like generations before them, most Americans also believed that a real lady was not only married but domestic as well. Never did Annie Oakley even hint that shooting should replace domestic endeavors in her life, or in the lives of other women, partly because she must have recognized the criticism that such a suggestion would bring and partly because she sincerely believed in the value of domestic work. Even when urging women to take up biking, shooting, and other forms of exercise, Oakley warned them not to slight their domestic cares. In 1899, she emphasized that it was not her intention to cause a woman to "neglect her home duties." Rather, Annie argued that time for both work and play should exist in every woman's life.

Given her peripatetic life, Annie did her best to put her own advice into effect. When a *New York World* reporter visited her apartment across from Madison Square Garden in 1887, he found it littered with shotguns, rifles, and revolvers, with gold and silver trophies covering the mantel piece and every tabletop. Annie herself stood in the small kitchen area, making tea and toasting muffins as serenely as any other housewife of the day.

Annie also exhibited mastery with the needle, a skill she learned as a girl when she worked at the Darke County Infirmary. She made most of her own costumes and cared for all of them so meticulously that some members of her family thought her overly particular and even touchy, liable to an occasional flare-up. But as a true lady, Annie could do as she pleased; the rules of domesticity supported her own inclinations. Her perfectionism might have annoyed those around her, but Annie could always justify her habits as ultimate domesticity.

Clearly, Annie carried her fastidiousness to an extreme. According to her niece Fern, Annie would never wear anything in less than perfect condition. "She never minded wearing the oldest clothes, if they had been made to look their best by either repairing or pressing." Fern added that Annie looked after Frank's clothing in the same finicky way. In her spare moments, Annie also pursued her love of fancy needlework, especially embroidery. Between shows, she regularly sat in a rocking chair in her tent, embroidery hoop in hand, producing a huge stock of exquisite linens.

Unfortunately, Annie lacked a permanent home in which to display her domestic talents. Still, she turned every boarding-house and hotel room, every tent, and every apartment into a home. She filled each with flowers, medals, gifts, and visitors, and when in one place for a period of time, she surrounded her current dwelling with beds of flowers that she cultivated herself. She also kept wine and such delicacies as ices and jelly cakes available for her and Frank's frequent guests. In 1893, one of these described her tent as "beautifully decorated" with a red brussels carpet, lounges, couches, rocking chairs, and satin pillows. Yet another praised her as "an accomplished housewife" because of the "neat and cheery appearance of her tent."

Despite the limitations of her tent, Annie proved herself an adept hostess. In 1887, a guest noted that Annie reigned within her flower-filled tent, holding a "sort of informal reception." She answered visitors' questions and told stories gracefully and graciously. Two years later, another commented that in her tent, Oakley "held a regular court where everybody paid homage — journalists of all nations, statesmen of all nations, soldiers of all nations." In 1892, Annie even successfully "entertained at tea" in her tent the count and countess de Paris, the duke of Orleans, and another unnamed prince. Frequently, however, entertaining seemed to be more of a matter of business and public relations to Annie than warm hospitality for personal friends.

Annie admitted as much. As early as 1889, she said she cared little for the show life and did it purely as a matter of business. If she had a choice, she would prefer a home in the country. Then in 1892, Oakley told an English reporter she was weary of moving about and wanted to settle down. That very year, Annie and Frank began building a handsome, three-story home with double porches and a five-sided alcove topped by a conical tower. Located at what is today 302 and 306 Grant Avenue in Nutley, New Jersey, it reportedly cost nine thousand dollars.

Lying roughly thirteen miles outside of New York City along the Passaic River, Nutley provided a country haven for writers, artists, and performers who, like Annie and Frank, needed proximity to the city. How the Butlers discovered Nutley remains unclear. Frank liked to joke that he found it when he got off a train at the wrong stop. Annie said they fell in love with the town when they happened to pass through. More realistically, they probably stabled horses, or even practiced Annie's act, at Eaton Stone's barn and stables north of town. Stone, the first circus performer to turn a somersault on a bareback horse and first to "ride" four horses by stepping from back to back, provided winter quarters for numerous showpeople.

Annie and Frank moved into their new house, which they sometimes called Oakley House, in December 1893. Both Annie and Frank made friends easily and were well accepted in Nutley. The Butlers joined the Nutley Rod and Gun Club, and Annie went sleighing with a group of young people. Annie and Frank also had many visitors, especially after Annie issued a blanket invitation to all friends and sportspeople to stop at her home. "They will find the latch string on the outside," she promised. It did not matter to her if guests shot a thirty-dollar or a three-hundred-dollar gun, but she hoped they would donate any specimen they had bagged themselves to her Sportsmen's Room, and she would put their name on it.

Among the first gifts was a huge stuffed owl that sat in state for nearly five years before moths attacked it. During the winter of 1899, Annie tied the owl to the roof to freeze out the moths. Although she tied it securely, its wings flapped in the wind and attracted attention. Local shooters broke windows and destroyed clothes hanging on the line by taking potshots at the bird, but the owl persevered. After the servants threatened to quit, Annie sent one of them out to remove the owl from its perch.

Sadly, home ownership failed to bring Annie the joy she had anticipated. The owl was the least of her problems. Perhaps because she had usually served as helper to her mother, Annie proved herself an indifferent cook. Because of her exacting nature, she lost not only hired cooks but seamstresses as well. She also felt ill at ease overseeing servants and preferred to leave managerial tasks to Frank, who had more experience and skill in giving directions, making requests, and initiating ideas.

According to Fern, Frank's brother always said that Annie and Frank had lived in a tent so many years that they no longer knew how to live in a house. In addition, Annie and Frank traveled so much that they had to either close up the house or rent it out while they were gone.

It is also likely that a large house, servants, and domestic management tried Annie on two fronts. She lost her usual tight control of her smaller and more manageable tent, hotel room, or apartment. Also, it became apparent that she lacked a crucial aspect of a lady's training; Annie had never been tutored in the art of handling servants. Annie's venture into home ownership and management may have proved to her that both her control and her ladyhood were more apparent than real and that she could best maintain the illusion of them on the road.

Finally, in 1904, Annie and Frank sold the Nutley house to Joseph Stirrat. (It was demolished in August 1937.) Next, the Butlers moved to the Pinehurst Hotel in New York City, overlooking Riverside Drive and the Hudson River. Annie spent the rest of her active career years until 1913 practicing her domestic skills in boardinghouse or hotel rooms, tents, or apartments. Although Frank sometimes longed to own a home once again, Annie tried to avoid it.

While living in Nutley, Annie publicly demonstrated that she possessed another crucial quality of a true lady—benevolence. In 1894, she agreed to take part in what one reporter described as "a mixture of circus, Wild West and indescribable feats by practiced amateurs." George H. Bayne and Frank E. Butler organized the Nutley circus, as residents called it, to be staged in March of that year in Eaton Stone's barn on Kingsland Road for the benefit of the Red Cross. Because Annie Oakley appeared on the bill, New York newspapers publicized the event and promised people that her performance alone would justify the one-dollar admission charge.

When the big night arrived, fifty electric lamps illuminated the barn, and red crosses adorned banners, programs, and even ten-cent bags of peanuts. While the local band played, the show began with a grand review; acrobats from the Orange and New York athletic clubs and the Newark Turn-verein followed. Others who appeared included Henry Cuyler Bunner, editor of *Puck* maga-zine, as ringmaster; young Al Stirrat on his pony; E. L. Field, with a bear and a monkey; a Professor Donovan, boxing with Alpheus Geer; Charles Smith, as a tramp riding Molly, the hat factory's delivery horse; and, of course, Annie Oakley, as "Ameri-ca's Representative Lady Shot."

Normally, however, Annie preferred to pursue her charitable works with much less fanfare. Through the years, she sent her mother and other family members money, material for clothes, and a variety of other gifts. Annie also sent regular gifts to her numerous nieces, nephews, grandnieces, and grandnephews. In 1977, Bess Lindsey Walcholz, the oldest grandchild of John Moses, Annie's only brother, remembered that during her childhood, her "Aunt Annie" often sent gifts of material for school dresses along with twenty dollars for buttons, braid, and other trimmings. Some packages also included children's books and cards picturing Sitting Bull and other Wild West stars. During wintertime, mit-tens, bathrobes, and "long-handled underwear" arrived. By the time Bess reached high school, Annie's packages included fine soaps and delicately perfumed face powder as well as white organdy for a graduation dress and money for a class ring and pin. Bess added that her Aunt Annie also enclosed a note, which invariably ended, "When you answer do not mention the money."

Frugal with herself, Oakley was seldom so with others. She wanted the best for her family and friends. In 1893, Annie ordered a dog collar for a hunting friend's pointer, Cyclone. "Get the finest and neatest collar to be had, regardless of cost." Annie also regularly contributed to local needs wherever she went. In 1891, for example, she sent a donation of two pound-notes (about ten dollars) to the Cardiff Infirmary while in Great Britain, and later her name turned up on the list of donors to the Keepers Benefit Society. When people asked Annie about her generosity, she would reply, "If I ever spend one dollar foolishly I see the tear-stained faces of little helpless children, beaten as I was."

By the time Annie visited a Mrs. J. J. Sumpter, Jr., of Hot Springs, Arkansas, in 1896, she was already well-known for her benevolent nature. The Hot Springs society column described Annie as "an accomplished and intellectual lady . . . known for her charity donations." Not surprisingly, many of Oakley's gifts went to children. According to Fern, Frank often said that Annie tried to ferret out all of the pathetic little waifs on the Wild West lot. In 1889, on location in Barcelona, Annie rescued a widow and her son Carlos from a mob of beggars to give them a basket of food, a practice she continued daily until she left the city.

In other cases, Annie sent gifts to her many namesakes. When a family in Spirit Lake, Iowa, named a daughter after her, Annie sent her a birthday gift for several years. In 1926, the woman—now a mother herself—wrote to Annie assuring her that the presents had "helped very much" in making her childhood days "happy ones."

Oakley also tried to help orphans. During her first tour of Europe during the late 1880s, Annie gave her first charity exhibition, in this case for the Vienna Orphan Asylum. Other similar exhibitions soon followed. Annie also encouraged the Wild West's orphan day performances. In 1901, for example, Cody and Salsbury invited orphans "to come and smell powder smoke and see Indians and be happy." In 1909, Oakley characteristically sent a check equaling 10 percent of her winnings from a match held the previous day to the *Winston-Salem Journal*, asking the paper to give the money to the pregnant widow and orphans of a man killed in a mine accident. Annie also challenged the citizens of Winston-Salem to follow her example, so as to "place the grief-stricken little widow, as well as the little life soon to begin, beyond want for awhile."

In addition to children, Oakley assisted a number of young women with schooling costs. Testimony from Annie's friends and thank-you notes from the women themselves indicate that she may have helped as many as twenty women. Among these notes was a postcard from "Bessie," evidently Annie's grandniece Bess Lindsey Walcholz, indicating that Annie was helping her through nurses' training school. In another document, Bess mentioned that Annie had sent her a heavy coat, a Spanish shawl, and a pale lavender dress. Although Bess received no financial help from her parents, she and Annie managed to finance her nurses' training, and she graduated in 1926.

Lest Oakley sound too good to be true, however, her gifts often had another side to them. With her gifts frequently came instructions and unsolicited advice. Annie's grandniece Bess, for example, revealed that Annie sent her special cosmetics along with directions. Annie noted, "You must be very careful what you put on your face, Dear." Annie also tended to use family members' homes as her own. On one occasion, she shipped a number of linen stage sets to her sister Hulda with a request to store them in Hulda's barn. Hulda eventually took the matter into her own hands; she cut up the linen, washed off the paint, and made a variety of towels and doilies from it. Clearly, although family members appreciated Annie's benevolence, they did not always follow the advice or orders that accompanied it.

Also, according to Irene Patterson Black, many family members took Annie's generosity for granted. They thought that because Annie earned substantial wages, gift-giving was easy for her. Few realized that Annie often denied herself to give to them. Moreover, in her last years, Annie occasionally spoke about the jealousy and divisiveness her gifts had caused among some family members, but she told Irene that she could not "deny" her relatives. Thus, rather than always causing her joy, Annie's benevolence sometimes marred her pleasure in her family and her visits to them.

Throughout her charity endeavors, Annie received Frank's full support. He best expressed his own attitude in a poem he wrote in 1911. Titled "What Did You Do?," it included these lines:

> Didn't you know it's the part of a brother of Man
> To find what the grief is and help what you can?
> . . . .
> Did you reach out a hand? Did you show him the road,
> Or did you just let him go by with his load?

Frank also abetted Annie in developing still another quality of ladyhood, the woman as a civilizing force. Because neither he nor Annie drank, smoked, gambled, or cursed, they were in an ideal position to act as models for the many performers who did all of those things.

Annie soon discovered that it was not always easy to maintain her exemplar position. For instance, because she practiced and worked outdoors, the vagaries of climate affected her disposition year round, sometimes for the worst. Constant travel must have taken its toll as well. And, in spite of Frank, Annie was probably lonely at times, for few other Anglo women traveled with the troupe, and Native American women lived in their own section of the camp. Newspapers were quick to comment if Annie happened to be the only white woman traveling with the show during a particular season. But her supporters often explained that despite the temptations and pressures, Oakley not only remained virtuous herself but exercised a moral, salutary effect on those around her.

Within the Wild West troupe, Oakley frequently acted as an example and guide to almost everyone. In 1899, she remarked that if any of the performers or crew met her "on the street, when they were with a man not of the highest character or slightly intoxi-cated, perhaps, they would all cross the street" out of respect. Annie added that not one of them had ever spoken a "rough word" to her. And in 1908, she reiterated, "Never has one of those cowboys made a remark to me which he would not make to an 8-year-old child." Annie's niece Fern painted a similar picture. She commented that if even the "roughest canvasman" happened to curse in Annie's presence, he would tip his hat and beg her pardon.

Predictably, Oakley's moral stance did not always serve her well. Some people found Annie prude-like and "holier than thou." Although they might have respected her beliefs, they sometimes jested about Annie's morals behind her back. Some members of the troupe even hinted that Annie's straitlaced behavior stemmed from stinginess rather than from true virtue, maintaining, for example, that Annie would drink a beer if someone else paid for it. People inside and outside the company also saved their off-color jokes and oaths for times when Annie was not present. In a way, then, Annie's morality increased her isolation and set her apart from the possibility of developing many intimate relationships. Surely she would have said that she cared little for relationships with such people, yet sitting in her tent, head bowed over her embroidery hoop, must have been less than riveting at times.

Once again, however, Oakley was well aware that she lived in the public eye and that her conduct had an impact outside the world of show business among the public. Because most people thought little of showpeople's morals, especially those of showwomen, Annie had the opportunity to revamp public thinking. Indeed, most people quickly saw the difference between her and other performers. In 1889, one fan was so taken with Annie's moral tone that he declared that she, "the circus-girl," fairly reeked "of beautiful purity and of maidenly dignity."

Annie also exercised her civilizing influence on the match and exhibition circuit. In 1897, for example, Annie maintained that few ladies shot because shooting grounds seldom made proper provision for them. Specifically, she continued, "A majority of club grounds have barrooms attached, and very often a part of the small clubroom is used for the sale of beer and liquors." Annie related her own experience at a recent tournament, where the shooters' room, a tent, had a bar in one end. Although the weather turned severe, she and many of the "gentlemen shots" preferred "to remain outside rather than risk the tobacco smoke and smell of whisky inside."

Apparently, Oakley's model proved effective, for growing numbers of women flocked to the shooting grounds each year. In 1902, one commentator remarked that because of Annie Oakley's example, many women had already taken up shooting. He concluded that "true sportsmen" were pleased, for these women would, like Annie Oakley herself, act as a civilizing force and "sweeten the joys of field sports."

This portrait of Annie Oakley as a Victorian lady runs counter to most people's imagined picture of her. Several people questioned for this study commented that when they thought of Annie, they envisioned male clothing, rough language, and a woman intent on smashing all barriers between women and men. One even styled Oakley a "woman's libber."

Nothing could be further from the truth. Annie not only rejected male dress and behavior but also refused to support the prevailing women's issue of her day, suffrage. Rather than using her reputation as a shooter and her dignity as a lady to further such a cause, Oakley disavowed it because she regarded it as unladylike. Annie also explained that she saw little value for women in such a reform.

In addition, Oakley would have disapproved of the way some women's rights leaders comported themselves. Newspaper accounts as well as gossip would have informed Annie that suffragists of the late nineteenth century were engaged in internecine warfare that often brought them scorn and disrepute. The fight had begun in 1869, when Elizabeth Cady Stanton and Susan B. Anthony organized the National Woman Suffrage Association, which excluded men from membership, published a journal called *Revolution*, and pressured the U.S. Congress to grant women the right to vote while Lucy Stone, Mary Livermore, and Julia Ward Howe formed the American Woman Suffrage Association, which welcomed male members, published *Woman's Journal* to offset the "radicalism" of *Revolution*, and lobbied individual states for suffrage. Perhaps as a result of this dissension, minimal progress occurred during the 1860s, 1870s, and 1880s. In 1867 and 1868, woman-suffrage amendments failed in Kansas. When, in 1869, Wyoming Territory granted women the right to vote, followed by Utah Territory in 1870, reformers hoped for a landslide, but the move toward suffrage failed to gain momentum.

Instead, in 1870, the sisters and influential reformers Catharine Beecher and Harriet Beecher Stowe collaborated in writing *Principles of Domestic Science*, which emphasized changes in the family rather than suffrage as the answer to women's problems. Then, during the 1870s, stockbroker and free-love advocate Victoria Woodhull, who ran for president in 1872, embarrassed suffrage leaders with what most people considered outrageous comments, unladylike behavior, and statements supporting free love.

During these upheavals, many women came to believe that access to the ballot box would simply bring corruption and vice to women as well as to their families. Oakley added another dimension to this thinking; she stated that she feared that not enough "good" women would vote. Even when the conflict between the two wings of the suffrage movement ended in 1890 with an uneasy truce and a merger between them, Annie remained aloof.

Of course, woman suffrage would have had little immediate

impact on Annie's life as a sportsperson and athlete. Rather, the changes taking place in women's sports at the time would have meant far more to her than suffrage. During Annie's formative years, American women had increasingly expanded their athletic activities. During the 1870s, they began to take up croquet, and soon they played alongside men. They also engaged in ice and roller skating and participated in archery tournaments, probably the first organized sport for women. In 1874, Mary E. Outerbridge of New York introduced tennis into the United States. Hindered by corsets, long skirts, and massive hats held to their heads by veils tied under their chins, women tennis players swung their rackets with ladylike grace but little athletic prowess.

During the time Annie was making her own mark in sports, the 1880s, 1890s, and early 1900s, women entered bowling tournaments, pedestrian races, and rodeos, especially as bronc riders. Socialite Eleonora Sears, great-great-granddaughter of Thomas Jefferson, toppled barriers to women's participation in organized events by winning more than 240 trophies in a variety of sports, including tennis and long-distance walking. She also shocked the nation in 1910 when she rode astride and competed against men on the polo field.

Still, despite the opportunities such changes created for Annie, she had no interest in emulating these "new women," as many Americans called them. Annie recognized that she already faced tough odds as a woman. Almost everyone who watched her shoot, or who heard about her, viewed her as a *woman* shooter. An 1888 judgment was typical: "Miss Oakley is a wonderful shot for a lady." Consequently, people watched how she, as a woman, reacted to various situations. She remembered that as she stepped up to the shooting line, both men and women observed her closely. Women especially looked her over, in her words, "sometimes disdainfully." She added, "If they wished to be friendly they could." If not, she convinced herself she did not care.

Rather than presenting herself as a new woman, Oakley chose to act like a lady on the shooting field. In one of her early matches, Annie competed against twenty-one shooters, all male. "When they saw me coming along they laughed at the notion of my shooting against them," she recalled. They were, she said, "less amused than they had been previously" when she captured the prize money. "It kind of galled me," Annie continued, "to see those hulking chaps so tickled in what was no doubt to them my impertinence in daring to shoot against them—and I reckon I was tickled too when I walked away with the prize."

Oakley similarly maintained her composure at a shooting exhibition she gave in 1886 at the Middlesex Gun Club in Dunellen, New Jersey. Members set the trap as tight as they could so that, according to Annie, they could "have a good laugh" at her. But, when the weather turned blustery and cold, Annie took heavy shells along and loaded her guns for fast clays. When the traps spewed out the first two try-out birds, Annie said that she just grinned and smashed them both. During her exhibition, she performed rifle and revolver stunts, then shot at fifty clays. In her last stunt, Annie sprang the trap herself, ran twenty feet, jumped over a table, picked up her gun from the ground, and aimed at two clay birds. Even when she slipped on the wet grass and landed on the ground, Annie reached down and caught her gun anyway. In her words, she "banged from a sitting posture" and hit one bird but missed the other. She picked herself up and tried again. This time she hit both birds. "That club was all right," Annie concluded. "They gave me a handsome medal and stated that the joke was on them."

The pressure on Oakley as a woman shooter abated somewhat during the 1890s, but she still disassociated herself from "new" women because of the public's and her own disapproval of them. In 1897, for example, a young woman diverted attention from the Wild West's opening parade in New York City because she sat mounted astride a handsome black horse. Agents of the show at first frowned at her, but then, according to one bystander, they "realized that she was one of the new women and they were all bound to see if she would flirt." In that same year, Annie was herself mistaken for a new woman while hunting in Crowson, Tennessee. One observer reported that when she first appeared in her "hunting suit," the others thought she was a new women. Annie soon proved them wrong but was nonetheless outraged by their mistake.

Despite her disavowals of suffrage, new women, and other women's issues of the day, Annie Oakley was what today many Americans would call a feminist. During her top career years of 1885 to 1913, Annie increasingly worked on behalf of women. As she matured and prospered, Oakley tried to use her success to open the way for others.

Surely Annie's childhood would have instilled in her a respect for women's contributions and abilities. Although as an adult, Annie either attended whatever Protestant church happened to be nearby or missed services, she prayed nightly and always maintained allegiance to such Quaker principles as a belief in women's essential worth. Too, she well remembered the strength the women of her family had exercised in various crises.

Annie herself had also demonstrated that women could achieve and excel. And because she had fought against prejudice and discrimination to earn a living, Annie recognized the constraints on women who wished or needed to work for wages outside their homes. Thus, in both example and word, Annie supported the advancement of women in certain areas of life. Rather than laboring in the political sphere for woman suffrage, Annie focused on economic rights and freedoms. Year by year, as she enhanced her own economic stability and earning power, Annie became increasingly vocal and adamant about women's right to hold employment, especially in arenic and other sports.

Oakley pursued her own brand of feminist reform under difficult conditions. Because she traveled regularly she could not join such women's clubs as sewing societies, where women discussed issues meaningful to them. Nor could Annie participate in women's rights groups or attend rallies, which would have given her information, purpose, and support. For most of the year, Annie operated in a predominantly male society of shooters, performers, and entrepreneurs. Even when she settled temporarily in Nutley, Annie continued this pattern by joining a gun club rather than a woman's group and by inviting shooters and showpeople to her home rather than reaching out to local women.

Only when her friend Amy Leslie or her niece Fern visited or when Annie returned home to see her mother, sisters, and neighbors did she experience a woman's culture. Susan's neighbor, Lela

Border Hollinger, recalled that during these visits, Frank often went hunting while Annie sat and chatted with the women. Although hardly liberals in their thinking regarding women's issues, Susan and the others offered Annie a sense of self, strength, and courage.

Gradually, Annie turned into a reformer for women's rights in the economic realm and in sports. The presence of a sympathetic and encouraging male in the person of Frank helped move Annie along the road toward activism. And freedom from domestic trivia and an appealing public persona gave her the opportunity to speak her mind.

Annie Oakley did this in a way that appealed to women and men alike. Alternately strong and self-effacing, Annie reached out to all who would listen. Annie especially proclaimed that she wanted "a fair chance" for her "sex" and gradually developed a tactic that might be termed subtle subversion. Like Sarah Josepha Hale, who as a well-educated lady and editor of *Godey's Lady's Book* gradually and tactfully initiated numerous reforms for women during the mid-nineteenth century, Oakley increasingly yet judiciously protested the boundaries of woman's accepted sphere during the latter part of the century.

Oakley worked her subtle subversion by charming both men and women with her ladylike demeanor and skill at firearms. As one viewer remarked in 1891, Annie entranced the "ladies" who had thought they would dislike the shooting in the Wild West show. She handled her guns with the same grace and dexterity "shown by themselves when yielding their less warlike weapon, the needle." Oakley especially captured the hearts of young women. In an 1892 letter from Sampson Morgan, editor of *Horticultural Times*, he described how his daughter enjoyed Annie's shooting and tried to emulate her. In England as well, Annie caused people to revise their opinions of women shooters. In 1892, one London newspaper announced that Oakley "won the hearts of the ladies" with her remarkable shooting and her demure appearance. "Where, after this, is the opponent of women's rights?" the article concluded.

Oakley picked an auspicious time to initiate a career in shooting and to reshape people's ideas concerning women in show business and in sports. The closing decades of the nineteenth century and the opening decade of the twentieth marked many firsts for women in every field. Among the achieving women were Mary Ann Shadd Cary, who in 1883 received a law degree from Howard University and established a successful practice in Washington, D.C., and Ella L. Knowles, who passed the Montana bar examination with distinction in 1889, thus becoming the state's first female attorney. During the 1890s, the names of such reformers as Jane Addams, Frances Perkins Gilman, Mary Elizabeth Lease, Mary Church Terrell, Lillian Wald, and Ida Wells-Barnett became well-known.

As a result, changes in women's status abounded in the United States. By 1890, almost four million women, approximately one out of every seven, worked for wages outside their homes. Then, Washington Territory gave women the right to vote in 1893 and Idaho followed in 1896. By 1900, the figure of employed women jumped to five million, or one out of every five. The Gibson Girl, a healthy, sensual, and rebellious female image first created by Charles Dana in 1890, captured many Americans' hearts and inspired some women to take unheard-of liberties. When Alice Roosevelt smoked in public, President Theodore Roosevelt simply shrugged and replied that he could do one of two things — be president or try to control Alice.

Obviously, times were changing for American women, and Oakley stood in the forefront of those changes. Her example encouraged a number of young women to leave home and join the show circuit as riders and shooters. As early as 1886, Cody and Salsbury added several women riders and shooters, besides Oakley, to the Wild West. Between then and 1900, probably more than a dozen women toured with this or other shows either part- or full-time. Many of them came from rodeos and local riding contests. Two of the more famous during the 1890s were bronc riders Annie Shaffer and Lulu Belle Parr, who left the rodeo to become full-time performers. But the best-known of the era's "cowgirls," other than Annie Oakley, was Lucille Mulhall, who made her debut in 1897 at age thirteen and by 1900 had proven herself a seasoned performer both in the arena and on the vaudeville stage.

During the early 1900s, many more young women followed the lead of these women. The pull of the circus and Wild West arenas on young men has been widely recognized, but women fled their homes as well. The influence of Oakley and others like her on the nation's women was widespread and not to be underestimated. A representative case was Jane Meekin, who in 1911 left her family in Wisconsin to take her chances on the show circuit. She called herself "Little Jean" and fired two pearl-handled revolvers. When Meekin's first season ended, she sought refuge with a St. Paul family who were longtime friends of her parents and whose sons had first taught her to shoot. When word of her whereabouts reached the Meekins, Jean's father and her older brother Austin went to fetch her. Jean arrived home in time for Christmas 1911; she married on February 22, 1912. The matter was never spoken of again except when she once confided her great adventure to her daughter.

As a role model and reformer, Annie must have occasionally felt lonely. Frank encouraged Annie, and her small community of women, including her mother, sisters, neighbors, niece Fern, and friend Amy Leslie, gave her what limited and intermittent support they could. But women's rights leaders of the day seemed oblivious of Annie and the changes she first modeled, then urged.

They spoke neither against her nor for her, nor did they include her in their accounts of suffrage and women's rights. Presumably, they regarded Annie as an entertainment star and little more. Even in the 1990s, few women's history handbooks and biographical collections include Annie Oakley. Those that do continue to overlook or undervalue her feminist impact.

Yet Oakley influenced the lives of thousands of women. One of her quieter campaigns was to encourage the 1890s fad of riding bicycles, which she considered an excellent sport for women. In 1892, Annie herself ordered a Premier Safety bicycle with solid tires from a firm in Coventry, England. She pedaled the thirty-five-pound vehicle around the streets of London for exercise and shopping, causing more than one eyebrow to raise as she passed. Annie later claimed that she was the first woman to ride a bicycle in London. When she prepared to return to the United States, she ordered her bike crated up. Annie maintained, "I am equally as fond of it as of my horse." In her view, both bicycles and horses provided pleasant and healthy exercise.

Concerned with maintaining her ladylike appearance, Annie soon devised a special outfit for cycling. In 1894, she explained that she "abominated" the bloomer costume that many women bicyclists wore; she considered bloomers both inconvenient and ungraceful. Oakley preferred instead the five-piece costume she had designed herself. On her legs, she laced gaiters about six inches above the knees. She then added a pair of knickerbockers (short, loose trousers gathered at the knee), a skirt extending halfway below the knee, a loose-fitting bodice of white silk, and an Eton-style jacket. Annie completed the tan-and-white outfit with matching tan shoes and tan gloves. Although this outfit may not sound unusual, Annie's special contribution to it lay hidden beneath the skirt. She sewed an eyelet to each gaiter and a corresponding elastic with a hook on the underside of the skirt. When mounting her bike, she gracefully hooked her skirt to the gaiters. While she rode, the elastic provided sufficient room for movement of the skirt but prevented it from rising above Annie's knees.

A few years later, in 1897, Oakley credited the cycling craze with opening the way for women shooters. Women who refused to shoot in their cumbersome Victorian outfits and feared wearing short skirts now had examples on nearly every street in the nation. "Ladies can be seen on the most crowded streets of our largest cities wearing dresses short enough to get through any brush or briars where man can." Annie hastily added, however, that she was not advocating the bloomer costume, for she thought "nothing so detestable."

By the end of the decade, Oakley had succeeded in drawing attention to the benefits of outdoor exercise for women. In 1900, one supporter pointed to her as a splendid example of "what athletic exercises and out-door life" was "doing for the American girl of this generation." He concluded that as a bicycle rider, Oakley had few equals. But cycling was not Oakley's major campaign. Rather, she intended to draw women into shooting. Annie used two arguments: that shooting provided fine sport and exercise, and that women could use skill with weapons to thwart life-threatening attacks on themselves and their families.

During Annie's first season in London, a number of society ladies asked her to give them shooting lessons. Annie remembered that she held her first classes on gunmaker Charles Lancaster's hunting preserve. She charged each of her five pupils five dollars. This endeavor proved so successful that Annie placed an advertisement in the London newspapers announcing that she would give lessons in the use of pistols, rifles, and shotguns "to ladies only." For this purpose, Oakley rented a private shooting ground in London or arranged to visit pupils at their private residences or country estates. Annie soon discovered that many women proved apt pupils and demonstrated that women could learn shooting quickly and well.

When she returned to the United States, Oakley continued to give lessons and to extol the virtues of women shooters. As early as 1888, one viewer remarked that the skill of some "ladies" at rifle ranges near Boston was not only "surprising" but often surpassed the efforts of some of the "sterner sex." In 1893, Oakley built on such observations by issuing a statement regarding women shooters: "I do not wish to be understood to mean by this that woman should sacrifice home and family duties entirely merely for outside pleasure but that, feeling how true it is that health goes a great way towards making home life happy, no opportunity should be lost by my sex of indulging in outdoor sports, pastimes, and recreations, which are at once healthy in their tone and results and womanly in their character."

Once again Annie sounded a great deal like editor Sarah Josepha Hale, who also emphasized women's domestic duties and family responsibilities at the same time that she pressed for an expansion of women's activities. Hale had also stressed the benefits of nature and health when arguing that women should walk or ride (sidesaddle, of course), and Annie did the same. She pointed out that shooting would take women out into the beauties of nature. There they would enjoy healthy and pleasurable recreation, which would engage their minds and bodies. Moreover, women shooters would gain confidence and self-possession, two crucial qualities in daily life.

In case this argument failed to persuade, Oakley added her second justification: a woman who understood guns could protect herself in time of danger. Annie took great exception to the common statement that "woman's only weapon is her tongue" but did admit that most women were "greatly handicapped when danger comes." They could remedy this by learning how to use a revolver, a weapon simple to operate and easy to carry.

Once she had established her arguments, Oakley continued to repeat them. In an essay written by "Gyp" around 1894, one suspects the fine hand and flowing writing style of Frank Butler but detects the thoughts of Annie Oakley. How could a woman stay behind when her husband goes hunting, the essay queried, just because of what the neighbors might think? If a woman's husband approves, then the woman should accompany him and "hang" the neighbors. Women would be healthier, and more marriages might be happier as well.

In 1897, Oakley restated her views. "I don't like bloomers or bloomer women, but I think that sport and healthful exercise make women better, healthier and happier." Also in 1897, the *New York Journal* ran a series of articles headed "Without Shooting Herself, Taught by Annie Oakley." In her newspaper instructions, Annie insisted that nervousness constituted the principal detriment to women's shooting. Since everyone expected them to shoot themselves—and the illustration accompanying the lessons pictured a female pupil wearing an unwieldy floor-length dress, a cape, and a plumed hat—it is little wonder that women exhibited nervousness. Oakley, however, assured all concerned that the sport of shooting was "one of the best kind of tonics for the nerves and for the mind." She recommended that would-be shooters begin with a .22-caliber, five-pound, 20-gauge or a six-pound, 12-gauge, hammerless shotgun. Annie also encouraged women to shoot at the traps and hunt alongside their husbands and sons. She could see no reason that they should remain housebound while their menfolk enjoyed the sport.

When, in March 1897, Oakley participated in the Sportsmen's Exposition in Madison Square Garden, she used her appearance as a forum to continue her campaign for women to learn shooting. Later that year, Annie warned women shooters to ignore the costumes advertised in fashion plates and newspapers. Anyone who wore them to shoot could not stoop, much less aim and fire. Instead, Annie advised women to select any one of the "natty" skirts, or gaiters and knickerbocker suits, worn for "wheeling" when they shot on a range or in the field.

The following year, as the nation tottered on the brink of war with Spain, Oakley took one of the most overtly feminist actions of her life. On April 5, 1898, she wrote to President William McKinley assuring him that she felt confident that his good judgment would guide America safely away from war. But, she continued, in case war did erupt, she was prepared "to place a Company of fifty lady sharpshooters" at his disposal. Annie guaranteed, "Every one of them will be an American and as they will furnish their own arms and ammunition will be little if any expense to the government." Annie sent this message on her special stationery, which featured a half-page letterhead declaring her "America's Representative Lady Shot" and "For eleven years, next to Buffalo Bill, the attraction with the Wild West." Apparently, these declarations failed to impress the president's personal secretary, who fired back his answer: he had forwarded her offer to the secretary of war.

This brush-off, coupled with public criticism from a Boston woman, must have temporarily dampened Annie's spirit for reform. In 1899, this woman chastised Oakley in an open letter to local newspapers: "Did it ever occur to you that you are wasting the best years of your life in the unwomanly occupation of shooting before the public? Take the advice of a well-wisher and renounce the gun, get married and lead a home life, and so give no reason for comments by anyone." Since Annie was already married and trying to lead a "home life" in Nutley, she probably ignored this attack.

Oakley also revealed her strength and determination by continuing to encourage women to take up shooting. In 1900, she argued that shooting need not detract from "a lady's qualities." She also remarked on the numbers of women who had taken up shooting and competed with men "on their own ground" during recent years. Then, in 1901, she declared: "Any woman who does not thoroughly enjoy tramping across the country on a clear, frosty morning with a good gun and a pair of dogs does not know how to enjoy life. God intended woman to be outside as well as men, and they do not know what they are missing when they stay cooped up in the house with a novel." Novel reading was an activity she deplored.

Also in 1901, a Mrs. Johnson publicly revealed her experience with guns. Although her husband had urged her to take up the sport, she had done so with great hesitation. Then, when it came her turn to shoot among a crowd of men, she felt "quite shaky." Her performance proved less than phenomenal, but she soon improved and eventually concluded that she had earned her "right to compete with the men."

Encouraged by such support, Annie Oakley stepped up her own efforts and reemphasized her dual theme. In 1902, she proclaimed that a woman who joined men in their outdoor sports approached "nearest to the highest development of the modern woman." Such a woman had learned to master all the minor difficulties that life put in the path of women and reached the peak of physical education as well. Annie further stated that "every intelligent woman should become familiar with the use of firearms" so that she could protect herself. Annie hoped that one day all women would be able to handle guns "as naturally as they handle babies."

Oakley recommended that every woman learn to use a revolver that she kept by her side, whether at home or on the streets. A woman equipped with a gun and the knowledge to use it properly, Annie said, could be courageous and self-reliant when home alone, for revolvers were "excellent life preservers." A woman who kept her gun in an accessible but safe place could easily scare off a robber or murderer or, if she wished to make him an example, maim him without killing him.

When a woman was in the streets, Annie urged during a 1904 visit to Cincinnati, she should not carry her revolver in her handbag but should have it ready at all times by concealing it within the folds of a small umbrella. Wearing a stylish, floor-length dress with full sleeves and a high collar, Annie posed for photographs showing women how to prepare themselves and their umbrellas to fend off thieves or "murderous attack." Annie also warned women to be "ready to shoot before the enemy shoots." Her concern was justified, for around the turn of the century, urban ills were increasing at an alarming rate while women were spending more time in city streets than formerly.

Home theft also grew at such a rapid rate that Oakley increased her attempts to get women to keep revolvers by their bedsides. A 1906 photograph shows her as a gentle, grandmotherly figure—a gray-haired lady in a dark dress with a full, ruffled, long-skirt—sitting by her bedside table loading a revolver to be placed in a nightstand drawer. Annie explained that she had no intention of encouraging women to make fools of themselves but that she wanted them to learn to protect themselves in an era when urban crime was on the rise.

Did Oakley's subtle subversion work? Did she successfully combine covert feminism and overt ladyhood to change people's minds about women's limitations? Perhaps the best answer appeared in 1896 when the *Philadelphia Inquirer* noted that although shooting was a strange career for a woman, no other young woman in the public eye garnered more plaudits and popularity than Annie.

Like Hale, Oakley, the true lady, attracted a wide audience with her skill and ladylike demeanor; Annie then proceeded to revise what the audience thought a woman shooter and a real lady should be. She not only pushed at the limits of women's sphere, she literally reestablished them. Even after Annie buried her mother in 1908 and thus lost an important personal supporter, she continued to work on behalf of women.

By the time Oakley retired from the Young Buffalo Show in 1913, women's choices included sport shooting as well as hunting. It was Annie's immense ability to wield, figuratively speaking, a needle with one hand and a gun with the other that endeared her to generations of Americans and allowed her to advance her causes. As shooter *and* lady, she annoyed some people but charmed a great many others, who often came to see things her way. Far from being tricked into accepting ladyhood, she used it to her advantage. She was clever not only in the arena but outside it as well.

CHAPTER 5

"Girl of the Western Plains"

STAGE lights glittered in the Olympic Theater and the audience applauded and cheered, but Sioux Chief Sitting Bull saw little to interest him. Ever since he had reportedly killed General George Armstrong Custer at the Battle of the Little Big Horn on June 25, 1876, he had been an object of curiosity and scorn. In recent years, he had made occasional trips to cities to slake his curiosity about white people and their way of life. Now, in March 1884, he was on a ten-day tour of St. Paul.

So far, Sitting Bull had visited a cigar factory, a millinery house, a school, and the *Pioneer Press* offices. He had also attended a couple of shows at the opera house and this evening was watching the Arlington and Fields Combination, which claimed in its advertising to have a remarkable "aggregation of talent." One would never know it from the chief's face. He sat stolidly through the Wertz brothers' acrobatics, Allie Jackson's singing, and Flynn and Sarsfield's minstrel act. Then Annie Oakley skipped onto the stage with rifle in hand, and the chief came to life.

Chief Sitting Bull understood Annie Oakley. She wore sensible clothes, handled a gun with great skill, and let nothing intimidate her. She knocked corks from bottles, snuffed out candles, and performed a variety of other stunts he had probably never seen before. Sitting Bull soon sent message after message to Annie's hotel asking to see her, but each time she refused. Oakley had a match to shoot and business to tend to. Then Sitting Bull sent sixty-five dollars and a request for her photograph. "This amused me," Annie said, "so I sent him back his money and a photograph, with my love."

Annie called on Sitting Bull the following morning. She thought him a kindly "old man," and he thought her a marvelous little woman. He was so pleased with her, Annie recalled, that he christened her "Watanya Cecilla," or "Little Sure Shot." He then insisted on adopting Annie to replace a daughter who had died after the Little Big Horn. To Annie, like the women on the westward trail who laughed when Indian men offered ponies in trade for them, the whole thing seemed just a lark. Annie knew she would never go to Dakota Territory, even though, as a chief's daughter, she could claim ponies, cattle, and other benefits.

Frank Butler proved quicker in recognizing the tremendous advertising possibilities in the incident. After all, if people all over the United States hoped to glimpse the chief whenever he left the reservation, why would they not throng to see his adopted daughter? This would prove to be the beginning of Annie Oakley as the "girl of the western plains," as many fans and reviewers liked to call her. Annie had already displayed a number of the qualities often associated with western women: she was independent yet was a helpmeet to her husband; she was aggressive yet was a civilizer as well. Now, a year before she joined Buffalo Bill, the great Sioux chief put her on the path toward identifying herself with the Old West.

Two weeks after the meeting between Annie and Sitting Bull, Frank placed an advertisement in the *New York Clipper* announcing that "the premier shots, Butler and Oakley," had made friends with the most fearsome Indian chief of all. Frank added that, in front of numerous witnesses, Sitting Bull had given them, along with other gifts, the pair of moccasins he had worn at the Little Big Horn. But the friendship was short-lived. Sitting Bull returned to the Standing Rock reservation in Dakota Territory and Annie turned eastward, first to visit her mother, then to join the Sells Brothers Circus for a season.

Frank had no hesitation about identifying Annie with the West to attract people caught somewhere between the disappearing frontier and the emerging machine age. Sitting Bull and Frank Butler ignited a flame that turned into a bonfire. Annie's relationships with Native Americans, her participation in the Wild West show, her stage appearances, and film and fiction between 1885 and 1913 fueled her western image into a blaze seen all over the world.

Annie and Sitting Bull reunited in 1885 after William F. Cody's press agent, John Burke, escorted Sitting Bull from Standing

Rock to tour with the Wild West. Legend has it that Sitting Bull leapt at the chance to be near his beloved "Little Sure Shot" every day, but the reality is far more complicated. Cody was not the first entertainer to think about taking Sitting Bull on the road. As early as 1883, Reverend Joseph A. Stephan asked the Indian agent Major James McLaughlin's permission to display the chief at his church fair in Jamestown in the Dakotas. McLaughlin refused the request and turned away other petitioners as well. McLaughlin had allowed the chief to visit cities only to impress him with the benefits of "civilization" so that Sitting Bull would encourage his people to engage in farming and start attending school. But McLaughlin feared that fame and publicity would make Sitting Bull conceited and unmanageable.

When Cody's request came in, McLaughlin refused permission as a matter of form. He noted that he had received so many similar proposals that they had become "considerable of a bore." McLaughlin did offer Cody a thread of hope, however. He wrote that if the "late hostiles" were ever given permission to leave the reservation with a show, he preferred to have them join the Wild West, which, in his view, presented worthy entertainment.

In the meantime, Stephan had taken over as head of the Bureau of Catholic Indian Missions and had persuaded Secretary of the Interior Henry M. Teller to allow him to take Sitting Bull on tour to benefit the missions. McLaughlin, who feared that the irascible chief and the touchy priest would ignite their own personal conflagration, decided to intervene. Handling Sitting Bull with great care and tact, McLaughlin encouraged him and eight others to tour on their own, as the Sitting Bull Combination, to twenty-five cities between Minnesota and New York. But when the group returned from the nearly two-month-long tour on October 25, 1884, they had little to show for their efforts.

McLaughlin believed that Cody and his flair for publicity could do far better by Sitting Bull. He gave his blessing to Cody, who on April 29, 1885, wired the secretary of the interior that Sitting Bull had "expressed a desire to travel" with him. Cody promised to treat the chief well and "pay him a good salary." The secretary directed the commissioner of Indian affairs, John Atkins, to "make a very emphatic No" to Cody. Atkins tried, arguing that the

Indians had to plant crops and could not travel and exhibit themselves "where they would naturally come in contact with evil associates and degrading immoralities."

Cody next rallied General William T. Sherman and Colonel Eugene A. Carr to his cause and petitioned again. On May 18, the secretary capitulated; he wired McLaughlin that Sitting Bull and a few other reservation Indians had permission to tour with the Wild West. John Burke picked up the men two weeks later. Burke brought with him a contract stipulating that Sitting Bull would receive a bonus of $125 in advance and a salary of $50 per week while the others would receive $25 per month. Apparently, Sitting Bull had thought of all the angles, for the contract had a handwritten note appended: "Sitting Bull is to have sole right to sell his own Photographs and Autographs."

When Burke arrived in Buffalo, New York, Sitting Bull in tow, he boasted: "He is ours. I have captured him." Burke and Sitting Bull must have made a startling couple, for Burke styled himself after Cody, including the long, flowing hair, whereas the chief wore a buckskin tunic weighted with beads, a forty-feather bonnet, a crucifix around his neck, and a medicine bag slung at his side. Sitting Bull probably looked as happy as Burke, however, for he believed he was about to make much-needed money and possibly get the opportunity to convey his people's troubles to what he called "the new White Father at Washington," President Grover Cleveland.

Annie welcomed Sitting Bull into the Wild West troupe. She marched up and asked him about some coins and a red silk handkerchief she had sent him. Through his interpreter, Sitting Bull replied that he had received the gifts but left them behind for safekeeping. He added: "I am very glad to see you. I have not forgotten you and feel pleased that you want to remember me."

During the following months on the road, Annie formed a fast friendship with Sitting Bull. She also listened to his complaints. Some members of the troupe claimed that Annie was the only one in camp who could lift Sitting Bull out of his frequent depressions. The chief's foremost grievance concerned army troops that trespassed on the hay and timber lands at Standing Rock. He feared that in a few years his people would face utter poverty. He also told Annie that cattle ranchers encroached on the reservation and counted twice each cow intended for Sioux consumption. And the agents, Sitting Bull confided, gave Indians "half-and-half instead of sugar—the other half being sand."

Annie also sympathized with Sitting Bull when he gave away much of his salary to the poor urchins who haunted every show lot. She understood his desire to help others. Too, Sitting Bull failed to understand the white people he met who, in his view, refused to take care of their own. He feared for the Indian, for what would such stingy, selfish people be willing to share with Native Americans?

Oddly enough, John Burke failed to turn the chief and Annie's friendship into a publicity gimmick. Neither did Oakley join the various publicity events that Burke staged for Sitting Bull that season. Since Burke never missed an opportunity, it is conceivable that Annie, out of respect for the chief, refused to cooperate.

After the final performance of the season on October 11, Sitting Bull told a reporter through his interpreter, "The wigwam is a better place for the red man." He added that he was "sick of the houses and the noises and multitude of men" who stared and poked their fingers at him. Sitting Bull went to Annie to say good-bye. Before he departed, in appreciation of her friendship, he gave her some invaluable Indian artifacts. In return, Annie wrote to Sitting Bull after he returned to Standing Rock.

But Oakley could not help the chief with the problems he encountered. Back on the reservation, McLaughlin judged the returned Sitting Bull a major nuisance. "He is," McLaughlin wrote, "inflated with the public attention he received and has not profited by what he has seen." McLaughlin claimed that Sitting Bull told the "most astonishing falsehoods" to other Indians and inflated his own authority over them. Consequently, McLaughlin refused to let Sitting Bull tour again the next season, arguing that the chief spent his earnings extravagantly to impress other Indians and was "too vain and obstinate to be benefitted" by the tour.

Oakley leapt to Sitting Bull's defense in 1887. She minimized her own contributions to the chief's welfare and said instead that he "made a great pet of me." Annie added, "He is a dear, faithful, old friend, and I've great respect and affection for him." She now regarded his adoption of her as a wonderful compliment.

But Indian-policy reformers of the time disagreed with Oakley's viewpoint and leaned more toward McLaughlin's. They believed that touring only "spoiled" Native Americans. Reformers were spurred on by Helen Hunt Jackson's poignant novel *Ramona*, which first appeared in 1884 and championed the rights of Indian women, and by the stirring speeches and writings during the 1870s and 1880s of a Paiute woman, Sarah Winnemucca. Consequently, reformers railed against the Wild West shows' representing Native Americans as primitive savages at a time when the Indian Bureau was trying to convince people that Indians were becoming productive and, according to Anglo standards, civilized.

Reformers feared that the public swallowed wholesale Cody's assurances that the Wild West presented Native Americans realistically. Before each performance, Cody himself denounced "rehearsals" and told the audience that what they were about to see was "an exhibition of skill" rather than a performance. And, in 1885 and 1886, Wild West advertising included part of a letter from General William Tecumseh Sherman, who praised Buffalo Bill's Wild West as "wonderfully realistic and historically reminiscent," and part of another from author Mark Twain, who stated, "Down to its smallest details the show is genuine—cowboys, vaqueros, Indians, stagecoach, costumes and all: it is wholly free from sham and insincerity."

In addition, other notables publicly praised the show and further verified its representation of Indians. For instance, Elizabeth Custer, widow of General Armstrong Custer who died at the Battle of the Little Big Horn, endorsed the Wild West's view of the battle and of Cody's taking Yellow Hand's scalp in revenge. As a consequence of such endorsements, scalping and other violent acts became acceptable family entertainment and were even considered educational. In 1895, the *Boston Sunday Post* made a typical observation about one Wild West performance: "Years of study could not teach what here may be learned in one night. If geography, history, climate, arts and industries could be taught to all the youths of Massachusetts in the manner of the 'Wild West' show, there would be no dull pupils."

Still, Cody's Wild West was the least of the offenders of the circuses and Wild West shows, partly because he had his own vision, both of the problem and of its solutions. The Wild West's historical reenactments always left the audience with the message that although Indians and whites had once been enemies, they now had to live together in peace. Cody believed he was helping achieve his slogan "An Enemy in '76, A Friend in '85," by showing Native Americans and Anglos how to live and work together in the Wild West troupe. Moreover, Cody seemed to have genuine concern and affection for most Indians, especially Sioux Chief Iron Tail. Reportedly, Cody once told M. I. McCreight, a shipper of buffalo bones from the plains during the 1880s, "Chief Iron Tail is the finest man I know, bar none!"

Because of the growing deterioration of Indian-white relations during the late 1880s, Annie never saw Sitting Bull again. When, in 1889, the Sioux Commission agreed to cede some land in western Dakota Territory, Sitting Bull opposed it. And when the Ghost Dance movement developed that same year, Sitting Bull encouraged the frantic dances that would bring an Indian messiah who would, in turn, destroy all Anglo Americans and restore Native American prosperity.

Fearing violence as a result of Sitting Bull's actions, McLaughlin requested authority to arrest the chief. At that point, Major General Nelson A. Miles, commanding general of the Division of the Missouri, interceded. He asked Cody, just back from his European tour, to go to Standing Rock and reason with Sitting Bull. On November 27, 1890, Cody and three friends arrived at Mandan, then went on to Fort Yates near Standing Rock. But, after much talking, drinking, and rescinding of orders, Cody returned to Chicago without seeing Sitting Bull. The climax of the contretemps came on December 14, when the Indian police tried to arrest Sitting Bull, and the chief's followers opened fire on them. Supposedly, at the sound of gunfire, the gray trick horse that Cody had given Sitting Bull sat down and lifted its front leg to shake hands. In the subsequent melee, Sitting Bull lost his life, as did seven of his men and six police officers.

Oakley immediately and publicly defended Sitting Bull. She declared that he had numerous good reasons to take up arms in his own and his people's defense. "His disposition was neither aggressive nor cruel," she continued, "nor would he have molested any one if he had not been first molested." Anyone who knew him would feel pity for his fate, Annie continued, to die knowing the lands of his people had been invaded and "their means of subsistence impaired, and faith not kept with them." Years later, shortly before her own death in 1926, Oakley still railed at the unfairness of the situation. "Had he been a white man someone would have been hung for his murder."

Cody too mourned Sitting Bull's death; he swore he could have saved him if given a proper chance. Yet Cody traded on the chief's growing reputation. Although his personal, humanitarian side sympathized with Sitting Bull, his entrepreneurial, entertainer side recognized the value of Sitting Bull's image. In addition, rather than heading off further trouble by replacing the Indians with actors, Cody continued his drive for authenticity and requested more and more Indians from McLaughlin.

In 1893, the Wild West played on a plot of ground outside the entrance to the world's fair. Because the Board of Fair Managers objected to Cody's representation of Indian history and culture, it refused to let Cody into the grounds of the World's Columbian Exposition. Cody's partner, Nate Salsbury, leased a fourteen-acre site outside the entrance and built stands designed to hold eighteen thousand people. Although the show already featured seventy-four Indians from Pine Ridge, Cody hired an additional one hundred from Pine Ridge, Standing Rock, and Rosebud. He also rode Sitting Bull's gray trick horse. After all, the tragic wars between whites and Indians during the 1880s and 1890s made Indians a premier attraction.

President Grover Cleveland opened the first show in 1893, and Cody introduced the Congress of Rough Riders of the World to American viewers. Despite the Panic of 1893, Cody and Salsbury enjoyed their most prosperous season ever.

Oakley found herself caught in a bind similar to Cody's. She clearly liked and respected Sitting Bull and other Native Americans, as well as sharing such values with them as honesty, hard work, and service to others. Should she, then, trade on Sitting

Bull's image, or should she let his memory rest in peace? No evidence exists that Annie protested or in any way objected to advertisements and posters to bill her as "Little Sure Shot," "Watanya Cecilla," and "Sitting Bull's Adopted Daughter." She also frequently spoke with reporters about Sitting Bull, his adoption of her, and his moccasins and other gifts.

At the same time, Annie seemed to care sincerely about Native Americans. She often tried to help those in the troupe with their problems. Because of her concern for them, many Indians went to Annie for advice or solace. Others asked her to help them navigate a show world filled with temptations and things they could not comprehend. For instance, Pawnee Long John, who had been, according to Annie, "shaking dice with a Mexican," asked her to hold his money for safekeeping so that he could avoid games of chance.

Frank Butler also supported and shared Oakley's attitudes toward Indians in the Wild West troupe. Some of Frank's contemporaries claimed that he learned to speak the Sioux language. He also liked to tell stories that placed Indians in a favorable light. For instance, when in 1894 the Wild West's weather forecaster predicted a tornado and ordered all the tents lashed down, Chief Rain-in-the-Face pointed out that the sky was clear of rain and wind. According to Frank, the practical-minded chief pronounced the "white men" big fools. Butler also developed a game for the Indians to play in camp, which involved pitching arrows at a bottle. Many of his native friends adopted it enthusiastically.

But Annie and Frank were not the only champions of Wild West Indians. During the 1890s and early 1900s, in show program after program, Cody expounded his philosophy regarding Native Americans and the misfortunes they had suffered. In his autobiography, Cody also spoke on behalf of Native Americans, imploring the U.S. government to treat them with justice and fairness. He argued that they had owned the land when Europeans arrived and thus had some claim to it, even though they were incapable "of developing it, or of really appreciating its possibilities." Besides, he continued, Indians are "real Americans" whose blood had "added a certain rugged strength to the characters of many of our Western citizens."

When Chief Luther Standing Bear served as interpretor of the Wild West Indians in 1903, he found Cody staunchly behind the native performers. On more than one occasion, Cody stated that the Native Americans were the "principal feature" of the Wild West and were not be be misused or neglected. After Standing Bear and Cody spent hours discussing tribal matters, Cody even offered to hire attorneys and bring Sioux grievances to the attention of President Theodore Roosevelt. Also, when Standing Bear and his wife bore a daughter in Birmingham, England, Cody served as her godparent and arranged for mother and daughter to earn extra funds.

When Annie joined the Young Buffalo Show in 1911, she again confronted the issue of "show Indians." Red Shirt and Flat Iron, also veterans of the Buffalo Bill Wild West, were among the cast, and the Indian-policy debate was escalating. By the time she left that organization in 1913, the debate had turned into a national outcry against "exhibiting" Indians in Wild West shows. Sioux Chauncy Yellow Robe, for example, pointed out that Columbus had staged the first Indian show by shipping Native Americans to Europe to amuse and amaze the nobility. Now the U.S. government, the supposed protector of Indians, let them participate in Wild West shows, fairs, and moving pictures that presented them to the public as savage beings. In 1914, another supporter of this position, E. H. Gohl, an adopted clan-member of the Onondagas, agreed that touring with Wild West shows was clearly "demoralizing and a menace to the Indians." Such "show" Indians hurt spectators as well, for viewers saw "burlesque" war dances rather than gaining any real knowledge of Indian customs.

Whether this issue influenced Annie Oakley's retirement in 1913 is unknown. But she seemed to distance herself from Indian concerns during following years, turning instead to raising money for the Red Cross during World War I, teaching women to shoot, and campaigning for women in shooting sports.

Annie's relationship with Chief Sitting Bull may have initiated in the public mind her identification with the Old West, but it was her participation in Cody's Wild West exhibition that clearly labeled her a western woman. In the days before radio, motion pictures, and television, the dime novel and other books, western art, and Wild West shows stood supreme as the mythmakers of the American West. Such authors as Ned Buntline and Prentiss Ingraham, along with such artists as Frederic Remington, did their part in making the West appear wild and woolly, but Cody and others took the image on the road.

Because Wild West shows presented clean, family entertainment, everyone could go and everyone could believe. After all, who could resist the appeal of a melodrama, a circus, the story of common Americans who overcame great odds, and a saga of patriotism and nationalism all rolled into one amazing tent show that came to your vicinity, whether you lived in a large city or a nearby small town?

Buffalo Bill's Wild West incorporated three major dimensions: exhibitions of cowboy and Indian skills, such as riding, shooting, lassoing, and racing on foot; historical reenactments of life in the Old West, such as the attack on the Deadwood Stage, the Pony Express, the burning of a settlers' cabin, and the Battle of the Little Big Horn; and western heroes in the guise of the Honorable William F. Cody, "Champion All-Round Shot of the World," Annie Oakley, "Little Sure Shot," Johnny Baker, "the Cowboy Kid," and Buck Taylor, "King of the Cowboys." Of these, Cody appeared as commentator throughout the show and also performed as a shooter, downing clay pigeons while holding his rifle in one hand, shooting from horseback with a Winchester rifle, and splintering glass balls with an ordinary Colt army revolver.

Neither Cody nor the Butlers ever stated that Annie hailed from the West beyond the Mississippi River, but audiences, fans, and reporters assumed as much. Annie's association with the famous Buffalo Bill Cody's Wild West sealed her identification with the Old West of Kansas, the Dakotas, or even Colorado in most people's mind. In reality, however, Annie traveled west of the Mississippi River only with the Wild West show. Route schedules of Buffalo Bill's Wild West during the 1880s and 1890s indicate that in the United States it toured largely in Connecticut, Delaware, Massachusetts, Maine, New Hampshire, New York, Pennsylvania, Rhode Island, and Vermont in the Northeast; in Illinois, Indiana, Michigan, Ohio, and Wisconsin in the Midwest; and in Kentucky, Maryland, Missouri, Tennessee, Virginia, Washington, D.C., and West Virginia in the South.

Presumably Cody preferred to play in highly populated areas of the country and to easterners fascinated by his romanticized version of the American West. Only occasionally during the 1890s did the Wild West venture as far west as Iowa, Kansas, Nebraska, and eastern South Dakota and as far south as Alabama, Georgia, North Carolina, and South Carolina. Finally, between 1898 and 1902, the Wild West ventured to the Southwest and the Pacific Coast, notably California.

In newspaper interviews, Annie always told reporters she came from Ohio, and she often talked about the family farm, the woods in which she first hunted, and her family back in Ohio. But even though the U.S. Census Bureau's frontier line had long since moved beyond Ohio and across the Mississippi River, and even though many Americans, especially Ohioans, realized that Ohio was no longer a "pioneer" state, Annie's fans continued to think of her as a frontier and western woman. New Yorkers seemed especially fond of viewing Annie Oakley as a "true" westerner, and from their perspective, Ohio probably seemed as far west as Colorado or Oregon. On May 13, 1894, the *New York Morning Journal* stated that Oakley was "a credit to the 'glorious country' beyond the Rockies" from which she came. Even reporter Amy Leslie, supposedly a close friend of Annie's, assured the public that Oakley had shot plenty of game, from coyote to buffalo, in the "high western mountains." Among the few American newspapers to counter this interpretation was the *Portland Sunday Times*, which in June 1900 emphatically declared Annie Oakley "not a western girl."

When the Wild West played London, reporters there tended to write even more outrageous copy than American journalists. After all, most Londoners knew the American West only through what they had read: the Leatherstocking tales of James Fenimore Cooper; the adventure stories written by Mayne Reid, Charles Sealsfield, and Friedrich Gerstäcker; or the writings of Karl May, often called Germany's Cooper, who did not visit the West until after he had written nearly all his "western" adventures. Londoners may have picked up additional ideas from viewing reproductions of the paintings of Swiss artist Karl Bodmer or American artist-explorer-naturalists George Catlin and Charles Bird King or perhaps from reading American history written by Francis Parkman. But too many of these pictures and books presented highly idealized western portraits that traded more in hyperbole than truth.

When the Wild West first arrived in England during the spring of 1887, Londoners soon accepted the exhibition as real western Americana. A member of a Wild West audience on May 14, 1887, admitted that he, an avid reader of Mayne Reid's tales and other similar books, was delighted to see Indians gallop into the arena "without a hitch" and pull up opposite the spectators with surprising suddenness. One always used to read of Indians riding up at a gallop, he remarked, and of pulling horses onto their haunches as they stopped; now anyone could go and see it done.

Londoners also accepted Annie Oakley as a true representative of the Old Wild West. One described her as "a Western girl with quiet, expressive eyes." During the following summer, many Londoners watched Annie ride on "the Row." Few would care to copy her style of dress, the *London Post* editorialized, but one had to admit that "her get-up" was "that of the real wild West."

When the Wild West returned to England in 1891, people welcomed the troupe and its star shooter by playing daily the "Wild West Waltz," dedicated to Annie Oakley, "Little Sure Shot," at the International Horticultural Exhibition. Even the London-based *Shooting Times* believed more than it should have. It flatly stated that shooting was the national sport in the United States and that guns were an integral part of all boys', and of some girls', lives. In fact, the *Times* continued, at one of Annie's U.S. exhibitions, "every man who passed through the gate" wore a pair of revolvers strapped to his waist, and some carried Winchester rifles.

The smaller English cities extended a similar suspension of disbelief to the Wild West exhibition. In August 1891, the *Nottingham Daily Express* said that Nottingham had "been to the Wild West, and found it good." People poured into the Wild West tent by the thousands, six or seven thousand for the afternoon performance and as many more during the evening. There, through the efforts of Buffalo Bill and his troupe, they were able to "conjure up scenes of prairie and frontier life such as novelists" had painted. Soon, the *Express* concluded, the "tomahawk and the hunting knife" would be extinct, and the American West would march only in Buffalo Bill's wake.

Having such a fascination for the American West, the English understandably continued to see Annie Oakley as an authentic westerner. Fans and reviewers alike referred to her as a "frontier" girl; some of those who had the opportunity to visit with her even thought she spoke with a delightful "western" accent. Thus did the Ohio farm girl become the model western woman.

In the meantime, William F. Cody had been in the gradual process of inventing the cowgirl, just as he had invented the cowboy, turning him from a rugged, often unsavory, manual laborer who worked at a low-paid, dusty, seasonal job into a cultural hero. Cody seemed to ignore the reality of the cowboy and the complaints against him. In 1881, for example, President Chester A. Arthur had asked the U.S. Congress to suppress not only Indians but also the desperadoes known as "Cow-boys" who ran rampant throughout the American West.

In a similar way, Cody created the cowgirl. If he hoped to attract women viewers, he would have to include women in the show. Moreover, rather than simply appearing as victims in the sketch about the burning of the settlers' cabin, women performers needed to be figures with whom a female audience could identify and admire. After all, the late nineteenth century was witnessing a drastic change in thinking about women and their abilities while the female work force was growing dramatically and women were breaking into virtually every professional field.

Also, because Buffalo Bill wanted to present an authentic portrayal of the West, he had to include women, for women did indeed ride and shoot in the West. Documented cases existed in Kansas, Montana, Wyoming, and Texas of women who ran ranches and drove their cattle to market or worked as partners with their husbands, performing a variety of jobs including wrangling cattle. In Wyoming, for example, Lucy Wells helped her unmarried brother develop a homestead into a ranch. She remembered that she "could handle the horses, milk cows, mow and rake in the fields," in short, everything there was "to be done on a ranch except plow."

Then, especially during the 1890s and early 1900s, a significant number of young women went west as "girl homesteaders." Land-office data from Colorado and Wyoming indicated that 11.9 and 18.2 percent of homestead entrants were females, more of them single than married. Data also revealed that 42.4 percent of the women "proved up" their claims, whereas only 37 percent of male claimants did so.

Consequently, even women who clung to the traditional female ethic of the Victorian era were curious about women who pushed at the bounds of that ethic. Thus, as Cody developed the cowgirl, he tried to shape the image of women performers the way he and, he hoped, potential audiences *wanted* to see western women.

One of the most popular acts in the Wild West that involved women was the Virginia reel on horseback, in which women rode as dance partners to the men. During her early years with the Wild West, Annie sometimes participated in the Virginia Reel, but it soon featured Emma Lake Hickok, daughter of Agnes Lake, a circus owner married to Hickok before his fatal shooting in Deadwood. Emma taught her horse to jump to music and stand on his hind legs to bow.

Of all the female performers, Annie captured first place in the public mind by personifying western women with unusual grace. She shot and rode with unusual skill. The first season with the Wild West, Annie began her act by shooting clay pigeons sprung from a trap; she then shot pigeons from two traps at a time, picked up her gun from the ground and shot after the trap was sprung, shot two pigeons in the same manner, and shot three glass balls thrown in the air in rapid succession, the first with her rifle held upside down on her head, the second and third with a shotgun. During following seasons, Oakley constantly practiced and regularly added new tricks to her repertoire.

Virtually all the women performers during the early years were Anglo women, often from rather conventional backgrounds and from areas outside the western United States. Shooter May Lillie grew up in Philadelphia and attended Smith College, whereas the "Texas Girl," Lillian Ward, had moved from Brooklyn to Texas for health reasons. Others accompanied husbands on the Wild West circuit. One of these was Minnie Thompson, who formed a partnership with her husband to run Wild West shows and circuses.

Women of other races and ethnic groups either had their own place in the Wild West shows or remained largely invisible. Native American women almost always appeared in limited roles; in the historical panoramas, they played torturers of white women or they appeared as "squaws" accompanying their men. Between shows, they provided back-lot attractions for curious visitors. African-American, Mexican, and Asian women seem to have been absent from the arena, at least during the early years.

As early as 1891, Cody's publicity used the term "cowgirls." Later, in 1898, the staff coined the term "rancheras" to describe the women riders in the show. The female riders Cody billed as "a bevy of beautiful rancheras, genuine and famous frontier girls in feats of daring equestrianism." But as more women joined the Wild West shows, the graceful term "rancheras" lost ground to the more descriptive "cowgirls." Even Annie Oakley's niece Fern came to think of her aunt as a cowgirl. She later wrote that as Annie rode into the arena, her long brown hair flying in the breeze, she "was typical of the Western cowgirl." Fern's words, of course, were inaccurate; her Aunt Annie, along with a few others, was only in the process of helping Cody *create* the typical western cowgirl.

Some of the cowgirls joined Wild West shows for excitement. May Lillie once said that being a cowgirl gave a woman far more enjoyment that "any pink tea or theater party or ballroom ever yielded." Many liked the opportunity to draw good pay or to work and travel with their husbands. Although some married couples attempted to bear and raise children on the circuit, childless married couples, like Annie Oakley and Frank Butler, were common.

At first, most cowgirls drew positive reactions from audiences. Cody and others billed them as prairie beauties, natural flowers of the American West, and Wild West show programs regularly denied that cowgirls belonged to the class of "new women." Cowgirls, promoters maintained, simply represented lively, athletic, young women who wanted the opportunity to develop their skills.

Such assertions sounded plausible; during the late 1890s most cowgirls still wore dresses or skirts and bodices, gloves, and hats with turned-up brims. Only a few rode their horses astride, and show programs explained that those cowgirls who adopted the "cross-seat" did so for safety and for freedom of movement. Even after the turn of the century, cowgirls who continued to work as "distaff" riders, appearing in historical sagas or horseback dances, or who sang songs around a campfire were generally well accepted.

By the mid-1890s, however, many cowgirls began to change their behavior and thus elicit negative comments. The image of cowgirls as tough women, unnaturally muscled and hardened in sentiment, began to emerge. Critics even viewed many cowgirls as potential corrupters of "good" women. This shift of opinion occurred partly because many cowgirls adopted masculine styles of clothing. At first, they wore divided skirts, which soon evolved into bloomer or trouser outfits bedecked with fur, feathers, beads, fringes, quillwork, and painted designs and set off by knee-high boots and Stetson hats. By the mid-1890s, a significant number of women in Wild West shows rode broncs, diving horses, and steers, as well as performed fancy roping and bulldogging. These cowgirls rode astride, which most Americans still thought immodest as well as potentially harmful to women's reproductive systems. A special saddle with a padded seat, a heavy roll of padding across the front of the seat, and thick, stiff leather between the saddle and the stirrup appeared, but most photographs and posters from the era show cowgirls continuing to use men's lighter roping saddles.

The majority of the criticism came from the public rather than from showpeople themselves. In August 1903, J. D. Tippett, an eighteen-year veteran with tent shows, wrote to Annie saying that he had always felt "touchy about what the world" called "show women," for he knew from his travels that they were "just as moral and respectable as any class of women on earth." Tippett's remarks about the public's attitude toward female performers, comments sent to Annie in reaction to the scurrilous article about her supposed use of drugs, places her own subsequent actions in a larger context. Her willingness to sue the newspapers reflected, at least in part, her determination to keep her reputation unsullied and to hold herself above the more disreputable cowgirls.

During the years Oakley pursued her libel suits, from 1904 to 1910, publicity became increasingly risqué. Posters picturing cowgirls engaged in unladylike activities alarmed many Americans even further. In 1910, a poster advertising a motion picture, *The Life of Buffalo Bill*, produced by the Buffalo Bill/Pawnee Bill Film Company, featured a cowgirl wearing trousers, a man's shirt and bandanna, a Stetson hat, and six-guns. Riding astride, she twirled a lariat above the horns of a massive, steam-snorting bull.

The following year, when Annie joined the Young Buffalo Show, the *Baltimore Evening Sun* described one cowgirl as wearing a "comic-opera costume" and displaying a pretty face turned as "hard as nails." With the Young Buffalo Show between 1911 and 1913, Oakley refused to model herself after such women. Annie, who continued to wear her usual conservative clothing, appealed to two types of viewers: those who admired her skill whatever her attire and demeanor, and those who appreciated her ladylike stance. She continued to draw audiences and garner favorable reviews, despite, or perhaps because of, the more modern dress and actions of her competitors.

Given Oakley's attitudes toward proper female behavior, she must have reacted with both amazement and displeasure to the changes she witnessed during the years between 1885 and 1913. At least seventy-two Wild West shows, and probably more than that, existed during this period. The shows literally saturated the nation with increasingly intrusive publicity. Their advance agents plastered publicity on board fences, billboards, and the walls of buildings from barns to outhouses, so that even if people did not attend a Wild West show, they still absorbed its images.

It was literally impossible to avoid such advertising. Agents had begun their publicity blitzes with a one-sheet bill, which measured twenty-eight by forty-two inches, but they rapidly progressed to two-, three-, four-, six-, eight-, twelve-, and six-teen-sheet posters. Among the grandest was the twenty-four sheet, which came in six separate sections and, when assembled, measured twenty-four times the size of the one-sheet. Agents gave young boys free tickets to distribute handbills house to house while they placed the smaller-sized bills in store windows, sometimes completely covering them. The twenty-four-size post-ers covered billboards at the cost of a small fee and farmers' barns for the price of a couple of free tickets.

It would have been difficult for anyone living in the United States to ignore the masculine images of women in such advertis-ing. During the early 1900s, Pawnee Bill billed his cowgirls as "Beautiful Daring Western Girls and Mexican Senoritas in a Contest of Equine Skill." Tiger Bill's Wild West went further; its posters pictured women shooters in the attack on the settlers' cabin. These women not only wielded guns alongside men but wore above-the-knee skirts, knee-high boots, and men's Stetson hats.

Other shows followed the trend. Owners, managers, and pub-licity agents, who realized that Wild West shows were losing ground to other mediums such as Owen Wister's novel *The Virginian*, published in 1902 and widely regarded as the "first" western adventure novel, or such as Edwin S. Porter's 1903 movie *The Great Train Robbery*, had to use every attention-getter they could devise. As a result, Tompkins Real Wild West and Frontier Exhibition issued posters that showed a woman riding astride, attired in a split skirt, her whip raised in the air, while another woman hung from a cross-saddle to retrieve something from the ground. Both rode amid men.

The Buffalo Ranch Real Wild West's advertising also portrayed women riding with men and participating in equestrian football and camel races. In other publicity, it claimed that cowboys, cowgirls, Indians, and Mexicans constituted the four elements of the Old West. It outreached Buffalo Bill Cody and his Congress of Rough Riders by presenting a Congress of American Cowgirls.

During these years, numerous Wild West shows expanded on the original western themes by adding "Far East" attractions. The Miller Brothers 101 Ranch Wild West, which included such spectacles as Cleopatra dancing and Julius Caesar fiddling, pictured in its advertising a woman charioteer whipping her four white horses as she competed against a male charioteer and his four black horses. She continued the race despite a lost wheel while spectators in the royal box waved and cheered.

Still other Wild West posters advertised shows that women owned and operated. As early as 1896, the Kemp Sisters Wild West entered the growing competition for audiences. In 1903, Luella Forepaugh-Fish's Wild West appeared, followed by Lone Star May's Wild West in 1909 and Prairie Lillie and Nebraska Bill's Wild West in 1912. Apparently, some of these women had risen from the ranks of Wild West performers into that of entrepreneurs.

In addition to handbills and posters, the rapidly growing number of Wild West shows gave away booklets called "couriers." Designed to attract customers, couriers often featured colored ink and line drawings. In 1899, Buffalo Bill's Wild West issued a sixteen-page, magazine-sized courier called the *Rough Rider*. As the annual editions of the *Rough Rider* continued into the 1900s, they grew longer in format and more elaborate in illustration and included more and more information about the acts and stars. Then, in 1909, the Buffalo-Bill/Pawnee Bill Wild West, called the Two-Bills' show, put out a thirty-page courier reproducing posters and other artwork, including Frederic Remington's *Buffalo Bill on Horseback*.

Advance agents gave stacks of these couriers to merchants and newspaper offices and sometimes distributed them house to house. If a person had somehow avoided Wild West images in handbills and posters, he or she could now peruse at leisure these extremely attractive and free couriers. Also, if a person attended a Wild West show, he or she could buy a souvenir program to study further at home and to pass around to family and friends.

Cody began selling such programs in 1883 for ten cents and soon added color-lithograph covers. For the first command performance in London, he and Salsbury ordered the programs with covers printed on silk. By the time the Wild West reached Paris in 1889, the program numbered forty-eight pages. When the Wild West returned to the United States from its second European tour in 1893, most Wild West programs used halftones rather than line drawings, were printed on good paper, and ran to sixty-four pages. In 1893, one program devoted a sizable segment to Annie Oakley:

> The first two years before the public she devoted to Rifle and Pistol Shooting, and there is very little in that line she has not accomplished. At Tiffin, Ohio, she once shot a ten-cent piece held between the thumb and forefinger of an attendant at a distance of 30 feet. In April, 1884, she attempted to beat the best record made at balls thrown in the air—the best record was 984 set by Dr. Ruth. Miss OAKLEY used a Stevens' 22 cal. rifle and broke 943. In February, 1885, she attempted the feat of shooting 5,000 balls in one day, loading the guns herself. In this feat she used three 16-gauge hammer guns; the balls were thrown from three traps 15 yards rise; out of the 5,000 shot at, she broke 4,722; on the second thousand she only missed 16, making the *best* 1,000 ball record, 984. Besides the thousands of exhibitions she has given in Europe and America, she has shot in over 50 matches and tournaments, winning forty-one prizes; her collection of medals and fire-arms, all of which have been won or presented to her, is considered one of the finest in the world.

If a viewer had not already learned a sufficient amount, he or she could also purchase a book featuring the various stars of the show. Cody started selling *Story of the Wild West and Camp-Fire Chats* in 1888 and even sent hawkers through the audience with stacks of the book. In 1893, John M. Burke added *"Buffalo Bill" from Prairie to Palace* to the books for sale, and in 1899, Cody's sister Helen Cody Wetmore released *Last of the Great Scouts*, sold on street corners for one dollar, with a ticket to the show included. During the 1910s, the Young Buffalo Show sold a ten-cent pamphlet of twenty-four pages titled *A Great White Indian Chief*.

The only such booklet that seems to have appeared about Annie was published in London in 1887. Titled *The Rifle Queen*, it ran sixty-four pages and sold for the bargain price of two cents. *The Rifle Queen* described Oakley's supposed childhood in Kansas (rather than Ohio), including her trapping wolves, foiling train robbers, riding out a blizzard, shooting a bear, and defeating a desperado. Many readers took the booklet as the truth, as did many reporters, who then reported Oakley's fictional exploits as fact.

By the turn of the century, courtesy of Buffalo Bill's Wild West and its far-reaching publicity, Annie Oakley had become the western woman and cowgirl par excellence.

Because Annie Oakley and Frank Butler had to earn an income during the Wild West's off-season—the late fall, winter, and early spring months—they sometimes tried to capitalize on her western image by taking it on the stage, much as Cody himself had starred in western melodramas during the 1870s and 1880s. Because western melodrama was a stock feature of theater offerings, Annie's efforts as an actress earned some money and lent additional credence to her reputation as a western woman.

Oakley first took to the boards in 1888 when she opened in *Deadwood Dick; or, The Sunbeam of the Sierras* in Philadelphia on Christmas Eve to less-than-enthusiastic reviews. "Bombastic" and "unreasonable" were among the terms applied to the show's plot. Other, kinder critics lauded Annie's dramatic ability and predicted a brilliant future for her or heaped high praise on the troupe, who played the roles of what some called "denizens of that far region," the American West, with realism and deftness. *Deadwood Dick* closed at the end of January 1889 after manager John Keenan decamped with the show's receipts.

Annie later claimed that the backer had guaranteed the play would be "first class." He had offered Annie good money, but she soon discovered that he was gambling on her reputation to clear a profit. She felt grateful that reviewers "abstained from vegetable throwing" and frequently gave her good reviews. Obviously, Annie and Frank recognized the appeal of western themes. As one reviewer sagely remarked, "Western drama never fails to find a sympathetic and appreciative audience." Annie and Frank simply needed to discover a workable formula for putting her western persona on the road and keeping it there.

During the fall of 1894, Annie and Frank tried again. The vehicle, *Miss Rora*, tried to capitalize on the nation's raging interest in the American West as well the growing allure of the Old South. Advance publicity described *Miss Rora* as a drama "illustrative of life on the frontier." Annie would star in the role of a "wild, wayward Western girl." Guaranteed to incorporate both pathos and humor, the story began at a silver mine in Arizona. Here the heroine, Aurora Blackburn, played of course by Annie, lived with her two "Daddies," miners who had rescued her after she survived an Indian attack that not only killed her parents but destroyed the entire party with whom they had traveled westward. At the urging of an itinerant minister who argued that the two miners might be doing Rora inadvertent harm by keeping her secluded in a mining camp, the men advertised in newspapers and located Rora's rich Louisiana grandfather, who duly appeared and took her back to his vast and prosperous plantation. Once Rora was in Louisiana, her two cousins attempted to destroy her, kill her grandfather, and break his new will, written in her favor, but she foiled all their attempts while winning the love of a handsome young planter.

Annie may have resented negative images of Native Americans, but she was unaware of other stereotypes. This play featured a "Chinaman" in the mining camp portion, as well as black servants who sang, danced, and played the banjo during the plantation scenes. Annie herself represented the West, wearing what one viewer termed "picturesque North American attire," shooting at glass balls and a variety of other targets, and riding her horse, Gipsy, on the stage, even though the horse's hoofs sometimes broke through the stage floor. Audiences seemed especially to appreciate the finale, in which Annie rode in a fox hunt with a pack of trained hounds and even jumped her horse over a hurdle.

Reviewers generally liked *Miss Rora* and judged Annie a good actress and a marvelous shooter. Still, many houses were sparse. The effects of the Panic of 1893 had hit with full force in 1894, with violent labor strikes helping to keep people at home. Also, *Miss Rora* had stiff competition for limited entertainment dollars. Among the year's attractions were Victor Herbert's first comic opera, *Prince Ananias*; Vesta Tilley, a celebrated male impersonator from England on her first American tour; and the opening of B. F. Keith's elegant vaudeville house, Boston's Colonial Theatre.

A final blow to *Miss Rora* in the United States came in November when the *New York Sunday World* caricatured Annie Oakley as a buxom woman wearing a dress with huge polka-dotted sleeves. She held her rifle in her hands and perched precariously atop a wooden rocking horse. Its caption read, "Annie Oakley, Late with Buffalo Bill, as Miss Roarer."

After the Christmas holidays, Annie and Frank took *Miss Rora* to England, where it did well throughout the winter and spring of 1895, generally playing to full houses. In her role of Rora, Oakley proved herself a poised actress, and her shooting exhibition usually brought down the house. When *Miss Rora* reached Nottingham, reviewers agreed that the play was "fun," but they criticized its slight plot, which would collapse without Annie's shooting exhibitions. In Wales, reviewers also loved Oakley's shooting, as well as the fox hunt finale.

Miss Rora traveled through Great Britain for ten weeks, but because of the depression that prevailed there as well as in the United States, the company made only enough to cover expenses. Annie ended her English tour at the Alhambra Theater, where she performed between acts of the ballet *Ali Baba* while stagehands moved the heavy, unwieldy scenery.

Given the outcome of *Deadwood Dick* and *Miss Rora*, Annie understandably limited her stage appearances to vaudeville and refrained from acting in another western drama for several years. Then, in November 1902, Annie opened in *The Western Girl*, written by the prolific and popular Langdon McCormick. She wore a curly brown wig to cover her white hair, and she appeared stouter. According to Frank, Annie had gained weight and now weighed 138 pounds, considerably more than usual.

The advance publicity, mostly newspaper advertisements and posters, employed terms similar to those used by Buffalo Bill's Wild West. It described *The Western Girl* as a portrayal of "the days of the Old West as never before attempted on the dramatic stage." Many notices featured Annie, one picturing her in a floor-length dress, with a Mexican style sash tied rakishly around her waist and a tilted sombrero on her head. Another showed a woman, presumably Annie, in the uncharacteristic position of riding astride, with her revolver pointed in the air.

Posters and other advertisement also announced that the play would feature Annie's own horses, especially Little Bess, "A Rocky Mountain Pet." Much like Cody's Wild West, the stage properties would include "The Old Historic MAIL COACH Procured Especially for this GREAT PLAY," which was the old Lead-ville stagecoach. It would be pulled by four horses with authentic western trappings. The spectacular scenery, painted on high-grade linen cloth, would reproduce the "days of the wild and wooly West." Including even the canyon of the Colorado River by moonlight, the scenery would add a touch of realism to this "startling picture of the Wild West."

According to the plot of *The Western Girl*, Oakley, as the heroine Nance Barry, foiled a half-breed bandit named LaFonde and defeated a variety of other villains. Predictably, Nance Barry and her confederate, Lieutenant Hawley, ended up in each other's arms by the end of the play. Along the way, the play featured Oakley shooting, riding, and defeating evil at every turn. In case all these elements did not suffice, the play also featured singing and yodeling specialties.

As products of their era, reviewers inevitably overlooked the play's many stereotypes, including a German scientist and an Irish miner with a talkative wife. In one especially classic scene, a Chinese laundryman rescued the heroine. Another stock charac-ter was a treacherous Mexican dance-hall girl, Pancheta, played by Jeannette Farrell, an Anglo woman born and raised in Syracuse, New York.

Nor did anyone question the authenticity of the play's represen-tation of the Old West. When *The Western Girl* played Atlantic City in December 1902, one reviewer applauded the play's re-creation of "the western hills in the days before the railroad brought civilization to the early pioneers, and bandits and out-laws had only the small check of scattered United States troops." Neither did critics question Oakley's audacity at presenting her-self as "the" western girl.

Annie either failed to notice the show's stereotypes or accepted them as show business conventions of the day. Oakley had a role to play and directions to follow, so rather than worrying about accurate images and portrayals, she was more concerned with giving a quality performance and continuing to perform under even the worst of circumstances. Whether she intended to or not, Annie thus reinforced her image as a strong, durable western woman. For instance, in Atlantic City during the fall of 1902,

Annie's spirited horse, nervous in small spaces, ran Oakley into a piece of projecting scenery that gashed her nose. Annie bled, reeled momentarily, then regained self-possession and rode off the stage. After a doctor in the audience hurried backstage to dress the deep gash and pull it together with adhesive, Oakley returned to the stage and, with what one viewer called "grit," continued the play, thus proving herself a courageous western woman in fiction and in fact.

Not surprisingly, audiences packed theaters to see Oakley as the western girl and often went wild with their applause, demanding as many as six curtain calls. The play succeeded despite some tough competition; in 1903, Victor Herbert's *Babes in Toyland* opened, and Millie De Leon launched her burlesque career by throwing garters to members of the audience. The *Wilkes-Barre Record* put its finger on the appeal of *The Western Girl*, saying the show was a "dashing, sparkling, not to say sensational, melodrama" that remained "clean and wholesome throughout."

Because the play proved less successful financially than critically, it closed in March 1903. The large cast and elaborate scenery cost a great deal to transport and often overwhelmed theater stages when they arrived. As a result, Annie and Frank disbanded the troupe and sent the scenery to Annie's sister Hulda to store on her farm.

Despite its short run, *The Western Girl* and its attendant publicity added one more building block to Annie's western image. The play presented Oakley as a western woman who demonstrated courage and toughness at the same time that she remained feminine, compassionate, and family-oriented. As Nance Barry, Annie provided a perfect heroine, one that both women and men could respect.

Combined with Oakley's association with Sitting Bull and Cody's Wild West, Annie's stage appearances, especially in *The Western Girl*, ensured her triumph as the archetypal western woman of the age. She represented a strong, brave, and self-reliant woman, yet a soft, pretty, and sweet one who fittingly ended her adventures in the arms of a deserving hero on stage and in those of her husband in real life. Oakley combined the best of older, revered American values with newer, expanded ideas regarding women and the West to establish herself as a virtually universal heroine.

In spite of Annie's widespread appeal, few films and books cast Oakley as their heroine between 1885 and 1913. Possibly, Annie's rendering of a western woman failed to generate enough excitement for novelists and scriptwriters. Certainly, Oakley's determination to remain ladylike must have made it difficult for authors to picture her as a rip-roaring, pistol-wielding western heroine. Especially after western writers turned away from James Fenimore Cooper's genteel heroines and replaced them with female desperadoes, usually attired in men's garb, Annie would have provided a poor fit. During the 1880s, 1890s, and early 1900s, Oakley's skirts, long hair, and demure behavior would have hardly been inspiration for western thrillers.

During the 1890s, however, Annie appeared in at least one motion picture. This came about as a result of Buffalo Bill Cody's close connection with Thomas Alva Edison, who designed the Wild West's six-hundred-horsepower electrical plant. Said to be the largest light producer in the world, the plant consumed two and one-half tons of coal in twenty-four hours and frequently required Edison's attentive presence.

When Edison invented his battery-powered kinetoscope moving-picture machine, he naturally turned to Cody and such performers as Oakley as subjects. In September 1894, Cody and fifteen colorfully dressed Native Americans went to Edison's "studio" in West Orange, New Jersey, to act before Edison's invention. The shoot took place in a "Black Maria," a frame building covered with black tar-paper, later referred to as the first motion picture studio.

Later that fall, Annie also traveled to East Orange, as did trapeze artist El Capitaine and the Gaiety Girls. Edison expressed particular interest in Oakley because he wanted to know if his invention could follow the flight of a bullet. Edison soon learned that his camera could reproduce Annie's shots, the smoke from her rifle, and the splintering of glass balls. Edison showed these early films, including those of Annie, in nickel-in-the-slot machines, called peep-show machines and later dubbed nickelodeons. Crowds lined up outside the kinetoscope parlors that had opened in New York in April 1894; slipping their coins in the slot, viewers pressed their eyes against the slit and watched a ninety-second "movie." Other parlors soon followed in such cities as Atlantic City, Baltimore, and Chicago.

Thousands of people who saw Annie Oakley in a peep-show machine would remember her as one of the first "western" figures caught on film. One scene showed her repeatedly firing a Winchester rifle to demonstrate rapidity, whereas another pictured her shooting at composition balls tossed in the air. People who had never seen Annie in one of her many live appearances could now view her at last, courtesy of Edison's invention.

In addition, Oakley appeared in at least one dime novel series. Given Buffalo Bill Cody's total of 557 original stories by twenty-two authors plus reprints, which amounted to 1,700 individual issues, it is curious that Oakley did not also star in many dime novels. Apparently, Annie did not fit any of the usual female types, ranging from victim to Amazon.

Because many dime novels appealed to a male audience, they frequently presented women as victims rather than as heroines. A representative dime novel released in 1899, Edward L. Wheeler's *Deadwood Dick's Eagles; or, The Pards of Flood Bar*, presented one such female victim. When a bully accosted her in quest of a kiss she cried out, "Are there no *men* among you who will help me?" After a stalwart hero saved her, he proclaimed that he "never hesitated to face death in defense of a woman."

Wheeler's female victims, however, often turned hard and bitter as a result of their mistreatment. As early as 1878, Wheeler created Hurricane Nell in *Bob Woolf, the Border Ruffian; or, The Girl Dead-Shot*. Nell swore vengeance against Bob Woolf after he burned her home and hastened the death of her parents. She soon appeared in Colorado mining towns dressed as a man. Then, in a reversal of the usual scenario, Nell saved the hero, killed three men with three shots, and won a shooting match. Wheeler followed Nell with Wild Edna, leader of a band of road agents in *Old Avalanche*, and with Calamity Jane (Martha Jane Cannary) in several of his "Deadwood Dick" series. In *Deadwood Dick on Deck; or, Calamity Jane, the Heroine of Whoop-Up* (1885), for example, Calamity Jane was another female victim who adopted male clothing, profane language, and a hard manner. Like Hurricane Nell, she too rescued the male hero.

In between the victim and the desperado were strong women who dressed and acted like women, rescued the hero, and then virtually disappeared from the story line. Wheeler wrote one such character into *Deadwood Dick's Eagles* (1899). When a young woman threatened Deadwood Dick at gunpoint and insisted he marry her, his wife, believed to be dead, appeared and challenged her husband's tormentor to a duel. In the resulting fight, Dick's wife lunged at her opponent, who fell back dead "with a blade run through her heart." In a later thriller, *The White Boy Chief; or, The Terror of the North Platte*, written in 1908 by an anonymous author known as "An Old Scout," a woman rescued the young hero from a band of "cussed redskins," then vanished from the story.

Annie fit none of these categories; she was not a victim, desperado, or minor character. It appears, however, that during the 1900s, Prentiss Ingraham patterned one of his capable women characters on Annie Oakley, perhaps in an attempt to create a new type of female heroine. In Ingraham's *Dauntless Dell* series, his new form of heroine proved herself the equal of any man.

In 1908, for example, in Ingraham's *Buffalo Bill's Girl Pard; or, Dauntless Dell's Daring*, Dell Dauntless of the Double D Ranch appeared on the scene dressed, much like Oakley in *The Western Girl*, in a knee-length skirt, "blouse-like waist," tan leggings, and "small russet shoes, with silver spurs at the heels." In one early scene, Dell chastised two cowboys because they had chased away two bandits whom the intrepid heroine had planned to capture by leading them into a nearby draw. As Dell slapped at her brace of holsters, she explained, much as Oakley might have, that she disliked rowdyism. "I try to be a lady, both at home on the ranch and when I'm abroad in the hills. But I don't think any the less of a lady because she's able to take care of herself."

Next, Dell set out to rescue her kidnapped friend, Annie McGowan. She enlisted the aid of Buffalo Bill and so impressed him with her abilities that he accepted her as his "pard." Watching her shoot and ride, Buffalo Bill asked himself, "Was there anything . . . in which Dell Dauntless did not excel?" Along the way, with the bowie knife that swung from her belt, Dell rescued a young Indian man named Little Cayuse. Cayuse rather rudely told Dell that "squaws" were supposed to boil water, make fires, and sew beads. After Dell replied, "I'm different from the ordinary run of squaws," Little Cayuse also accepted Dell as his "pard."

In subsequent chapters, Dell shot a rifle out of a villain's hand, rode important dispatches through armed Apaches, and broke out of Fort Grant. Dell had indeed proven herself to Buffalo Bill, "the king of the scouts," who concluded that Dell ranked "Class A among Western girls."

The story sounds improbable today, but then it taught such important virtues as bravery, assertiveness, ladyhood, loyalty, the importance of friendship, and the triumph of good over evil. More than just an adventure tale, this dime novel instructed readers in morals and values. Although most readers of dime novels remained male, some young women also read these western adventure tales. Perhaps Ingraham hoped to attract additional female readers with his creation of Dauntless Dell, who was clearly a laudable woman. Even the name Dauntless Dell carried a message; it indicated that some women were as fearless and capable of heroic deeds as men.

Because this book also impressed on readers' minds the courageous nature of such western-style performers as Annie Oakley, it helped legitimize the activities of show cowgirls and added women to the saga of the American West. Of course, Dauntless Dell was not an average western woman. Dell not only wielded firearms but also failed to end up in the hero's arms. As she assured Little Cayuse, she was different from ordinary women. Still, Dell showed readers that some women could act on their own behalf and could demonstrate bravery, decisiveness, and strength. Much as the real Annie Oakley helped open show business and sport shooting to women, her fictional prototype gave readers uncommon ideas regarding women.

During the early 1900s, Annie Oakley occasionally mentioned the possibility that she would star in a Hollywood motion picture. Although Annie appeared in at least one screen test, the project never materialized. Annie's comments indicate that she clearly realized that the nature of entertainment had undergone radical changes during the late nineteenth and early twentieth centuries; she may even have retired from the Young Buffalo Show in 1913 because she recognized that the popularity of Wild West shows had peaked.

According to Oakley, "Fancy sometimes helps us out in this big round world." But she must have been appalled and amazed at certain entertainment innovations of the day. For instance, burlesque performers now tickled viewers' imaginations by stripping off pieces of clothing. Then, in 1913, the celebrated Palace Theatre opened in New York, setting a standard for all vaudeville theaters that followed, while Al Jolson and Eddie Cantor astounded Broadway audiences and the motion picture *Uncle Tom's Cabin* attracted crowds of viewers.

In light of these changes, Annie retired just in time to keep intact her reputation as a great shooter and her image as a model western woman. Had she continued to work in the arena after 1913, she may have been overshadowed by other forms of entertainment. As it was, all that remained after 1913 was for Annie Oakley to put the finishing touches on her sparkling image. She would prove as adept at that as at almost everything else she tackled.

CHAPTER 6

"Why did I give up the arena?"

AS early as 1887, Annie Oakley had assured a London reporter, "I do not intend remaining in the profession until I become an old woman." Yet it was October 1913 before she, at fifty-three years of age and with silver-white hair, finally said good-bye to the Wild West circuit.

Within a few years after leaving Vernon Seavers's Young Buffalo Show, which had taken her to 139 towns in seventeen states, Annie posed the question, "Why did I give up the arena?" She answered in her usual succinct manner, "Because I made hay in the hay-day of my youth, and felt that I had earned a change."

But what would "change" mean for a woman who had retained her youthful agility and her athletic skills, so that she could still shoot, ride, and twirl a lariat with the best of them?

Because Annie Oakley had already become a legend in her own time, she had no further need for publicity. Her name would go down in history in many ways, for example as the term for free passes to shows. Because passes had to be punched to differentiate them from paid tickets, they were as full of holes as the playing cards, decorated with hearts and Annie's picture at one end, at which Annie shot and then threw into the audience as souvenirs. After one man said a pass looked like Annie Oakley had been shooting at it, the term "Annie Oakley" caught on in the theater, baseball, and circus worlds.

Nor did Annie Oakley have any need for further income. Because she and Frank Butler had planned well for retirement, they could choose a life of total leisure if so inclined. But the Butlers were both doers rather than watchers; they viewed retirement as anything but sitting and observing others. Instead, retirement offered the opportunity to pursue the interests and activities often denied them by their life on the road. The nature of their activities changed somewhat, but active the Butlers remained.

The years with the Young Buffalo Show had taken Annie and Frank to a beautiful waterfront town in Maryland. When Frank saw Cambridge, he turned to Annie and said that he would like to live there someday. In 1913, then, they began building a house on the shore of Hambrooks Bay at the mouth of the Great Choptank River. Annie requested square rooms with no projecting closets, a sink low enough for a five-foot-tall woman to work at in comfort, and a host of other amenities. From the home's front porch, the Butlers and their guests could watch oyster boats, a ferry, and the swaying buoys that marked the boundaries.

Just as he hoped, Frank loved Cambridge and their new home. He could boat, fish, and hunt until satiated. To him, Cambridge provided a "sportsman's paradise" that lay only "two hundred miles from Broadway." He completed the picture one day when he found a black, white, and tan purebred, soulful-eyed English setter languishing in a none-too-clean kennel. Frank bought the dog, brought him home to Annie, and named him Dave after Dave Montgomery of the comedy team Montgomery and Stone.

When a friend, Dr. Samuel Fort, visited the house on Hambrooks Bay that year, he found Frank "genial," Dave "a member of the family," and Annie "still the same patient, cheerful, kindly little woman." Then Annie's niece Fern visited the Butlers during the summer of 1913. She thought the place wonderful and especially liked to sit on the porch and "look over the bay and dream." Fern also enjoyed the boating, fishing, and hunting, but she noticed that Annie displayed a "restless spirit." Fern later recalled that she and Frank wondered how long Annie would enjoy life in Cambridge, despite its vast fields and hills for shooting and hunting.

Annie herself admitted that although they had "settled down" and expected to live happily, she could not do it. Years on the road had accustomed her to structured days, activity, admiration, and a rich social life. Now Annie faced a life that must have seemed to her erratic, boring, and out of her control. The domesticity that she liked to practice in a tent or hotel room now dominated her life. Instead of counting her achievements in numbers of shots made or quail downed, she found herself in charge of producing meals and clean laundry and planning social events.

Predictably, just as she had years earlier in Nutley, Annie failed at running a home. "I went all to pieces under the care of a home," she explained. Frank agreed. She was a "rotten housekeeper," he said without even a stab at tact. He added that Annie's "record in this department" was "seven cooks in five days." Because her fastidious nature about her clothing and costumes extended to her house and meals, Annie frequently drove both domestic helpers and Frank to distraction. Also, her attention to detail, which served her so well in the arena and on the hunting grounds, proved difficult to maintain in a less-formal, domestic setting. And the confidence and patience she exhibited with a rifle in her hands dissipated the moment she exchanged gun for domestic utensil. Evidently, domestic life was less suited to Annie's perfectionist and achievement-oriented personality than life on the road.

Also in 1913, another visitor arrived who may have exacerbated Annie's apparent wanderlust. George Widows, the young man who had run off to South America when he learned Annie was married, arrived bearing exotic presents. Frank had corresponded with George for years, and now George repaid the friendship with gifts of unusual animal horns and tales of his hunts and other adventures.

Still, despite Annie's restiveness, the Butlers spent a peaceful and productive year hunting, fishing, and writing. Frank, who was now sixty-three years old, looked back in verse on his life as a sportsman. "A hunter now old and gray sat musing on his sports of long ago . . . and sighed because his hunting days were o'er." Other poems he dedicated to Annie. "Her presence would remind you / Of an angel in the skies."

Annie wrote as well. In between hunting and shooting at their own clay pigeon trap and or at the Du Pont shooting grounds in Cambridge, donated by the Du Pont family, she composed the pamphlet *Powders I Have Used*, published by the Du Pont Company. She also contributed articles, arguing for women as shooters and hunters, to such journals as the *Sportsman's Review*. Then, in 1914, Annie sent one of her open letters to *American Field*. She noted that Dorchester County officials had issued more than seventeen hundred game licenses and that "a great deal of game" was bagged there. But she added, "I am pleased to say there is plenty left over."

By 1915, the retired life seemed good, at least to Frank, who at sixty-five years of age appeared more ready for retirement than his fifty-five-year-old wife, who seemed to want more variety in their lives. In response to Annie's restlessness, that summer, Frank loaded her and Fern into their automobile and toured them across the country. Along the way, Frank noted the changes that had overtaken circuses and Wild West shows. Despite a healthy economy, he counted six stranded traveling shows, one standing six feet under water. And when they ran into Buffalo Bill Cody, who had sold the Wild West in 1913 to cover some of his extensive debts and who now performed in shows he did not own, hoping to raise some money to buy his own show again, Frank Butler judged William Cody "quite feeble" and near the end of his days. Frank remarked that show business was in "very bad straits"; retirement had come at just the right time for him and Annie.

Annie, however, believed she might find a place in new types of entertainment, especially films. She commented that she had retired only until movie producers were "willing to pay" the salary she wanted. In 1915, rumors of a movie deal circulated. Oakley assured a reporter that she had received the offer of "several positions" in films but had turned them all down. "They don't want to pay enough and until they do I will not be seen in the movies." About this time she ordered two new guns from the Ithaca Gun Company; it shipped the first, a 12-gauge double-barreled field gun, to Cambridge in September.

Unlike Annie, Frank had little desire to exchange retirement for erratic schedules, travel, and more public exposure. As a result, he relied heavily on his and Annie's friendship with Fred Stone and his family to keep Annie amused. Certainly, Fred Stone and his partner, Dave Montgomery, especially in their colossal hit *The Red Mill*, kept half the nation amused.

Rather than telling Annie jokes, however, Stone engaged her attention by inviting her and Frank to his farm on Long Island. There the Butlers shot on the trap range Stone had built after his friendship with them had encouraged him to become a devoted trap shooter. Stone also shot at local gun clubs wherever his current hit played and once commented, "[I] got more pleasure out of breaking 100 straight in a 100-target match at the Chicago Gun Club than I did out of all our Chicago *Red Mill* notices."

Still, Annie remained unsettled. With Susan dead, family members busy with concerns of their own, and former neighbors dead or dispersed, Annie's desire to make frequent visits to Ohio dwindled. Also, some of Annie's nieces and grandnieces seemed to vie with each other for her favor, so that jealousy may have marred her visits home. At the very least, Annie's community of women back in Ohio had largely dissipated.

Yet the leisure that she and Frank had saved and planned for was not enough for Annie; she longed for more action and perhaps more contact with people. Thus, besides hunting near Cambridge, the Butlers began to spend the quail season in Leesburg, Florida, where they had first hunted in 1911. Photographs show a happy Annie and Frank in front of the Lakeview Hotel, a large two-story building fronted by a wide porch, and at Kamp Kumfort on Treasure Island, a private retreat owned by the mayor of Leesburg.

Frank loved Leesburg, which for him was, like Cambridge, a "sportsman's paradise." The Lakeview Hotel, he said, knew how to "cater to sportsmen." The hunting proved good; Annie and Frank bagged so much game that they distributed it to the other guests or ordered it served for dinner. Good company proved abundant as well. One Leesburg resident remembers that Annie called his father, John Jacob Stoer of Philadelphia, the "best quail shot" she had ever hunted with.

But Leesburg was not total heaven. Annie also bagged huge rattlesnakes, and Dave battled fleas and ticks. In addition, Annie seemed to need more structure and activity in her days. As a result, the Butlers turned to the resort town of Pinehurst, with its dozen stores, three schools, a library, a post office, four hotels, a clubhouse, two golf courses, a skeet and target range, plentiful kennels and stables, and one weekly newspaper, the *Pinehurst Outlook*, published every Saturday.

As early as 1908 and 1909, the *Outlook* had revealed that Annie and Frank had gained local favor. In January 1909, the newspaper described the hundreds of people who witnessed Oakley's exhibition, the opening event of the Midwinter Handicap, and concluded, "No one went away disappointed." Among other feats, Annie clipped a potato off a stick piece by piece; shot through the ace of hearts; sliced with bullets four cards held edgewise; smashed pieces of coal, brass discs about the size of a quarter, and marbles; and finally aimed at .22 cartridges tossed in the air, driving each out of sight. The *Outlook* also described Frank Butler as "one of the most popular shooters in the country."

Then the *Outlook* announced on December 11, 1915, that the Butlers were "spending the winter at The Carolina." Frank took charge of the traps and hunting, and Annie offered to teach some of the other women guests how to shoot. Because Annie had agreed to help female guests at the Carolina learn the proper handling of rifles and shotguns, there was "an unusual interest" in the sport. The *Outlook* noted, "Many of the girls are acquiring a skill in potting the bric-a-brac pigeons which may tax the ability of the old hands to excel."

Annie and Frank had picked the finest hotel in Pinehurst. The Carolina stood four stories high and provided its guests with electricity, central heating, and telephones in every room. The Carolina attracted wealthy northerners, who began to pour into its grounds during the early fall months to enjoy golfing, shooting, hunting, horseback riding, and other sports. Among the celebrities that Annie and Frank visited with there were Alexander Graham Bell, Edgar Guest, Senator Warren G. Harding, John D. Rockefeller, Will Rogers, Theodore Roosevelt, John Philip Sousa, Walter Hines Page, and Booth Tarkington.

Of course, Oakley and Butler themselves added to the sparkle of the guest list. When Harding first met Annie, he told her, "I feel highly honored at meeting Ohio's most distinguished daughter." She responded, "I am equally pleased to meet our next President." When he blushed and replied, "I'm not so sure," she shot back, "I am."

Annie seemed contented at last. She often joined early morning fox hunts, raced at the Pinehurst jockey club, hunted quail, entered at least one dog show, and went on weekly hunts that kept her, in her words, "vital." She also enjoyed the company of women guests. One day, she took three of them hunting and for lunch put a bird on a stick, placed a piece of bacon inside for flavoring, and broiled it over the fire. She later remarked, "How they did enjoy that meal!" On another occasion, Annie overheard a New York woman complain, "My, how I wish I were a man so that I could shoot." Annie assured her that gender did not prevent her from learning to shoot and led her to the range. Annie placed a .22-caliber rifle in the woman's hands and taught her how to stand, load, and aim properly. By the end of the lesson, the woman hit a perfect bull's-eye. After that, Annie devoted two hours to classes every morning. She charged no fee and only hoped that women would become "shooting enthusiasts."

Frank liked the Carolina as well. Apparently, one sportperson's paradise was as good as another, especially if his beloved Annie found happiness there. Frank rode, hunted, canoed, and took local Boy Scouts on outings.

Then, during the summer of 1916, Frank and Annie moved to a summer resort, Newcastle-by-the-Sea, near Portsmouth, New Hampshire. At a hotel owned by Harry Priest, the manager of the Carolina Hotel, the Butlers gave trap-shooting lessons. It appeared that the Butlers could happily shift between Cambridge, Pinehurst, and New Hampshire indefinitely. Still, what Annie was thinking remains unclear. She evidently intended to continue an active retirement and still considered the possibility of making films; in January 1916 another special gun had arrived from the Ithaca Gun Company, this one a #4-grade single-barrel trap gun.

As the year unfolded, Annie received more than one portent of coming changes. Newspaper headlines kept the European war, begun in 1914, in everyone's minds. And when Annie and her niece Fern visited Buffalo Bill Cody in New York City, Cody, according to Fern, got tears in his eyes and said, "Annie, I have come to this." The Wild West, victim of a bankruptcy engineered earlier by *Denver Post* tycoons, was no longer Cody's. Both Annie and Fern realized that Cody's end was near.

The year 1917 proved a significant one in Annie's and Frank's lives. They especially grieved the fate of their old friend and champion, William F. Cody. Cody had spent Christmas at his ranch near

Cody, Wyoming, then returned to Denver and, on the advice of his physician, took the waters at Glenwood Springs. After a few days Buffalo Bill, a bitter and defeated man, returned to the home of his sister, May Decker, on Denver's Lafayette Street. Cody's wife, Louisa, and daughter, Irma, had rushed to his side, as did Johnny Baker. When news spread of his impending death, Boy Scouts stood watch on May's porch. Hourly bulletins on Cody's condition went out while letters, telegrams, and telephone calls poured in. Then, on January 10, 1917, Buffalo Bill Cody died of uremic poisoning.

Cody's death jolted Annie and Frank as well as hundreds of others who had known, worked for, or loved Cody. One of these was Milt Hinkle, a bronc rider with rodeos and such shows as the Buffalo Bill Wild West and Miller and Arlington's 101 Ranch Real Wild West. Hinkle remembered that he was riding horses through sales inspection in Denver in 1917. When he came out of work the night of January 10 and walked toward the stockyards cafe, Hinkle heard newsboys shouting: "Extra! Extra! All about the death of Buffalo Bill!" Hinkle bowed his head in respect for Cody, whom he called "the greatest showman of all time."

Neither Annie nor Frank went to Denver for Cody's funeral. According to Hinkle, Cody lay "in state" in the capitol, and the Elks and Masons gave him a grand funeral. A long procession wound its way through the streets of Denver while Cody's "white horse, with pistols and rifle hung from the empty saddle," walked riderless, and "about one hundred of us cowboys on foot, followed the remains of Colonel Cody." Cody's body then lay in a vault for months while family members argued about where to bury him. Some argued for his birthplace, Iowa; some for his adopted home, Nebraska; and some for the town he founded, Cody, Wyoming. Finally, the *Denver Post* came to the rescue by paying for Cody's burial on Lookout Mountain. According to Hinkle, "It was another scoop for the Denver *Post*."

Annie vented her grief over Cody's death by composing a long, stirring eulogy, which was published in many newspapers, including the one Cody founded, the *Cody Enterprise*. Probably inadvertently, she helped perpetuate the myths that surrounded Cody and his version of the West during his lifetime. And, as astute as ever, Oakley recognized Cody's heroic image and the impact it would have on people's thinking about western men for generations to come.

> He was the kindest, simplest, most loyal man I ever knew. He was the staunchest friend. He was in fact the personification of those sturdy and lovable qualities that really made the West, and they were the final criterion of all men, East and West. Like all really great and gentle men he was not even a fighter by preference. His relations with everyone he came in contact with were the most cordial and trusting of any man I ever knew.

Another part of Cody's mythical western bearing was his legendary generosity, based on, according to Annie, the charitable philosophy "of the plains and the camp." It was no wonder to her, and others who knew him, that he died a poor man. As Annie wrote, "The same qualities that insured success also insured his ultimate poverty." Cody was so generous and kind-hearted that he could not resist any "mortal in distress"; he even borrowed money to give away to tramps and others in need.

Cody fulfilled beliefs about a true westerner in another way as well. He treated all equally, whether a band of cowboys or an emperor with his entourage. "A teepee and a palace were all the same to him," Oakley remarked, "and so were their inhabitants."

It was little wonder, then, that Cody inspired great loyalty. Oakley stated that she had traveled with Cody for years and watched all kinds of people join and leave his troupe, every one devoted to him. "His word was better than most contracts," she explained. "Personally, I never had a contract with the show after I started. It would have been superfluous."

Oakley also emphasized Cody's ability as a showperson. At the beginning, she wrote, the Wild West was just a loose conglomeration of people and animals who went into a town and gave a show, but "the essential truth and good spirit of the game made it the foremost educational performance ever given in the world." Cody had such a widespread effect on the entertainment industry that "he had hundreds of imitators" even though he "was quite inimitable."

Oakley concluded that Cody's "heart never left the great West." At the end of each day, he sat and watched the setting sun, and he returned home — to the West — every time he had the opportunity. "The sun setting over the mountain," Annie finished, "will pay its daily tribute to the resting place of the last of the great builders of the West, all of which you loved and part of which you were."

Cody's death marked the passing of the Wild West era. The halcyon days were done, and Annie's stardom was a thing of the past. If Cody's death was not enough to make Annie feel her own age and mortality, the *New York Tribune* tactlessly stated on January 11, 1917, that she was no longer a "dashing girl of the plains" but a little, old, silver-haired lady who sat and knitted. In an indignant letter dated January 20, Annie responded by detailing a few incidents from her life. "I have," she wrote, "never knitted." Instead, she taught women to shoot for "pleasure" rather than for compensation; she also rode and hunted. According to her, a twelve- or fifteen-mile trip made her "sleep and dream over again of the days when [she] ran bare-footed over hill and dale chasing the wild bees and butterflies or climbing nimbly up a dog-wood tree to pick the finest of blossomes [*sic*]."

Annie added that she had waged a hard fight for recognition in the arena. It had been "uphill work," for there was prejudice against women "to live down." But, thanks to the many "good American people" who gave generously of "their approval and applause," she had surmounted gender barriers. She hoped that her story gave an encouraging message to others who were "just beginning the great battle of life."

Clearly, Annie was far from ready to follow Cody. Nor did she want anyone to think she was an aged has-been, sitting at home knitting. Demonstrating her energy in a series of shooting exhibitions, she essentially gave notice that she remained robust and had no intention of following Cody anytime in the near future. Within a few weeks, another *Tribune* columnist remarked on Oakley's continuing vitality, perhaps by way of apology. On February 8, 1917, he wrote that he could hear the "sharp crack of Annie Oakley's rifle" all the way from Pinehurst, North Carolina.

Then, on February 11, nearly four hundred people assembled at the Pinehurst gun club to watch Oakley shoot. Among them was Martin G. Brumbaugh, governor of Pennsylvania, and his wife, whom Annie regarded as her cousins because her stepfather,

Daniel Brumbaugh, had come from Pennsylvania. According to the *Outlook*, Annie shot up "the entire neighborhood of F. E. Butler, including his cigarettes [which he held in his mouth as targets] and his money [which he held in his fingers] without apparently disconcerting him the least." Annie also shot a potato off Dave's head, scrambled five eggs in midair, cracked nuts, and shot backward by aiming in a mirror. The *Outlook* reporter was even more stunned by her reply to his request for a program. They had no plans, she answered; they just put together "an impromptu shoot" and ran the stunts as long as the audience wanted them.

For the time being, Oakley had forced Americans to remember her. Impending world war would offer another opportunity to exhibit her skills and continuing vitality. The war in Europe continued to pull at the United States, and on April 6, 1917, America declared war on Germany. Americans, hopeful of spreading democracy around the world, described their offensive as the war to end all wars. On June 5, 1917, the first selective service draft registered over nine million men. Food rationing went into effect as well, with President Woodrow Wilson repeatedly calling for an end to "wastefulness and extravagance." The observance of wheatless, meatless, and butterless days soon spread over the nation. At the Carolina, one March day in 1918, a woman guest gave a stirring speech while three others passed "a bushel basket each" and asked other guests for donations. They raised four hundred dollars for the war effort.

Annie Oakley and Frank Butler also expressed their deep concern regarding the war. In a 1918 poem, titled "Come Across," Frank stated that the issue went beyond democracy; Americans were fighting "For the honor of Old Glory, And to save the U.S.A." A reporter at the *Philadelphia Public Ledger* claimed, probably inaccurately, that Annie had once had the opportunity to avoid the war by hitting Kaiser Wilhelm rather than the cigarette he held in his mouth: "An American Woman Who Could Have Shot Kaiser, She Leveled Her Rifle Directly at His Head but Hit Only His Cigarette." Frank quipped that he wrote to Kaiser Wilhelm saying that Annie wanted to repeat the shot but that he never got a reply.

On a more serious level, Annie again offered, as she had in 1898, to raise a women's regiment to fight in the war. Although she still withheld her support from women's suffrage, she argued for women's rights in employment, sports, and self-defense. Consequently, Oakley wired Secretary of War Newton D. Baker, "I can guarantee a regiment of women for home protection, every one of whom can and will shoot if necessary." This time she received no answer; both President Wilson and Secretary Baker opposed her plan. Neither they nor most Americans were ready to accept women in combat.

At this point, Annie reportedly volunteered her services to the government as an instructor without cost and offered to go to camps, posts, or anywhere to demonstrate to soldiers the right way of firing, loading, and handling firearms. According to legend, when a lower-echelon officer's rejection of her proposal leaked to the press, Annie received offers from vaudeville to give shooting exhibitions for as much as one-thousand dollars per week. She would be billed as the shot the U.S. government turned down.

Instead, Oakley and Butler visited camps through the auspices of the National War Work Council of the Young Men's Christian Association and War Camp Community Service. At army posts, Annie gave exhibitions and talks. She and Frank carried their own equipment and supplies; they also paid their own expenses. Soldiers in camps everywhere rewarded their efforts. For instance, on May 22, 1918, at Camp Crane in Allentown, Pennsylvania, Annie drew "cheer after cheer from the soldier boys" as she performed all her usual stunts and then splattered a tin can with a "dum-dum" bullet used by German soldiers. Annie also received numerous letters of thanks for her war service.

Because she had the opportunity to contribute to the war effort, Annie said she was the "happiest woman in the world." Her time in the camps proved even more exciting than her days in the Wild West arena. But sometimes Annie added that she wished she could go to the front so that, instead of shooting at tin cans and other targets, she could knock down what she called German "square-heads" as fast as they advanced. Annie explained that anyone who visited army camps could not escape without catching the "On to Berlin" spirit and predicted that American troops would have the kaiser "on his knees" in no time.

During the war years, Oakley and Butler also worked to raise funds for the Red Cross. During 1918, Dave became "The Red Cross Dog" by hunting out money that people wrapped in handkerchiefs and hid within one hundred yards of the performance area. Blindfolded, Dave sniffed out the hidden money, which all went to the Red Cross. Annie and Frank always promised to give a like amount to the Red Cross themselves if Dave failed, but he never did.

When Kaiser Wilhelm II abdicated on November 9, 1918, and an armistice was signed on November 11, Annie, Frank, and Dave celebrated in their own way. Two days after peace, they staged a shooting exhibition. The excitement had ended, and to Annie's despair, they soon returned to retirement.

Life resumed its pleasantness at the Carolina. Along with the other guests, the Butlers participated in the hotel's many theatricals and balls. On Valentine Eve 1919, Annie appeared at a costume ball as Sitting Bull Jr. Dressed in an outfit that included a headdress of pheasant feathers and layers of beads wrapped around her neck, Annie captured first prize.

Annie also continued shooting. On March 19, 1920, at Pinehurst, she marked pennies with bullets and sold her autographs for the benefit of the Farm Life School in Eureka, North Carolina. A few weeks later, Annie and Frank traveled to Montrose, North Carolina, to give an exhibition for a tuberculosis sanitorium. This disease especially interested Annie because it had claimed her sisters Elizabeth and Lydia (Lyda), so she ordered many of her gold medals melted down and then contributed the proceeds to a sanitarium near Pinehurst.

Annie gave lessons as well. One observer claimed that at Pinehurst, Oakley instructed as many as two thousand ladies a year; on April 8, 1921, the *Pinehurst Outlook* reported that Annie had taught thousands of women since 1915, including some eight hundred in 1921 alone. Although many of these women now wore the new calf-length dresses, along with shoes supported by chunky two-inch heels, Annie still favored ankle-length dresses with flat-heeled shoes for teaching. For hunting, however, Annie sometimes wore skirts that fell just below the knee. She had also adopted the cross-saddle, for riding astride, but on those occasions a long flowing skirt, probably a split skirt, and high leather boots covered her legs and ankles.

Sometime during this period, a laudatory article, "Greatest of Modern Dianas," noted that the thousands of sportspeople who left the snow and cold of the northern winter behind in favor of Pinehurst's moderate climate made the acquaintance of a "motherly woman" and "estimable lady," Annie Oakley. It quoted Annie as saying that she had used approximately forty thousand shells a year for thirty years, or 1.2 million shot shells, and intended to keep going, for shooting kept her young. When one wealthy Philadelphian saw Annie shoot, the article went on, he wanted to buy Annie's horse, Fred Stone, and her dog, Dave, who held chalk in his teeth and an apple on his head for Annie to shoot at, then caught a piece of apple in his mouth, just as the poodle George had done those many years ago when Annie had first met Frank. When the man gave Oakley a signed check and told her to fill in the amounts, she said there was not enough money in the world to buy Fred and Dave.

Clearly, in retirement, Annie continued to hone her skills and attract attention. As a girl, Annie had learned to fight for what she wanted. Then, as an adult, she had learned that control and middle-class living gave her ease and pleasure. Thus, in retirement, she also continued to regulate closely her life and her environment. She and Frank lived well but watched their budget, exercised, and monitored their diet. The butcher Roy Lyons remembered, for example, that whenever Annie and Frank returned to Ansonia, Ohio for a visit, they purchased meat from him, always specifying the cut, thickness, and quality. They even taught Roy and his family the precise way they preferred to prepare their steaks.

Unfortunately for Annie, she was unable to control all aspects of her life. Consequently, the year 1922 turned out to be another critical, and very tragic, one for the Butlers. It started exceptionally well; in Pinehurst on April 16, 1922, Annie hit one hundred targets in a row, a record believed to have never been duplicated by a woman. The following day the *New York Times* announced that Annie Oakley had just set a new world's record.

That summer Annie and Frank spent a great deal of time with the Stones and furthered their friendship with comedian Will Rogers, who lived across the road from the Stones and may have taught Annie the art of lariat twirling. They also expressed enthusiasm as Fred Stone organized a charity circus, the Motor Hippodrome and Wild West Show, to be staged at the Mineola Race Track in Long Island for the benefit of the Occupational Therapy Society, which ran training programs for disabled soldiers. On July 1, 1922, the show attracted four thousand society people.

The show began with a parade led by Annie Oakley and Fred Stone. Then came a cavalcade of trucks, each with a stage mounted on it. On each stage, actors performed as they rolled passed the grandstand. The Friars, for example, produced a mystery melodrama written by George M. Cohan. Next, Stone did some trick riding while Annie gave what Stone later called "her last great shooting exhibition." Annie skipped into the arena wearing a knee-length skirt and khaki silk blouse, a red tie, and a hat with a broad brim. She put on her spectacles, then signaled Frank to begin. Among other things, he threw into the air three plates and swung a ball on a cord in a circle around his head while Annie caught the plates and ball with bullets.

The show ended with an attack on a stagecoach by what Stone called "a band of redskins." As in Buffalo Bill's Wild West, cowboys drove off and defeated the attackers. Even the stagecoach was as authentic as Cody's "Old Deadwood Stage." Stone had gotten this particular stage, which was built in 1832 and used in Dakota Territory, from Joseph P. Kennedy, later an ambassador to England. After the show, Stone gave it to Will Rogers, who later donated it to the Smithsonian Institution.

After the final applause died down, reporters crowded around Annie while a swarm of photographers snapped picture after picture. Her 1917 nemesis, the *New York Tribune*, reported that "the star of the occasion," which earned eleven thousand dollars for charity, was "the brisk and agile Annie Oakley, who cavorted around the ring, skipping and blowing kisses with the coyness she learned 40 years ago." In spite of her age and eyeglasses, she could still shoot. "The balls looped up against the sky and fell in showers of black pieces." How she shot, even leaning back over a chair, made no difference; she hit all her targets. A film clip captured part of her performance that day at the Mineola Fairgrounds. In spite of its choppiness, the film reveals her extraordinary agility and litheness. Annie raised her guns to her shoulder just as she had when a young woman.

During the weeks following the Motor Hippodrome and Wild West Show, rumors circulated that Annie might make a motion picture in earnest. Even before Stone's charity show, on June 28, 1922, the *New York Herald* had predicted, "If the taste of publicity she [Oakley] gets next Saturday (at the Hippodrome) proves agreeable she may say yes and move to Hollywood." Annie still struggled against retirement, but although she made a number of screen tests, she never made a feature film.

In addition, that fall Annie continued to thrill audiences. On October 5, 1922, Annie shot at the Brockton fair in Massachusetts, which attracted some one hundred thousand people. She shot five exhibitions of five minutes each and earned seven hundred dollars, her first paid performance in years. Afterward, as she watched the surging crowds and listened to the escalating noise, she commented: "All this has its glamour. All this has its lure, especially after 38 years of it, but still, home is best." The old ambivalence about retirement evidently still gripped her.

Then, in November, any dreams she may have harbored about a comeback abruptly ended. On Thursday, November 9, the car in which Annie rode on the way to Leesburg overturned. From the accident on Dixie Highway, an ambulance rushed Annie to Bohannon Hospital in Daytona. Annie and Frank had been traveling with friends, a Mr. C. H. Stoer and his wife, to spend the winter in Florida. When a passing automobile forced the chauffeur-driven Cadillac into the sand, the driver tried to get the car back on the highway but overturned it instead, pinning Annie under the car.

For six weeks afterward, Frank lived in a room across from the hospital and visited Annie daily. She suffered from a fractured hip and a shattered right ankle. When Annie moved from the hospital to her own bed, her half-sister, Emily Brumbaugh Patterson, came to care for her. As Annie learned to get around on crutches, with a steel brace supporting her right leg, she wrote a letter of thanks to the readers of *American Field* for the "nearly 2,000 letters and telegrams" as well as the "loads of flowers" she had received. She finally graduated to a cane, but the brace remained in place.

Unfortunately, Annie's and Frank's sorrows spilled over into 1923. Although on February 4 Annie wrote to a friend in Newark, New Jersey, that she had been out to dinner and "out of bed 7 hours to day," her joy was short-lived. On February 25, as Frank walked and Dave cavorted, an automobile struck and killed "The Red Cross Dog." The *Leesburg Commercial* eulogized Dave and re-marked, "Having no children, Mr. and Mrs. Butler had made of 'Dave' a pet, a hero, a pal, and in his death they feel the sorrow that parents would feel for the loss of a child."

This was true; for years Annie had signed Christmas cards with Dave's name and had written letters to friends on his behalf, letters she signed "Dave Butler." Annie and Frank had also reveled in newspaper accolades that called Dave a "great actor" and an animal with "almost human intelligence." Now, Annie and Frank buried Dave in a peaceful orange grove and planned to erect a small monument. They also issued a public announcement, say-ing that Dave had worked "through the cantonments for sixteen weeks, doing his bit for his country, and bringing sunshine to the hearts of thousands of our dear boys." Their animal companion, they continued, was "more [comforting] than some humans," for he had sat by Annie's bedside every day of her convalescence, both at the hospital and at home. They concluded that Dave's memory was "one of the sweetest" they had ever known.

Letters of condolence poured in. One friend assured Frank that Dave had embodied "character, intelligence and devotion." An-nie's grandniece Bess Lindsey Walcholz, who later described Dave as the "love" of Annie's and Frank's lives, tried to console Annie. Annie replied to Bess that she felt certain she would see Dave again, in heaven. She added some advice for Bess that sounded more like advice for herself in her time of despair: "Don't get discouraged. Work for all good. Pass all else by."

Frank also vented his grief by writing; he created "The Life of

Dave, As Told by Himself." When Dave's story appeared in the *Newark Sunday Call* on June 24, 1923, the *Call's* editor explained that the piece was about Frank and Annie's dog. "Wherever they lived . . . Dave was ever a third guest. Everywhere that Annie went the dog was sure to go." But "The Life of Dave" was about far more than that; it revealed the warm spirit of the Butler family — Annie, Frank, and Dave — and provided a retrospective of their retirement years together.

According to Frank's story, Dave especially remembered the summer of 1917, when Annie, Frank, and he went to New Hampshire and the air crackled with news of the U.S. involvement in the war. Later, the Butlers worked in cantonments, and Dave earned $1,629 for the Red Cross. Dave had learned a lot on his travels and had even developed his own philosophy: "I know during my travels I have met all kinds of dogs — good, bad and very bad. My master tells me, however, that humans are the same. He also told me I could save a lot of trouble by minding my own business, which I tried to do, but many times when I had little curs running and snapping at my feet I found it very hard to live up to it."

Dave's life story, as told by Frank, also revealed an Annie who was as kind and patient when at home as when she was before the public or giving interviews to reporters. Although Annie may have been incapable of managing a home, in Frank's view she proved herself empathetic and loving when managing family members. After nearly fifty years of marriage, Annie retained her luster in her husband's eyes.

After Dave's death, Annie and Frank continued to live at the Lakeview Hotel and never returned to the Cambridge house, which they had sold in 1921 or 1922. At the Lakeview in 1923, Annie grieved for Dave and hoped for the best in light of doctors' predictions that she would never shoot again. She also showed glimmers of her will to fight; daily she worked her legs painfully and haltingly.

Then, one March day in 1923, Annie and Frank drove to Cooke Field in Leesburg, where members of the Philadelphia Phillies were in spring training. As Frank set up targets and Annie laid out her guns, the Phillies took seats in the bleachers, accompanied by the small boys who always seemed to line the practice field. With her right leg encased in its steel brace, Annie stood on her left leg and raised her rifle. In rapid succession, she winged pennies and sent the boys in the grandstand scrambling for them. When, using her left hand, she shattered the five eggs Frank tossed into the air, the Phillies broke into applause.

Annie intended to control her own life. Despite the steel brace, she refused to give in to age and time. Annie also evidenced her old perfectionism. When, also in March, she viewed some photographs of Philadelphia's Drexel Institute girls shooting, she remarked that she wished she had time to give them "a little instruction." Although the young shooters were undefeated, Annie felt they did not hold their guns "quite right" and could benefit from her coaching.

When Annie and Frank visited Pinehurst that October 1923, Frank told people that Annie was fast recovering from her injuries. Annie herself scoffed that although doctors had told her at three different times in her life that she would never ride again, she always had. She remarked that she fully intended to resume her schedule of charity exhibitions.

That same month, the *Philadelphia Ledger* quoted Annie's advice for the "modern girl." "Learn to ride a horse—not merely to hold one," Annie advised. She added that girls should learn to shoot and to occupy their minds with "other people's troubles" so that they would have no time to grieve over their own. Annie had lost none of her true grit; she was still highly motivated and disciplined—the model western woman.

By the time Annie and Frank reached the home of her niece Bonnie Blakeley, and Bonnie's husband, Rush, near Ansonia, Ohio, where they planned to spend the winter, Annie displayed good spirits. Annie and Frank paid the Blakelys thirty dollars a week for their room and board. In addition, Annie, as neat and orderly as ever, washed, ironed, and mended clothes, as well as helping Bonnie cook. To Rush, it seemed as if Annie "was always doing something," and to Bonnie's daughter, Beatrice, it seemed as if the two women always produced exceptional meals.

Frank spent a good deal of his time walking, without Annie because of her brace. But when with Annie, Frank was as devoted as ever. Sometime during this period, young Hazel Moses, grand-daughter of John Moses, visited Annie and Frank. She remembered that Frank sat at his wife's right and was "very attentive" to Annie. After dinner, Annie and Frank prepared a bowl of scraps for their current dog, Dave II.

In the spring of 1924, Annie and Frank came out of total retirement once again. They traveled to another North Carolina resort, the Mayview Manor in Blowing Rock. Here, at ages sixty-three and seventy-three respectively, Annie and Frank planned to help establish a new gun club. The *Charlotte Observer* described Annie as "a frail little woman with a bright, infectious smile" and Frank as "hale and hearty." Only eighteen months after Annie's accident, she shattered nintey-eight out of one hundred pigeons and established a new club record.

Rather than collapsing in exhaustion at the end of the season, Annie and Frank visited friends. In October, the Butlers stayed at the Hotel Robert Treat in Newark, New Jersey, while visiting Dr. Edwin Betts, a Newark resident, and Fred Stone, who was in Newark with a show. Annie now looked thin and of indeterminate age, yet she still followed the latest fashions, including wearing cloche hats.

During these years, Annie displayed the same spirit she had as a girl when she refused to let adversity defeat her. She tried to keep moving, although now, at age sixty-four, she lacked the strong body to go with her determined spirit. One can only wonder whether she had left something in her life unresolved or unaccomplished, something that drove her on. Apparently, she failed to recognize the significance of her own achievements, for she seldom spoke of them and gradually dispersed her possessions and documents.

Only as her health declined did Annie gradually accept some of her own limitations. She and Frank decided to return to Ohio to be near her family. They arrived in Dayton in December 1924, where they first rented an apartment, then moved into a two-story white house with a commodious front porch on Lexington Avenue. The following spring and summer they took an interest in local shooting matches, especially those at the nearby Vandalia shooting grounds. According to Oakley's grandniece Bess, who attended a match with Annie and Frank, Annie happily offered tips to various shooters. "She hadn't been out of the house for a long time except to the doctor and the market," Bess explained, "and it was a joy to see how happy she was."

During 1925, Annie continued her modified activities. In August, the Butlers attended the Grand American Trapshoot in Vandalia. Although Annie took an inconspicuous seat on the veranda, reporters and photographers flocked around her. Annie even raised a gun to her shoulder and posed for one of the photographers. On October 6, 1925, Annie posed again, this time dancing a jig, leg brace and all, for a *Newark Star Eagle* photographer.

Privately, however, Annie recognized that her end was nearing. On October 7, she and Frank went to the Essex County Surrogate Court, where they each signed a last will and testament. Among other bequests, Annie Oakley Butler left one thousand dollars each to her half-sister, Emily, her sister Hulda, and her brother, John, and distributed other amounts to her sister Ellen, to her nieces Fern, Bonnie, Irene, and grandniece Elsie, and to six nephews, all for a total of thirty-five thousand dollars. Frank Butler gave money to his first wife, Elizabeth, now married to Howard Hall of Camden, New Jersey; to his daughter, now married to a Philadelphia man; and to his godchild, the former Gladys Baker, daughter of Johnny Baker. He designated that his jewelry and guns go to his brother, Will, of Joliet, Illinois.

After the Butlers returned to Dayton, Annie received a letter in December from the Amateur Trapshooting Association in Vandalia. The ATA wanted to purchase the log house that had once been her home near Greenville, move it to the ATA grounds, and preserve it in honor of what she had "done for the shooting game." Unfortunately, the project never materialized, and the house was eventually demolished.

Also, Frank urged Annie to write her memoirs, and early in 1926, he contacted a Mr. Shaw in New York City to help. On March 3, 1926, Shaw responded with pleasure; he expressed his approval that Annie did not intend to present her experiences "in the light, sensational style of a good many writers of today." But the idea of collaborating with Shaw to write her memoirs, like the ATA plan to purchase her girlhood home, never materialized.

Annie began to write a very brief autobiography on her own, reaching only the year 1890. In it, she spoke little of her personal relationships. She condensed her long career into a few pages and confused some dates and events. She also minimized the importance of her achievements and looked instead back to what she remembered as the simpler times of her childhood. "I wish I could live over again those days of simplicity when God was consulted. It far surpassed being bowed to and complimented by the crowned heads of all the world!"

In other ways, however, Annie looked ahead. Although she and her brother, John, had had a falling-out, perhaps over Annie's rejection of the name "Moses," she now purchased from John two burial plots in the family cemetery near Brock, Ohio. As Frank listened to Annie speak of her impending death as the path leading to the gates of "God's Great World," he too decided he wanted a place in the Mosey family plot. After all, over the years her family had become his family.

That May, the *Dayton Daily News* honored Annie and Frank with a series of articles, titled "From Circus Fame to Lace and Silver Hair." The *News* published a drawing of Annie and Frank, both dark-haired and vital, during their early years on the stage, alongside a recent photograph, in which they both appeared white-haired and frail. The *News* reviewed Annie's career and passed on her advice to its women readers, advice as meaningful as when she had first offered it during the late 1880s. In the article, Oakley repeated her long-standing dual themes, women as sport shooters and women as protectors of themselves and their homes. In the matter of shooting, Annie said, gender made no difference. "It is largely a matter of determination and practice that makes good marksmen and women." Most women feared the very sound of gunfire because they lacked experience "in any kind of outdoor sport." But after a little instruction, women could shoot well and were "keen to excel." If women and girls would learn the skill, Annie noted, "they would add to their happiness by falling in love with one of the finest of outdoor sports."

Oakley added, "Women should be prepared; not necessarily for war, although it would not be undesirable to have them ready for extreme emergencies in war time, but to defend themselves." Even in the most civilized of countries, occasions for self-defense arose. She claimed to have taught fifteen thousand women to shoot, most recently at Wentworth, New Hampshire, during summers and in Pinehurst, North Carolina, during winters, totally without compensation. "Because I had an ideal for my sex, I have wanted them to be capable of protecting their homes."

Annie also related one of her favorite stories regarding a woman shooter. One wealthy Back Bay woman from Boston came to Annie very much frightened of firearms, but after a few lessons, she did so well that her husband presented her with a "fine pistol." When the woman returned home one day to find a thief stealing the silverware, she held him at bay with her gun while she called the police. Although it turned out that her careful husband had removed the cartridges to avoid an accident, the result proved satisfactory, and the woman credited Annie Oakley with her capture of the thief. Understandably, Annie also railed against state legislation prohibiting firearms in private homes. To her, such laws protected the burglar, who had the advantage because he carried a gun while most people would obey the law and not have one handy when the thief arrived on the scene. Home accidents with guns could easily be avoided by training both children and adults in the careful use of firearms.

The *News* tribute was not the last. In a column about Annie, which appeared on April 30, 1926, Will Rogers remarked that he had visited Annie in Dayton and found her "a wonderful Christian character," in fact, a "greater character than she was a Rifle shot." Emily Brumbaugh Patterson's daughter, Irene, who as a young nurse helped care for Annie, remembers that Annie never complained about her pain or the weight of the steel brace she wore. Irene remarked that for Rogers's visit, Emily had dressed Annie in pink and fixed her silver hair. When Rogers came downstairs after his visit, tears filled his eyes, and he told Emily and Irene that he had never expected to see an angel on earth but that he had just seen one in the person of Annie Oakley.

Rogers's subsequent newspaper tribute honored Annie, now

bedridden and largely forgotten. Her exemplary life, he wrote, had established "a mark for any woman to shoot at." He suggested that people write to Annie in Dayton. Rogers's paean also marked changes in entertainment and media. As Annie's life faded, so did the era of shooters, vaudeville, circuses, and Wild West shows. Rogers used the growing power of the print media to revive Annie's former fame and glory.

As a result of Rogers's syndicated column, letters from fans deluged Oakley throughout the spring and summer of 1926. Many of them, in various ways, recognized Oakley's four major dimensions: entertainer, sport shooter, lady, and western woman. For instance, a Cleveland man remembered Oakley primarily as an entertainer. He had first seen her with the Wild West in 1897 or 1898 and thought the show a "wonderful whirl" and her a "trim little lady" who did not miss a single shot. Women too remembered Annie from the arena. A Florida woman who had seen Annie with the Wild West recalled her own "amazed delight" in Annie's "wonderful handling of a rifle," for she herself was an "indifferent but enthusiastic" shot at the time.

But people also remembered Oakley as a sport shooter. A Florida man reminisced that as a boy, he had put clay pigeons in a trap in a New York match where she, the only female competitor, captured first prize. "I always thought it a great honor to do that for you." Others noted Annie's skill at exhibitions and hunting, as did the New York man who had seen her shoot at Fred Stone's farm. "So many people love you and think of you," he wrote.

Others thought of Oakley primarily as a great lady. When a Washington, D.C., man sent her a necklace, he commented that it was not really good enough for "such a lady as you." As part of Annie's ladyhood, many people remarked on her beneficence. A New York woman reminded Annie that, just as she had once made so many less privileged people happy, she had the strength and "true values" to carry herself forward through her illness.

Many more thought of her as a western woman. A California man described himself as "an old Westerner" who first went west in 1881 and was one of her many fans. He too, he wrote, was nearing "the end of the trail"; he liked to let his memory wander to the "days of the old west" when he had "punched cows, mined in Idaho and followed the gold rush into Alaska in 1900" and lived as "full a life as possible" for anyone. And a California woman, born in a covered wagon in 1851 on the way west, never saw Annie in person but felt akin to Annie because they had both shared in "the era of the Wild West."

Yet other letters asked Annie questions, requested favors, or gave advice. One inquired if Annie remembered Lillian Smith, "quite a noted shot before your time." That must have tickled Annie, since Smith always claimed to be younger than Oakley. Another writer even asked for Annie's prayers because he believed he was in more dire straits than she. Many of these letter writers recommended that Annie look on the bright side, think only good thoughts, pray, and read the Bible. Several others advised her to try Christian Science; another offered to give her a blood transfusion if she needed one.

Annie answered many of these letters, sometimes with information but more often with clippings. She especially liked to send copies of Dave's life story to her well-wishers because it summed up the family history after she left the public eye in 1913 as well as conveying her and Frank's values.

Sometime during the summer of 1926, Annie returned to Bonnie and Rush's farm near Ansonia, Ohio. Although Frank enjoyed only slightly better health than Annie, he hoped that he and Annie would be able to travel to North Carolina for the winter, but Annie urged him to go on without her. Although Frank too felt unwell, he headed south to please her. Frank went to New Jersey first, where in late August he attended a shooting match in Morristown. While there, he wrote to a friend that Annie was in poor health. He noted, "Doctors don't give me *much* hope." Frank added that he feared he and Annie could not afford Pinehurst that winter because the doctors' bills had "put a lump" in their bank account.

Because Frank did not feel well enough to go to Pinehurst on his own, either he or a friend wired Fern in Michigan for help. When Frank arrived at Fern's, she immediately realized that he was far too ill to travel south or even to return to Annie in Ohio. Fern put Frank to bed and took care of him, just as Annie had always asked should the necessity arise.

Meanwhile, Annie's condition continued to worsen. She finally accepted the inevitably of imminent death and decided to prepare for it. In a letter she dictated to her nurse on September 11, 1926, Annie told a friend that the ordeal of her own and Frank's illnesses, which she believed caused mental instability in him, had nearly overwhelmed her. "I am just exausted [*sic*] and confined to my bed," she confided.

When Annie's doctor decided that her condition required his full-time supervision, Annie planned yet another move and began to distribute her prized possessions to family members and friends. In October 1926, an Indian pipe went to her nephew C. G. Moses of Kansas City, the son of her only brother, John Moses, now of McCurtain, Oklahoma. With the gift was a clipping showing Sitting Bull with the pipe in his hands and a letter saying that Frank was in Detroit and "in a bad condition both physical and mentaly [*sic*]." In addition, Annie gave C. G. and his brother, Lee Moses, each a cut-glass decanter and other crystal pieces given to her by the kaiser and kaiserin of Germany and divided between them a set of silver from Queen Victoria as well as photographs, newspaper clippings, and old advertising lithographs.

Annie's sister Hulda soon moved Annie to the Zemer and Broderick Home on 225 East Third Street in Greenville. According to Bess Edwards, Annie's grandniece, Annie hoped to go south for the winter and thus had dresses fitted by the Zemer and Broderick sisters. During this time, Annie's doctor visited regularly, and Reverend Christian C. Wessel, pastor of the Lutheran Church of York township, called often and listened to Annie's longings for the "simple life," the days of her childhood as she now remembered them. Another caller was a woman embalmer, Louise Stocker, chosen by Annie because she wanted only a woman to handle her body. Sometime in late October, Annie gave Louise explicit instructions and showed her the dress she wanted to wear.

On Wednesday, November 3, 1926, at about 11 P.M., sixty-six-year-old Annie died in her sleep. Her doctor listed the cause of death as pernicious anemia, but some of her friends and family would later say that she had finally worn down and worn out; others believe the cause may have been something other than anemia, perhaps even lead poisoning induced by years of handling weapons and lead shot.

After Annie's death, Louise Stocker went to the house to pick up the apricot silk dress Annie had designated and then began to dress her. Louise put Annie's wispy hair in a chignon and patted some makeup on her withered face. On the morning of November 4, the news of her death went out over the Associated Press wire. The Darke County girl, Annie Oakley, "the friend of monarchs and the confidante of Sitting Bull," was dead.

On Friday, November 5, in the home of family friends Fred and Hazel Grote of Greenville, Reverend Wessel conducted a private ceremony. The Grotes had announced the service for Saturday but held it on Friday to thwart curiosity seekers and intrusive reporters. Annie's body lay on a bed, for she had instructed Stocker to send her body to Cincinnati for cremation. When the ashes came back in an urn, which Fern claimed was the silver loving cup that the French people had given Annie and that Annie had ordered fixed with a screw top, Fred Grote made an oak box for the urn and placed it in the vault at Stocker's Funeral Parlor until Frank joined her in death.

Annie's family began to disperse her remaining things according to her wishes. Annie's clothing, jewelry, and other personal items were to go to her three sisters—Ellen Grabfelder, Hulda Haines, and Emily Patterson—and to her nieces—Fern Campbell, Bonnie Blakeley, Irene Patterson, and some others. A paper-wrapped box went to Fred Stone at the Globe Theater. When he opened it, reportedly on stage, Stone discovered Annie's typewritten autobiography and a series of scrapbooks and pictures.

Newspapers announced that the rest of Annie's estate, mostly securities and real estate, had appraised at $42,448.68, which she left to family members. Annie had named Spencer S. Marsh, vice president of the National Newark and Essex Banking Company, and either William Longfellow or William Longfelder of Nutley as executors. Although the will itself reads William Longfellow, newspapers reported William Longfelder. Longfelder seems more likely because the Longfelders were longtime friends of Annie and Frank's from Nutley.

In the meantime, Frank, still at Fern's in Michigan, languished.

Fern later said that Frank "never ate a bite" after he heard the news of Annie's death, but other family members believe that he was already too weak, or perhaps mentally disoriented, to fully absorb the news. Frank, at seventy-six years of age, died on November 21, eighteen days after Annie. In Fern's view, Frank died because of internal injuries she believed he had received in the 1922 accident in Florida and because "his heart was broken" after Annie died. Frank's death certificate simply listed senility as the cause.

On Thanksgiving Day 1926, Reverend Wessel officiated at the burial of Annie and Frank in the family plot at the Brock cemetery near Greenville, Ohio. Legend says that the box containing Annie's ashes lies in Frank's casket, but some family members believe it lies in her own grave. Both are marked with handsome red granite stones, one reading Annie Oakley and the other Frank E. Butler, each with the two simple words "At Rest," chosen by Annie.

Almost immediately, tributes to Annie began. Newspapers termed her remarkable, marvelous, and wonderful. One Annie would have especially appreciated came from the *Springfield Republican*; it described her as a "quiet, modest little figure" of a woman. Will Rogers penned one of the most extensive tributes. In 1927, he wrote that whenever he thought of that marvelous woman, Annie Oakley, he realized, "It's what you are and not what you are in, that makes you."

Annie's family and friends reminisced as well. Her nephew C. G. Moses told reporters that his aunt used to shoot pennies off his head when he was a boy. "I wasn't frightened. . . . She never missed." And William Longfelder's wife claimed when Annie had astonished her by doing somersaults around her living room after the 1922 accident and had talked about going into movies. Years later, in his 1945 autobiography *Rolling Stone*, Fred Stone recalled his amusement when he watched people meet Oakley for the first time. Although they expected a "big, masculine, blustering" woman, they got, much to their surprise, a "tiny woman with the quiet voice." Stone also told about the day, as he entertained friends by shooting down targets that Frank tossed into the air, when Annie asked if she could have his gun for a minute. With her snow-white hair and petite frame, she hoisted the gun to her shoulder and shot down all five targets that Frank had tossed up in a bunch. She returned the gun with thanks and turned to rejoin the other women making dinner in the house. As he watched her depart, one man wiped his brow and asked Stone, "My God, Fred, was that your mother?"

Dorothy Stone also had fond memories of Annie. During a 1950s interview at her home in Encino, California, Dorothy recalled the summers Annie had stayed with the Stones in Amityville, Long Island, summers when Annie taught Dorothy to shoot and gave her a gun with a gold plate on the stock inscribed "To Dorothy from Annie Oakley." Annie also gave Dorothy one of her saddles, complete with hand grips for stunt riding in Wild West shows and with the name "Annie Oakley" tooled in leather in the rise of the seat. Dorothy described Annie as a "sweet and retiring person" who never looked people in the eye while talking with them and made people uncomfortable by staring at the top of their heads or at their ears. Yet Dorothy added that "shy" Annie often closed her act with two rather dramatic actions: she ran and slid on her stomach to hit the last ball before it hit the ground, then she ran around the arena with her arms up in the air holding her rifle.

Shy in person and bold in public, Oakley was a study in contrasts. Yet it is not surprising that a person from humble beginnings who was also a woman living during the late nineteenth and early twentieth centuries would be somewhat reserved. Given the expectations of her era regarding women, Oakley's ability to discard her reservations when she picked up a gun or mounted a horse is more surprising than her shyness.

Of course, Annie's death had a different impact on different generations of people. To older people, who had seen her in the Wild West or perhaps watched her shoot in a match or an exhibition, her passing seemed momentous and profound. But to younger people, who associated Annie with their parents' or grandparents' day, her death meant little. They were more wrapped up in listening to the 2.5 million radios in America; in worshiping swimmer Gertrude Ederle, boxing champion Jack Dempsey, baseball player Babe Ruth, and aviators Charles Lindbergh and Amelia Earhart; in humming the music of George and Ira Gershwin, Richard Rodgers and Lorenz Hart, or Jerome Kern and Oscar Hammerstein II; or in following the lives of film stars Charlie Chaplin, Douglas Fairbanks, and Mary Pickford, whose motion pictures showed in the more than twenty thousand theaters that then spread across the nation.

Despite youngsters' lack of interest, Annie Oakley's image refused to fade. Family members and friends told stories, gradually honing their tales to include what they wanted to remember and believe about Annie and Frank. Even today, those people who remember Annie and Frank reveal their recollections guardedly and are usually careful to put the couple in the best light.

In addition, the very media that replaced the Wild West era and the very stars that eclipsed Annie Oakley's fame eventually created elements of an Annie Oakley legend. The motion picture industry, which Annie never conquered, offered its version of her life, as did authors, reporters, illustrators, collectors, and museum exhibits. Promoting Annie Oakley turned into a small and ongoing industry, one that frequently skewed her image in a different direction than she would have chosen. Media and myth often portrayed her as swaggering and brassy, adding a dimension that is far from what she intended to leave behind as part of her legend.

CHAPTER 7

The Legend

ONE of Annie's admirers wrote in 1926 that "nobody" could take Oakley's place. In her eyes, "only one" Annie Oakley would ever exist. Yet today, although nearly everyone recognizes the name Annie Oakley, few people know who Oakley was, either as a person or as a symbol. Frequently, people confuse her with another woman of the era, Calamity Jane (Martha Jane Cannary), even though the two were radically different.

Annie and Jane shared only one thing: both women appeared with Wild West shows during the 1890s and early 1900s. Calamity Jane performed briefly with Kohl and Middleton's Palace Museum in Minneapolis, Minnesota, in January 1896, which advertised her as "The Famous Woman Scout of the Wild West." Kohl and Middleton also claimed that Jane had lived through a "thousand" thrilling adventures, was the "terror" of evil-doers in the Black Hills, and had ridden with Buffalo Bill Cody and Wild Bill Hickok. Jane also appeared briefly with a variety of other shows, including burlesque and freak shows, which often billed her as "The Wild Woman of the West."

Apparently, in the arena Cannary did little more than appear in a buckskin outfit, revolvers at each side, and tell stories about what the show's publicity called her "daring exploits." The Palace Museum's poster, which pictured Jane dressed like a man and grasping the barrel of a rifle, suggests that she appeared more as a curiosity than a full-fledged performer. Later, Jane joined Colonel Frederic T. Cummins's Wild West and Indian Congress; at the 1901 Pan-American Exposition in Buffalo, New York, she appeared as an authentic western character and sold a less-than-authentic autobiography in which she claimed to be "the Woman Scout who was made so famous through her daring career in the West and Black Hill countries."

Despite the differences between Annie and Jane, they are often linked in the public mind. In 1948, for example, author Stewart H.

Holbrook included Calamity Jane in a book titled *Annie Oakley and Other Rugged People*. Holbrook described Annie as "a merger of dainty feminine charm and lead bullets," but he viewed Jane as a "singularly unattractive" woman and a "camp follower." To him, Jane was little more than "an able consumer of liquor" and "one of the great and indestructible phonies of the West."

More recently, novelist Larry McMurtry also included both Annie and Jane in *Buffalo Girls*, a 1990 western. When Jane supposedly sailed to Europe with Cody's Wild West during 1886, she found Annie a rather stiff, even "steely," woman, who had little time for her. This seems plausible, for Jane spent a good deal of time frequenting saloons, an activity that Annie deplored, while Annie spent time practicing, exercising, and resting, pursuits that seemed pointless to Jane.

Contrary to McMurtry's account, Jane never appeared in Cody's Wild West. Consequently, Annie probably never met Calamity Jane; undoubtedly, she would not have liked Jane if she had. These women fell at opposite ends of the spectrum. Yet many people lump them together as daring western girls—cowgirls of the Old Wild West.

In part, people's confusion regarding Annie and Jane reveals the numerous changes American women experienced after Oakley's death and the longevity of the myth of the American West, as well as the literary license both these phenomena encouraged. Because Americans altered their views of women, they also rewrote Annie's story. And because they often saw the Old West more as popular culture than factual history, they shaped and bent it to fit their needs. In the process, the heroic, as well as the not-so-heroic, figures associated with the Old West received their share of shaping and bending as well.

As a result, Annie Oakley's legend has not always been what she would have desired. Her story has strayed from the truth—sometimes very far from the truth—and has changed to fit the values of a particular era. Since Oakley's death in 1926, Annie's image has metamorphosed a number of times. Her characterization began as that of a talented woman who was willing and capable of challenging barriers to women's participation in Wild West shows and sport shooting, but it soon changed to that of a woman who purposely lost a shooting match to win a man.

More recently, Oakley's portrayal has shifted back to an achieving woman forging a path for other women. This process demonstrates the way legends — and images of the people behind them — ebb and flow. Except during the World War II years, narratives of Oakley's life changed to fit what Americans believed about women and about the American West at a given time.

Annie's legend began to develop as early as 1927, only one year after her death. Oakley's first biographer, Courtney Ryley Cooper, whose *Annie Oakley: Woman at Arms* was released in 1927, had the advantage of writing during a time when American women were exploring numerous activities and areas. In 1920, women had gained the right of suffrage through the Nineteenth Amendment to the U.S. Constitution. During the following decade, significant numbers of women moved into paid labor, the professions, and myriad organizations and reform movements, including the League of Women Voters, the Women's Trade Union League, the American Birth Control League, and the antilynching crusade. In 1927, a special issue of *Current History* devoted to "The New Woman" revealed that such leaders as Charlotte Perkins Gilman applauded women's progress in politics, reform, jobs, and professions. In the same month, an issue of *Harper's Magazine* indicated that younger women now wanted everything — careers, marriage, and the right to individual expression.

Given these attitudes, Annie Oakley provided a perfect role model. To the older group, she stood as an example of achievement and benevolence. To the younger group, she supplied a case study of a woman who had successfully combined marriage, career, and her own talents and interests. Consequently, Cooper was able to present a reasonably genuine Annie Oakley. First, Cooper emphasized Oakley's benevolence. "[She] had done naught but kindness . . . [and] had given of her store of wealth that suffering might be alleviated, the uneducated benefitted by the advantage of books and schooling." Next, he described the hardworking girl and the achieving woman and, in his conclusion, claimed that American men who had seen Oakley perform would always remember her as their first love.

Thus did Cooper's Annie become a success story for women of

the late 1920s. She had worked hard, remained true to her humble beginnings, treated everyone fairly, and achieved money, recognition, and love. Along the way, however, Cooper supplied a number of fabrications regarding Oakley. By drawing liberally and literally on her unfinished autobiography, he repeated inaccurate dates and anecdotes, some of which are still taken as truth.

Soon after Cooper wrote, Hollywood made its first contribution to Annie's legend. Unfortunately, the decade of the 1930s was a less-than-propitious time to make a film about a strong, successful woman like Oakley. Thanks to such stars as vamp Theda Bara, girl-next-door Lillian Gish, sexually free Gloria Swanson, "It Girl" Clara Bow, and "America's Sweetheart" Mary Pickford, women in films appeared youthful, innocent, feminine, and kittenish rather than secure and successful.

Nor did Oakley's stance as a demure lady fit well with Hollywood images. A 1929 study indicated that Joan Crawford was the leading model for young American women. The chorus girls and flappers she portrayed established a standard of behavior, dress, and makeup for an entire generation of female movie-goers. As one sixteen-year-old girl commented, "These modern pictures give me a feeling to imitate their ways."

Oakley's demeanor as an athlete also appeared stodgy during the 1930s, an era when women sports figures contributed to the nation's growing fascination with female freedom and sexuality. Among such stars were Alice Marble and Helen Wills, who excelled at tennis, Eleanor Holm and Helen Madison, who established swimming records, and Mildred "Babe" Didrikson Zaharias, who mastered women's basketball, track, and golf. At the same time, women's softball and basketball teams also flourished. Along with women's sports came light tennis dresses, tennis shorts, and satin shorts for basketball players; women's bare legs soon became a common sight.

Even Annie's persona as a western woman had questionable appeal during the 1930s. Because the Dust Bowl, the wind-eroded area that produced migrants referred to as Okies, came to symbolize the West in many people's minds, the American West increasingly appeared bankrupt. The combination of overcultivation and drought had caused bare dirt to lie dry and vulnerable to ravaging winds, especially in Kansas, Oklahoma, and Texas. Despite relative prosperity in the Southwest and Pacific Northwest, novelist John Steinbeck's *The Grapes of Wrath* and Dorothea Lange's touching photographs impressed on Americans the tragedy suffered by land, animals, and people in the central West. Other media reported that westerners by the thousands were abandoning their worn-out lands while western states were applying for one federal subsidy after another.

What, then, could a movie version of Annie Oakley's life say to American viewers? It had to portray an attractive woman interested in love and able to get her man, despite the costs. It also had to picture the Old West of opportunity and success rather than the Dust Bowl West of disaster and despair. And, given Hollywood's penchant for the dramatic, it would be wise to incorporate more conflict than Annie's life had included.

The result was Barbara Stanwyck's 1935 film *Annie Oakley*. The film's promoters billed Stanwyck as "Queen of the Roaring 80s" and promised that *Annie Oakley* would "thrill" viewers with a "drama of fighting men and red romance." Despite this turgid publicity, Stanwyck's portrayal of Oakley was spunky enough to gain approval from Annie's supporters. When the movie premiered in Annie's hometown of Greenville, Ohio, a viewer who had known Annie declared Stanwyck "just like" her.

The movie's plot, however, retold Annie's story in a way that suited the times. It focused on Annie's shooting match with Frank and their subsequent love affair. Borrowing heavily from Cooper's account, the film set the match in Cincinnati in 1876. Toby Walker, the film's name for Frank Butler, was a handsome, arrogant devil. With a sleazy blond woman on his arm, Toby arrived for the match dolled up in a fringed, white buckskin shirt punctuated by shooting medals. Toby provided a stark contrast to Annie in her gingham dress, nondescript hat, and lack of medals or jewelry.

At first, Walker refused to shoot against Oakley, but she eventually goaded him into a match. As Oakley was about to defeat Walker, her mother whispered that she hoped Annie would not cause the "nice young man" to lose his job. Of course, during the depression of the 1930s, lost jobs posed a great concern to American men, who often watched helplessly as women supported families with meager wages from menial work. Thus, contrary to what Oakley had done in real life, Stanwyck's Annie threw the match. Toby won the shooting match and retained his job with Buffalo Bill's Wild West.

Because Stanwyck's Annie was infatuated with Toby, she too accepted a job with Buffalo Bill's Wild West so that she could be near Toby. Cody's partner broke the news to the all-male troupe by introducing Annie as a "high-minded" and "uplifting" woman, the kind who helped "civilize" the West in thousands of other Hollywood productions. Naturally, Toby returned Annie's interest, even though she was not much of a lady. Stanwyck's Oakley wore short skirts, rode astride, revealed that she had *let* Walker win the Cincinnati match, and continued to outshoot him.

When Cody, characterized as a nice guy and the ultimate entertainer, pitted Oakley against Walker (in fact it was Johnny Baker) in the arena for the "championship" of the world, Annie outshot Toby. After Toby's shooting grew worse from an eye injury and Cody banished him from the show, Annie traveled through Europe with the Wild West, astonishing audience after audience with her shooting feats but yearning for Toby. When the troupe returned to New York, Sitting Bull reunited the pair. Annie fell into Toby's arms, thus creating yet another happy Hollywood ending.

Because Annie, and Frank as well, failed to fit prevailing gender expectations of the 1930s, Hollywood had to alter their images and their stories. Annie became so love-struck that she lost a match and took a job to gain the man in question. Similarly, Toby became slickly handsome and aggressively dominant. And rather than focusing on her career or their long marriage, the film concentrated on their love affair. The film's conclusion implied that love would conquer all and that Annie and Toby would work things out. Of course, Toby's damaged eyesight made it acceptable for him to drop into a secondary position and Annie to continue shooting, if that was what viewers wanted to believe. By ending with Annie in Toby's arms, the film also avoided following the life of a childless career woman with a manager-husband in an era that deified motherhood and assigned men the breadwinner role.

Despite these and other distortions, the film had several admirable qualities. It presented Annie as a woman who could outshoot men. It allowed Toby (Frank) to say he was proud of Annie's achievements. And, if viewers cared to look beyond Annie's and Toby's superficial characteristics, the film portrayed Annie as a clean-cut, talented woman and Toby as a sensible, caring man at a time when most western women in films and literature were "good" women, including the ultimate civilizer, or were "bad" women, including prostitutes, femmes fatales, and vamps, while western men were typically presented as heroes, villains, or buffoons. When compared with subsequent western women in films—notably Marlene Dietrich, who in 1939 played the sexy Frenchy, the owner of the Last Chance Saloon in *Destry Rides Again*, or Jane Russell, who in 1943 played the sensual Rio, primarily a sex object for Billy the Kid, in *The Outlaw*—Stanwyck's *Annie Oakley* had much to recommend it.

Stanwyck herself came to like and respect Oakley. When she learned that the town of Greenville planned to erect a bronze plaque in Annie's honor near Annie's girlhood home, Stanwyck sent a one-hundred-dollar check to Mayor Frazer Wilson of Greenville. Stanwyck may have diminished Oakley somewhat in her screen role, but she honored her by supporting the plaque.

During World War II (1941–45), however, Annie's incipient legend almost disappeared. Such concerns as raising troops, recruiting industrial workers, and producing armaments claimed Americans' attention. A massive shift in ideas regarding American women began soon after the bombing of Pearl Harbor on December 7, 1941. The U.S. government called women from their homes to provide a temporary labor supply while men went to the front. Although women had absorbed numerous messages telling them that wife- and motherhood gave meaning to their lives, the War Manpower Commission created Rosie the Riveter to persuade women to rethink employment outside the home.

Soon, posters featuring Rosie covered buildings and billboards across the country. Dressed in overalls, her hair in a bandanna,

Rosie also appeared in advertisements, newspapers, and magazines. Songs called "Rosie the Riveter" and "We're the Janes Who
Make the Planes" went to the top of the charts. Even Hollywood
pitched in with such films as *Swing Shift Maisie*.

Oakley, who had championed women as workers and suggested
that they participate in World War I, would have approved of the
consequences for American women. Between 1940 and 1945,
women in paid employment increased by more than 50 percent.
In 1940, 11,970,000 women worked outside their homes, but in
1945, 18,610,000 did so. Most of the other two-thirds of the female
population worked by volunteering for the war effort, especially
in such organizations as the Red Cross and the Office of Civil
Defense, and by raising victory gardens, growing and canning
their own foods, collecting tin cans and newspapers for reuse,
selling war bonds, and entertaining troops in USO canteens,
much as Annie had done during World War I.

At the same time that women's visibility increased, the West
regained some of its importance in American eyes. It supplied not
only troops but also foodstuffs and mineral resources to both the
U.S. government and the Allied powers. Still, most Americans
paid less than full attention to western heroes, either historical or
current. Instead, books, radio programs, and moving pictures
emphasized the war. Romance and conflict continued, now set
against the background of a defense plant or a military hospital.

In spite of the rising importance of both women and the West,
few people thought about Annie during the war. Those who did
remember Oakley focused more on her patriotic value and expertise with firearms than on her achievements as a woman or a
westerner. One of Oakley's few recognitions came from the U.S.
Maritime Commission (now the Maritime Administration), which
named a ship after Oakley on September 12, 1943.

This was one of the "Liberty" cargo ships, first produced in
1941 after German submarines had badly crippled the merchant
shipping that supported the Allied war effort. The Liberty ships—
simply designed, mass-produced cargo ships—were all named
after famous Americans, beginning with Patrick Henry. The
California Shipbuilding Corporation at Los Angeles completed
the *Annie Oakley* on August 21, 1943. Under the Lend Lease

program, the British Ministry of War Transport took command of the vessel. The ship served under the British flag until April 1945, when a German torpedo sank it in the English Channel.

In that year, as World War II ended, another organization paid homage to Oakley's memory as an expert shooter. At the home of the American Trapshooting Association in Vandalia, Ohio, near Dayton, officials inaugurated a special event in honor of Oakley's memory. The ATA urged other gun clubs across the country to hold similar memorial shoots.

When the war ended in 1945, Annie's legend revived, but in an altered milieu. Beginning in 1945, American women lost their fleeting recognition. As they returned from the front, men pushed women out of their wartime jobs. Soon child-care facilities closed. In 1945, the U.S. Women's Bureau reported that 80 percent of working women wanted to keep their jobs; when laid off, they turned instead to clerical, department store, and service work.

Rosie herself hung up her acetylene torch and headed home. Thousands of posters, advertisements, and pamphlets informed American women that the crisis was over; they could return home to produce a new and larger generation of children to replace the many Americans killed in the war. The back-to-the-home movement had begun.

At the same time, the American West gained increased recognition and importance. During the postwar years, many people questioned traditional institutions and social values, worried about ethnic and racial problems, and lamented the power of the welfare state. As a consequence, Americans increasingly longed for what they believed were the good old days. For many, the good old days meant the Old West, an era that exercised the power of nostalgia and now appeared to be a perfect past.

With women's stock falling and the West's rising, the Annie Oakley legend faced difficulties. Would it play more to prevailing beliefs regarding women or to those regarding the West? In 1946, Oakley's niece Anna Fern Campbell Swartwout took the first tack. In her version of Annie's life, *Missie: An Historical Biography of Annie Oakley*, Fern portrayed her aunt as a woman rather than a pseudo-westerner. Fern described Annie as a woman of "rare genius," a person of "tireless energy," and the most "unselfish character" she had ever known.

Unfortunately, Fern lacked a sense of chronology and occasionally revised events according to her own standards of propriety. Fern also drew heavily on Annie's autobiography, which she may have helped her aunt write and which she edited for newspaper publication shortly after Oakley's death. Or perhaps Fern copied directly from the autobiography, for the same incidents, and even some of the same wording, appear in both the autobiography and *Missie*. As a consequence, Fern's book is strongest in conveying her own memories of time spent with Annie and Frank.

Like Fern, brother-and-sister writing team Dorothy and Herbert Fields played the women's more than the western angle when they wrote a "book" about Oakley's life. Titled *Annie Get Your Gun*, the story was intended for production on the musical stage. The Fields explained that they "dreamed" up the show for the "wonderful Merman," actress Ethel Merman. When producers Richard Rodgers and Oscar Hammerstein II agreed to produce their version of Annie's life, the Fields were delighted. They said they appreciated Rodgers and Hammerstein's assurances that the stage play would remain true to the book, but they never explained why they took Annie's story one giant step further away from fact.

On May 16, 1946, Ethel Merman opened as Annie at the Imperial Theater in New York City. She played to viewers who were eager to escape to simpler times, before mass death, war camps, and atomic bombs, and who also longed for such traditional values as honesty and hard work. Many viewers, in the throes of the back-to-the-home movement, also believed that women should marry and bear children. Little wonder, then, that the playbill pictured a girlish Merman who wore a short-sleeved, knee-length, fringed dress with dark stockings and moccasins and who looked more like Peter Pan than Annie Oakley. As the play progressed, Merman switched to a fringed and sequined suit with hat, gloves, and boots to match. Given Merman's very feminine character, it is unsurprising that the show featured Annie's supposed loss of the shooting match to Frank.

Reviewers in Nutley, New Jersey, Annie's one-time hometown, proved critical. One claimed that if Oakley's hardships were known, she would seem even "more fabulous" than the show portrayed her. Merman replied that she had no desire to replicate Annie's difficulties. "If the show included all of Annie's hardships it would be a melodrama, and I'd be a wreck." Another Nutley reviewer titled his critique "Pistol Packin' Annie" and interviewed Annie's friend, Mrs. William Longfelder, who portrayed the real Annie as a quiet, soft-spoken, and unassuming person. But, Longfelder noted, the real Annie would not score a hit on the musical comedy stage.

In fact, the musical wowed audiences. The Fields gave the public the Annie they thought it wanted, and they were obviously right. The show ran for three years, for a total of 1,159 performances. Decca Records also released a six-record set of 78-speed phonograph records of the original cast singing the show's score. And, beginning in 1947 at the Texas State Fair, Mary Martin took the show on a road tour and later presented it on television.

The following year, in 1948, Stewart H. Holbrook, author of *Annie Oakley and Other Rugged People*, credited *Annie Get Your Gun* with "bringing back" Annie Oakley, whom he described as "a combination of Lillian Russell and Buffalo Bill . . . draped in gorgeous yellow buckskins and topped with a halo of powder-blue smoke." Of course, Annie never wore buckskin and would have blanched at being compared to either Russell or Cody, but Holbrook was right about one thing: the musical *Annie Get Your Gun* kept Annie's story in the public eye. Many of Annie's achievements, including her influence on American women, had disappeared in the process, but Annie herself lived on the musical stage.

Also in 1948, a comic book released by National Comics in New York presented Annie as a feminine, glamorous figure. Here, an accidental blow to Dale Evans's head turned her into the long-dead Annie Oakley. As Oakley, Evans, who wore makeup and feminine clothing and who looked, according to one of the male characters, "real purty," became the "Two-Gun Terror of the West." She single-handedly destroyed a violent gang and cleaned up Boom City. By rolling Ethel Merman, Dale Evans, and an imaginary western gun moll into one character, this rendition of Annie Oakley fulfilled the era's definition of feminine women and the comic-reader's need for thrills and excitement.

During the 1950s, the saga of Annie Oakley underwent further modification. This occurred, at least in part, because ambivalence concerning women rent the decade.

On the one hand, back-to-the-home advocates lauded the virtues of traditional womanhood. In 1956, *Life Magazine* described the ideal American woman as a wife, hostess, volunteer, "home manager," and "conscientious mother." In addition, such long-running televisions series as *I Love Lucy* and *Father Knows Best* portrayed women as homebodies while actresses Doris Day and Debbie Reynolds revealed women's innocent side.

On the other hand, women were leaving their homes by the thousands for paid employment. In 1950, women accounted for 29 percent of the paid work force in the United States; by 1960, this figure jumped to almost 35 percent. At the same time, the number of working mothers rose by 400 percent. Women themselves obviously had reservations about the back-to-the-home message.

Could the authentic Annie Oakley fit into this contradictory situation? Sometimes. In 1954, Ohio author Walter Havighurst's fictionalized but reasonably accurate account *Annie Oakley of the Wild West* presented a feminine yet strong woman who survived both hardships and accidents. Annie worked hard, adhered to her principles, and succeeded in both her marriage and her career.

In Hollywood, however, motion pictures, which catered to what the public wanted and seemed willing to pay for, had no place for such an Annie. Most filmmakers wanted more romance; others tried to please as many viewers as possible with their portrayals of both women and the West.

As a result, in western films during the 1950s, most actresses, notably Dale Evans, Rhonda Fleming, and Ruth Mix, played sidekicks or, in other words, proper helpmeets to their men. An occasional exception occurred when such major stars as Joan Crawford or Barbara Stanwyck played tough-minded women who controlled their own lives. Yet, even in these films, landing a man and marrying proved paramount. Thus, in 1954, in *Johnny*

Guitar, Crawford waged a battle with Mercedes McCambridge over railroad land *and* the love of Sterling Hayden. Also in that year, Barbara Stanwyck, playing opposite Ronald Reagan in *Cattle Queen of Montana*, helped capture a gang of rustlers *and* won a husband.

Because the stage Annie, who could both achieve career success and land a man, fit the latter type, it seemed an ideal time to revive *Annie Get Your Gun*. In 1950, Betty Hutton and Howard Keel starred in the MGM "musical western," which implanted inaccurate ideas about Annie into millions of people's minds. Billed as "The Biggest Musical Under the Sun in Technicolor," *Annie Get Your Gun* led to original cast albums released by MGM records and grossed over four million dollars. Although such a sentiment would have been anathema to Annie, few Americans escaped the message that "you can't get a man with a gun."

The film version of *Annie Get Your Gun* also dressed Annie in 1950s fashions. Although for the initial match with Frank Butler, Hutton's Oakley appeared in tattered buckskin laced together with rawhide, her appearance changed when she joined the Wild West. Much as women of the 1950s donned full skirts supported by crinoline petticoats, adopted the baby-doll look, and struggled with girdles and merry widow corsets, Hutton's Annie adopted the latest in feminine attire. She sported an outfit composed of a short, tight-fitting jacket and a slim, knee-length skirt, both decorated with gold braid. Instead of Oakley's leggings, Hutton wore nylon hose that revealed her legs between the bottom of her skirt and the tops of her high-heeled boots. Her jaunty hat sat atop her blond, curly hair. Throughout, Hutton wore makeup, including dark red lipstick, and in the ballroom scene she wore a décolleté ball gown decorated with medals, even though Annie had neither approved of such outfits nor worn her medals in public.

Moreover, according to this version of Annie's story, Frank quit the Wild West in a pout because Annie outperformed him. After touring Europe without the petulant, dandified Frank, Annie ran into him again at Cody's homecoming ball. They decided to shoot it out for the championship, but when Sitting Bull suggested to Annie that she purposely lose, she took his advice. Hutton thus once again reinforced the idea that a true woman must never defeat a man—and that a real man could not accept or love a woman who did so.

A Nutley critic protested, "They wronged our Annie in Technicolor fantasy." He added that the latest film version of Annie "wore dresses up to her knees and sang like Betty Hutton." Those "varmints out in Hollywood" had given a "torchy" side to Annie Oakley, even though her Nutley friends remembered her as a "distinguished lady."

Of course, most films of the time emphasized strong, heroic men and weak, dependent women. Audiences expected men to be "masculine" and women "feminine." Men triumphed while women depended on men for their ultimate happiness. Given those expectations, Frank had to be Hollywood-handsome and macho, whereas Annie had to be soft and pliant. Most Americans were unwilling to recognize the possibility that shooter and athlete Annie Oakley achieved a successful career and that her husband managed that career. They felt far more comfortable with a cute, cuddly Annie who let her man carry off the honors.

Other western women, notably Calamity Jane, also fell victim to this film genre. In 1953, when Doris Day starred in *Calamity Jane,* her version of Jane had to hide her inner self to get a man. Rather than portraying Jane as a wild woman or a hell-raiser, Day characterized her as a blustery woman who backed down when a man was at stake.

Young audiences of the 1950s, however, received a slightly different vision of Annie Oakley. While their parents laughed, applauded, or sighed along with Oakley's antics on stage and screen, young people followed the adventures of a pretty and domestic but also an independent and strong-minded Annie. This began when Gene Autry's Flying A Productions, one of the era's most prolific creators of western adventures, produced the series *Annie Oakley and Tagg* for television.

When *Annie Oakley and Tagg* premiered on CBS in 1954, it attracted both girls and boys as viewers. Wearing her blond hair in pigtails, Gail Davis played Annie Oakley until 1956 in eighty-one episodes. According to Autry's usual restrictive contract, Davis, although in her twenties, had to keep her blond hair in pigtails for all public appearances until 1960. Autry clearly wanted to preserve the image Davis projected of Oakley as a girlish, feminine woman who could also ride, rope, and shoot expertly.

Davis's Annie lived on a Texas ranch with her younger brother, Tagg. With the assistance of her love interest, deputy sheriff Lofty, Annie protected the nearby town of Diablo from outlaws and other villains. Wearing a bandanna, boots, and a fringed vest and split-skirt outfit, Annie jumped from horseback to stagecoach, shot while standing on horseback, and performed other marvelous feats.

In this series, Annie routinely exhibited such "female" characteristics as sensitivity and benevolence. But, unlike Merman's and Hutton's Annies, Davis also clearly exhibited such "male" characteristics as aggressiveness and toughness. In one episode, titled "Trouble Shooter," Annie championed convict laborers working on a nearby ranch, a "female" cause that involved a great deal of "male" shooting. In another, "Twisted Trails," Annie defended a rodeo performer, and in yet another, she protected a Dutch gunmaker from discriminatory treatment.

Davis's Oakley thrilled a generation of youngsters but also gave them important ideas regarding women. Granted, like any good woman of the time, Davis's Annie pursued admirable goals and relied on men in her quests. But she also ventured beyond the era's prescriptions for women, acting like a strong-minded woman who outrode and outshot everybody. Her male confederates defended her on this count. According to Tagg and Lofty, Annie could "do everything."

The books and comics that resulted from this series carried a similar double-sided message. In Dell Publishing Company's "Annie Oakley" comics, Annie charmed men, championed all sorts of causes, and cooked expertly. But Annie also shot, rode hard, and performed other masculine feats.

The feminine/masculine Annie also appeared in Whitman Publishing Company's 1955 release *Annie Oakley in Danger at Diablo* by Doris Schroeder. In its first few pages, the feminine Annie protected her brother and whipped up rabbit stew and dumplings to succor him. At the same time, the masculine

Annie drove a wagon through the southwestern desert and bagged the rabbit with a Springfield rifle, which she carried in addition to the army Colt revolver she wore in a holster marked "U.S.A."

Evidently, because the fictional Annie Oakley presented to young people during the 1950s was a western woman, she could exhibit strengths and skills forbidden to most women. In 1956, for example, author Edmund Collier's *The Story of Annie Oakley* gave young readers a nostalgic, fictionalized account that not only lionized Annie but also characterized her as a child of the frontier. According to Collier, the young Annie even slept under a buffalo hide blanket, even though buffalo never roamed in Ohio during Annie's lifetime.

Meanwhile, in Greenville, Ohio, the "Annie Oakley" patrol of Girl Scouts sang the "Ballad of Annie Oakley" to the tune of "Davy Crockett, King of the Wild Frontier." Especially written in 1956 for the Greenville Girl Scouts, the song deified Annie as the "Queen of the Wild Frontier" in an epic that avoided mention of love and marriage.

> Lived in a cabin in O-hi-o
> Shot up a storm not a century ago
> She got more game than with a bow
> And said I'll get good as soon as I grow
> Annie — Annie Oakley, Queen of the wild frontier.
>
> When she was eight she saw in the sky
> A nice bunch of quail flying by
> Up went her gun aimed rather high
> And down came a bird shot thru the eye
> Annie — Annie Oakley, Queen of the wild frontier.
>
> To match after match away she would go
> She could hit the mark both high and low
> And with her gun beat any Joe
> Which got her a job in the Bill Cody show
> Annie — Annie Oakley, Queen of the wild frontier.
>
> With Buffalo Bill she crossed the sea
> To give their show in each country
> She gained much fame as we can see
> And earned the command of royalty
> Annie — Annie Oakley, Queen of the wild frontier.

Chief Sitting Bull was her good friend
Upon her word he could depend
The bow of friendship he did bend
With "Little Sure Shot"—right to the end
Annie—Annie Oakley, Queen of the wild frontier.

During the closing years of the 1950s, juvenile literature regarding Annie Oakley continued to give its readers a much stronger
character than the one their parents and other adults watched on
stage and screen. In 1958, Shannon Garst's *Annie Oakley*, which
perpetuated many fabrications and included fictitious conversa-
tion, represented Oakley as a woman who exhibited a good deal of
true grit, and Ellen Wilson's *Annie Oakley: Little Sure Shot* offered
a fictionalized account of an Oakley who was strong and purpose-
ful, even as a child.

During the 1960s, some of the nation's thinking about women was
resolved, perhaps by some of the very young people who had
grown up with the strong Annie Oakley portrayed on television,
in comic books, and in young people's literature. Early in the
decade and alongside the conflict in Vietnam came a host of
reform causes: civil rights, antiwar, poverty, environment, sexual
behavior, and contemporary feminism. Many people gradually
turned away from traditional definitions of femininity to wider
ones that allowed women to demonstrate nondomestic skills and
achievements. In 1960, Esther Peterson, head of the Women's
Bureau, stated that "homemaking chores" were "no great challenge" to competent women. Three years later, Betty Friedan
enlarged on Peterson's warning in *The Feminine Mystique*.

The growing belief in women's capabilities allowed a more authentic Annie to reappear from the welter of images ranging from
Stanwyck to Hutton. Oakley's legend moved toward an Annie
Oakley who provided a model well worth emulating. As early as
1961, *Annie Oakley: The Shooting Star*, by Charles P. Graves, showed
evidence of a revised message. Graves told his young readers that
because Oakley excelled in her profession and also did good for
others, she was exemplary. Then, in October 1964, the annual Annie
Oakley Trapshoot began in Pinehurst, North Carolina, to recognize
Oakley as an athlete rather than a show business star.

But Broadway and Hollywood proved tough adversaries. Ever since 1946, *Annie Get Your Gun* had experienced numerous revivals. Although such productions probably intended to honor Annie's memory, the gave their audiences fanciful images of westerners and of Annie rather than the genuine article. Each version took its own liberties. An English production arrayed Annie in a bustle outfit with high-top boots while it made Cody a virtual caricature, Sitting Bull a cigar-store Indian, and Pawnee Bill a mountain man. A German company cast Annie as a dirty, ragged, blond urchin and Frank as a handsome, mustachioed, devil-may-care fellow. When, in 1966, Ethel Merman revived *Annie Get Your Gun* in celebration of the twentieth anniversary of the play's first run, twenty-nine-year-old Bruce Yarnell, wearing a fringed shirt and a white Stetson hat, played Frank opposite the aging Merman's Annie.

Would the truth about Annie and her life triumph, or would the romantic, conflict-based western fantasy hold sway?

During the early 1970s, American views of both women and the West altered significantly. In particular, the feminist movement cast women as assertive, capable beings while historians started to rethink customary interpretations of the West. Scholars began to reject famed historian Frederick Jackson Turner's 1893 description of western settlers as men; they came to recognize that women played significant roles in the West as well. The mid-seventies marked the beginning of a virtual outpouring of books and articles concerning the roles and contributions of women in the Old West.

Hollywood was in turmoil as well. With feminists demanding newer, stronger images of women, directors and producers had to revamp their films. Westerns especially had to change. Critics scoffed at old stereotypes of good and bad women, ladies of the night, civilizers, and strong women. As they called for fuller, more complex characters, male and female directors began to respond. As early as 1971, Julie Christie in *McCabe and Mrs. Miller* portrayed a capable heroine. But the era still seemed confused about a strong woman's ability to sustain a relationship; thus Christie's character had to forgo the affection of Warren Beatty's character because she was the stronger of the two.

Then, in 1976, a turning point occurred in *Buffalo Bill and the Indians; or, Sitting Bull's History Lesson*. This Robert Altman film, based on the Arthur Kopit play *Indians*, starred Paul Newman as Buffalo Bill Cody, Geraldine Chaplin as Annie Oakley, and Burt Lancaster as Ned Buntline. By spoofing Wild West shows, Altman attempted to totally debunk hero-worshiping Westerns. He called the film a "Bicentennial gift to America," presumably meaning that it gave Americans a chance to reassess their history, especially western history.

Instead, Altman remythologized the West, generally in a negative manner. He painted Cody as an inept manager, as well as an egomaniac, coward, and drunkard. Chaplin, as Annie, accidentally shot Frank through the shoulder at close range at about the same time that a female troupe member informed Frank she was carrying his child. Burt Lancaster, as Buntline, acted, according to one critic, "like an unemployed mortician." Although the reviews of *Buffalo Bill* were generally favorable, the audiences were scant.

Along with such other films as *Soldier Blue*, *Little Big Man*, *The Wild Bunch*, *Butch Cassidy*, and Clint Eastwood's westerns, Altman's film seemed to provide a necessary low point of disillusionment with American institutions, heroes, and values. Hollywood appeared to regroup and grasp at a more balanced view of the past, resulting in more authentic women characters than the civilizers and femmes fatales that had dominated the screen in the past. In 1978, for example, Jane Fonda played an independent woman in *Comes a Horseman*; the following year, Conchata Ferrell in *Heartland* met challenges with bravery and stamina.

The way was at last open for the genuine Annie to emerge. In 1973, author Isabelle S. Sayers's well-researched and factual pamphlet-sized *The Rifle Queen: Annie Oakley* appeared. Then, in 1979, Clifford Lindsey Alderman, author of *Annie Oakley and the World of Her Time*, won the distinction of being the only Oakley biographer to link the woman to her era. Alderman maintained that Oakley's life and career reflected the nation's fascination with westward expansion and prosperity. He concluded that Oakley's story of "struggle and triumph," as well as her spirit of energy and ambition, mirrored "America's golden era."

By the early 1980s, Annie Oakley began to attract increasing interest, and her legend started to gain more authenticity. Gradually, many Americans had come to esteem career women and those who entered male-dominated fields. Thus, Americans of the 1980s could admire the original Annie—the woman who defeated a man in a shooting match, handled firearms better than most men, and built a successful career yet bore no children. At last, they could also respect Frank Butler, the man who managed his wife's career. Frank's choice of vocations was no longer atypical and suspect.

Because Annie and Frank fit 1980s expectations of women and men, their lives could be celebrated rather than revised. Thus, Annie soon became an example for aspiring girls and women. In 1981, Isabelle Sayers's *Annie Oakley and Buffalo Bill's Wild West* presented, in text and 102 illustrations, a woman of courage and conviction. In 1985, Ideals Publishing Corporation published Jan Gleiter's and Kathleen Thompson's *Annie Oakley: Great Tales*. Intended for young readers, the slim book described Annie Oakley as a modern-day Abraham Lincoln—honest and hard-working as a child and therefore successful and famous as an adult. In both text and illustrations, Annie emerged as a contemporary heroine who had "shot straight for twenty-five years and never hurt a living soul."

Also in 1985, actress Jamie Lee Curtis starred in a one-hour version of Oakley's life story. As part of the series *Tall Tales and Legends*, this rendition offered an accurate, fully developed picture of Annie from girlhood to later life. In response, the theater journal *Variety* described Curtis's Oakley in modern terms indeed: a "media superstar" and an "independent, strong-willed woman who never forgot her roots."

In 1989, in *True West* magazine, historian R. Douglas Hurt similarly took a contemporary, straightforward approach. In "Annie Oakley: An Enduring Western Legend," Hurt described Oakley as an honest entertainer who never employed trickery. Although not born in the West, Oakley showed the world "a glimpse of American life as it once was." Because Oakley established her reputation at a time when the Wild West was becoming the New West, she herself came to represent an "America of a bygone age."

Also in 1989, a book for young readers debunked the usual Annie Oakley myth. Ellen Levine tried to tell Oakley's true story in Scholastic Press's *Ready, Aim, Fire! The Real Adventures of Annie Oakley*. Levine explained that writers and producers had thought that audiences might not like Annie if they knew she outshot Frank. They also might dislike Frank if they realized that he married the woman who had defeated him. But, Levine concluded, Frank loved Annie for herself. In fact, "Frank was more interesting than the writers pictured him, and Annie was true to herself."

Granted, the genuine Annie achieved recognition during the 1980s, but the mythical West continued to exert an influence. For many, Annie Oakley still symbolized the Old Wild West. Typical of the materialism of the 1980s, some people even began to use Oakley's image and memory to sell western products. In an advertisement for Justin Boots, John Justin proclaimed, "When Annie Oakley began performing sharpshooting tricks in 1885, my grandfather had been making boots for 6 years." Another repre-sentative advertisement appeared in 1988 in *Guns & Ammo*. Below a picture of Annie and her guns it declared, "Used To Be Only Legends Could Nail a Rattler At Ten Paces." But now any upstart could hit a rattlesnake with CCI ammunition. The advertisement refused to guarantee that readers would become legends like Oakley but did assure them that they would "sure shoot like one."

In addition to advertisements, a number of writers also contin-ued to associate Oakley with the mythical West In 1988, Robert Quackenbush's *Who's That Girl with the Gun? A Story of Annie Oakley*, one of Prentice-Hall's Books for Young Readers, de-scribed Annie as a wonderful product of the "frontier," where "pioneer life was hard." The author concluded that Annie ranked among "America's real-life folk heroes," including Davy Crockett, Daniel Boone, and other famous "frontier" people. Still, Quaken-bush probed for Oakley's true story, which he believed captured the "American spirit."

More recently, in 1991, a publication for children, *Cobblestone* magazine, devoted an entire issue to Annie Oakley. One author pointed out that Oakley "brought the excitement and romance of the American West" to audiences at home and abroad. Another stated that audiences flocked to see shows about the American West "by people who had been there." Of course, Annie had spent little time in the West, yet her western image prevailed.

Another 1991 publication, by Tom Tierney for Dover Publications, a cut-out book titled *Annie Oakley and Buffalo Bill: Paper Dolls in Full Color*, further demonstrated the importance of Annie's western reputation. In between pages of seventeen costumes for Annie, Tierney stated that Oakley's costumes had "become the prototype for women's Western wear for years to come." During the 1890s, Cody and Oakley had created the western cowgirl. Now they appropriately stood together—in full color—as the fashion leaders of the Old West—and of the contemporary West as well.

In 1992, a Rabbit Ears Productions cartoon also presented Annie as a western heroine. Riddled with such factual errors as the claim that Cody hired Annie immediately and that Annie always opened Wild West performances, this rendition also misrepresented Annie Oakley as a homely woman with a large nose.

As the 1990s unfold, the fascination with Annie Oakley—both the woman and the westerner—continues and even grows. Moreover, accounts of Oakley's life and career are more realistic and revisionist than ever. For instance, journalist Shirl Kasper's 1992 *Annie Oakley* set a new standard in myth-busting. By using newspaper clippings in a meticulous and thorough fashion, Kasper pinpointed many formerly unclear events of Annie's life and career. Instead of repeating stories, Kasper detailed Oakley's achievements in a way that far exceeded that of any other biographer.

In addition, for those who wish to pursue Annie Oakley's life and career, several organizations have collected and make available to researchers and other visitors Annie's belongings and documents. This bodes well for the future of the Annie Oakley legend, for when authors, television scriptwriters, and movie producers are ready to reject the Oakley myth and pursue the reality, information is available.

One such organization is located in Annie's hometown of Greenville, Ohio. Here residents have worked to preserve Oakley's artifacts and spirit, on some occasions more successfully than others. For instance, although some Greenville citizens hoped a rifle club might purchase Oakley's childhood home when it went on the auction block in 1939, a Fort Recovery man bought the homestead instead. A decade later, however, the Darke County Historical Society initiated a fund-raising campaign to collect one hundred thousand dollars for a statue of Annie Oakley. More recently, in 1966, the Greenville Chamber of Commerce inaugurated Annie Oakley Days, which include a parade, an Annie Oakley shooting contest, an "Olde Time Melodrama," western square dancing, a "National Fast Draw Competition," and other events.

The 1980s saw even more advances. In July 1981, Greenville placed a memorial on the site of Annie's birthplace. In February 1988, after many years of fund-raising, an 840-pound statue of Oakley finally arrived in Greenville. The sculptor, Terry Mimnaugh of Lakeview, Montana, produced a larger-than-life bronze statue of Oakley wearing her skirted shooting dress, with her cowboy-style hat on the back of her head and her rifle in hand.

In addition, the Darke County Historical Society, located in the Garst Museum in Greenville, has a sizable Annie Oakley room. Many of the artifacts displayed here came directly from Annie, who frequently gave or lent out artifacts or curios. In 1907, she and Frank gave the Greenville Library an autographed photo of Annie taken in London and one of Cody. They also lent to the forerunner of the Garst Museum many Sioux Indian artifacts, including a pair of beaded buckskin moccasins supposedly worn by the celebrated Chief Sitting Bull at the Battle of the Little Big Horn, a muslin jacket worn by the Sioux messiah "Short Bull" in his ghost dances, a beaded buckskin arrow pouch worn by Chief Red Cloud, a beaded tobacco pouch carried by Chief White Eagle, and an ornamental headdress worn by Sitting Bull.

Also in Greenville, the Annie Oakley Foundation and its newsletter, *Taking Aim*, work to preserve the facts about Oakley's life and to clear up "the fictions of the 'Annie Oakley legend.'" The foundation disseminates information, offers slide lectures, and holds such Oakley artifacts as silver pieces that Queen Victoria gave Annie, crystal decanters presented to Annie by the German kaiser; a variety of coins including a commemorative coin from the 1893 Chicago World's Fair, and the 1883 Parker Brothers shotgun that Annie called her first gun of "quality."

Another agency that devotes space to Oakley holdings is the Nutley Historical Society in New Jersey. When, in 1945, Nutley organized a historical society dedicated to collecting "available historic materials," to helping genealogists, and to writing a history of Nutley, Annie's years in Nutley played a prominent role. Today, the society sponsors an annual "birthday party" for Annie every August and displays Oakley's memorabilia, including gadgets, photographs, letters, and the two pistols, one a Colt six-shooter and the other a horse pistol, that Annie gave to John Donaldson, former Nutley station agent.

Besides Greenville and Nutley, the Buffalo Bill Historical Center in Cody, Wyoming, holds a sizable and important collection of Oakley correspondence, ephemera, artifacts, and weapons. Among the weapons are a Francotte double-barrel, 12-gauge shotgun, which is a lightweight but expensive Belgian trap gun with elaborate engraving and inlays, and two of Oakley's 1892 Winchester rifles, one an engraved .25–.20-caliber rifle that Annie purchased in New York City. Recently, a private collector has donated to the Buffalo Bill Historical Center one of Oakley's Smith & Wesson .38–.44 revolvers with pearl grips, a Colt .38 revolver, two shotguns, and three of the hand-blown glass balls—filled with red, white, and blue feathers—that Annie blasted into smithereens during her performances.

On exhibit at the Buffalo Bill Historical Center are two Winchester Model #92, lever-action carbines. One is a .44-caliber with a twenty-two-inch octagonal barrel, a checkered stock, and a receiver with floral engravings; the other is a .32-caliber with a twenty-one and three-eighths half-octagonal barrel and animal engravings on the gold-plated receiver. Also on display are a pump-action Remington .22 and a pearl-handled, nickel-plated revolver, as well as Oakley's trunk and other belongings.

Still more Oakley memorabilia is exhibited at Oklahoma's Cowboy Hall of Fame and California's Gene Autry Museum. In addition, family members and individual collectors hold such other items as crystal, china, cabinet photographs, coins, Wild

West programs and artifacts, jewelry, guns, medals, and numerous Native American artifacts that Oakley dispersed before her
death or in her will. One of these collectors prizes a .38-caliber
semi-fluted Colt conversion six-shooter. An antique weapons
collector in San Francisco has purchased three of Annie's guns,
engraved gold-plated Smith & Wesson revolvers with pearl han-
dles; according to an 1899 newspaper report, the Smith & Wesson
Company made these three guns specially for Annie.

The multitude of books, articles, plays, films, television programs, artifacts, and other information that survived Annie Oakley indicates that she was a woman of success and of substance.
But reading about Annie Oakley or visiting museum exhibits is
one thing; distilling her essence from them is quite another.

Consequently, Annie's legacy is controversial, and the real
Annie remains somewhat clouded. People continue to confuse
Annie with Calamity Jane, and *Annie Get Your Gun* still enjoys
frequent revivals. According to Annie's descendant Irene Patterson Black, Annie was such a special person that she simply cannot
be described. Perhaps so, but given Oakley's effect on show
business, the sport of shooting, American women, and the American West, assessing Annie Oakley remains a worthwhile and
instructive endeavor.

Conclusion

Who Was Annie Oakley?

IN her own day, the late 1800s and early 1900s, Annie Oakley represented certain virtues and characteristics that many Americans valued yet feared losing: hard work, simplicity, modesty, friendliness, femininity, frugality, ambition, the ability to succeed, and a love of animals and nature. In decades marked by decreasing open spaces in the United States and the prevalence of robber barons, labor union riots, yellow journalism, cooch dancers, a soaring divorce rate, world war, and a host of other ills publicized in the nation's newspapers and foremost in people's minds, Annie Oakley symbolized what many people believed America had been and could again be.

People found it easy to admire and believe in Oakley, who was genuinely a hard-working, generous, friendly, and compassionate person. Although she may have seemed too straitlaced and diligent to some, others respected her moral stance and the hours she spent practicing her craft. While some may have thought her too frugal and particular, others lauded her for being generous with her time, money, and energy. Even though she was sharp-tongued at times, on numerous other occasions she went out of her way to smooth over difficult situations. And in spite of her tendency to guard her privacy so much that we will never understand her real feelings about her childhood or her relationship with Frank, she welcomed children into her tent and gave money, gifts, and her possessions to family members, neighbors, and admirers.

One key to understanding Annie was her integrity. She constantly sought authenticity in the arena and in her personal life. Throughout her career, she demanded honest applause for genuine feats. Oakley seems to have told only one lie—that her birth date was 1866 rather than 1860—and it is doubtful that she initiated the falsehood. Rather, she perpetuated it, probably for show business reasons rather than personal vanity. In her autobiography, she returned to the truth; she gave her birth date as 1860.

Annie's integrity also had its difficult side. Like so many admirable human qualities, Annie's honesty sometimes led her to take actions she might otherwise have disdained. For instance, she occasionally made public sport of reporters who embroidered their stories. In addition, according to neighbor Lela Border Hollinger, Annie hated itinerant "gypsies," whom she judged insincere and even dishonest. Clearly, Annie had little tolerance for those who failed to adhere to the same standards in which she believed.

A second insight comes from an examination of Oakley's generosity. Rather than providing herself with an abundance of luxuries, she spent a great deal of money on others. Poor in her youth, as an adult she preferred to lavish things on others rather than on herself. Her grandniece Bess Lindsey Walcholz remarked that even "the last days of her life were spent in wrapping packages for friends all over the world . . . she forgot no one."

On the negative side, however, Annie was what one relative called "particular" and a "stickler," even concerning her generosity. As a case in point, Dorothy Stone described Annie as "a bit austere in some matters," especially because Annie once gave a Victrola to a children's hospital and, hearing nothing more about it, proceeded to investigate. When Annie discovered the Victrola in the nurses' office, she seized it and took it home. She wanted her gift to be used for the young patients and was not above rescinding it when someone disobeyed her instructions.

A third clue to Oakley's personality lay in her inability to understand the extent of her historical significance, or perhaps to diminish and deny it. Even though Americans were beginning to laud some women as significant and influential, Oakley failed to put herself in that category. Instead, Annie saw herself as a skilled wage-earner and a reasonably good stage performer. According to Annie's descendant Beatrice Blakeley Hunt, Annie and Frank never spoke of her fame to family members or acted like she had achieved more than the others. Although Annie wanted to leave an unsullied reputation behind her, she rejected conceit and an enlarged notion of her own impact on the world. Oakley would, I believe, be surprised at the number of plays, films, books, statues, and organizations perpetuating her life story.

The unfortunate side to this character trait was that Annie seemed unable to enjoy retirement as a reward for a job well done but was anxious to add more items to her list of credits. Moreover, she failed to keep a diary or journal, preserve her correspondence, or save any memorabilia other than several scrapbooks of newspaper clippings. She put off writing an autobiography until near death and dispersed her possessions with little thought to the historical record. In September 1926, for example, she sent a friend a packet of photographs and an Indian sketchbook drawn by the man Sioux Indians believed to be the messiah. Annie even melted down most of her medals for charity. As a result, it is impossible to grasp the essence of the "real" and inner Annie Oakley.

We can, however, assess Oakley's contributions. Although her death in November 1926 ended her immediate influence, her legend grew to proportions she would never have imagined. The story of Annie Oakley—the dazzling entertainer, exceptional athlete, true lady, and model western woman—lives on in articles, books, movies, and television shows. Her impact appears in everything from free passes called "Annie Oakleys" to women's sports participation, from Annie Oakley celebrations and shooting contests to children's books, statues, and museum exhibits.

Many of the above reveal Oakley's importance in helping widen society's images and expectations of women. What Buffalo Bill Cody did for Wild West shows and rodeos, Annie Oakley did for women performers, athletes, and sports enthusiasts. But, by refusing to act like a "new woman," Annie maintained universal appeal. In addition, unlike Cody and others, Oakley was a successful, significant performer who remained happily married, sober, and solvent. For women, Annie provided the Horatio Alger story of the day.

Yet perhaps her most significant contribution was the integral role she played in the world's great love affair with the American West. She represented the best of the West: she was "just folks" who came from humble beginnings and dressed and acted simply throughout her life. Like a "true" westerner, she shot and rode with great skill. And like a "good" western woman, she asserted herself without sacrificing virtue, sweetness, and domesticity.

Today, Annie Oakley lives in the world's memory as a westerner, but one who clung to ladyhood. Consequently, both her own and current generations can welcome Annie Oakley into their hearts without censure or regret.

How much of this was happenstance and social milieu and how much Oakley's personal choice? Certainly happenstance and milieu dictated many of the options available to Annie. As a woman, a Quaker, and an Ohioan, she was not likely to become a hard-bitten, rough-riding buffalo hunter or Indian scout. Still, Oakley exercised a great deal of agency in endeavors accessible to her. Annie especially demonstrated her will as an entertainer and sport shooter; here she smashed barriers holding back women. At the same time she more or less accepted two prevailing social judgments of the time—the ideal attributes of ladies and of westerners. But, while accepting them, she also turned them to her advantage; she enhanced her image and appeal by acting like a lady and a western women.

Thus, Oakley chose to break bounds in some areas while adopting them in others. She fought for goals important to her—earning a living as a shooter and participating in sports—at the same time she adopted, and used, such prevailing concepts of the time as ladyhood and the mythic West.

Because Annie successfully combined her talent with such beliefs, she appealed to virtually everyone. Rather than being like the irrepressible and infamous Calamity Jane, Annie Oakley was more like Maria Martinez, a western potter who strove for beauty and accuracy, like Amelia Bloomer, a western reformer who worked to improve the lot of women, and like Mary Austin, a western writer who desired justice for Native Americans. In addition, Annie had the stage presence and appeal of Jenny Lind, a Swedish singer who toured the United States, the honesty of Sarah Winnemucca, a Paiute woman who revealed the truth even if unpleasant, and the generosity of Mary Ellen Pleasant, a California entrepreneur and philanthropist. If Annie had negative traits as well, they simply made her human.

Today, Oakley continues to have widespread appeal. A century after her prime, the United States is a more mature, responsible nation than during the 1890s. Yet the 1990s bear many similarities to Annie's times. The "good old days" of family farms and simple virtues are fast fading. In their place are stock market scandals, racial riots, tabloid journalism, exposé talk shows, AIDS, a soaring divorce rate, global warfare, and a plethora of other social problems. Today, Annie Oakley still embodies largely middle-class values and standards, including hard work, honesty, and humility, which numerous Americans believe in and hope to restore.

Oakley is thus part of a larger phenomenon; she personifies the longing of a nation to return to certain elements of its past, a past characterized by the Old West. The West endures because it is a useful and attractive part of Americans' collective past, a part characterized by many successes and associated with virtues many people think of as peculiarly American. For those Americans who continue to demonstrate a fascination with the positive side of the Old West, Oakley provides a fitting symbol.

Because the Old West cannot survive when stripped of its heroes, Oakley is an extremely important figure of the enduring West. She allows people to return without guilt or remorse to the days of the Old Wild West. One can condemn aspects of the conquest of the West without rejecting Annie or her compelling achievements and qualities.

In truth, Annie Oakley became a westerner by affinity rather than by birth, and she created a model western woman. As a result, she has become a western heroine for all time—she has proven as enduring as the West itself.

Note on Sources

BECAUSE Annie Oakley had little sense of her own historical significance, she kept few of her letters and personal documents. The two best
sources for Annie Oakley's words and memories are Annie Oakley,
"Autobiography," undated, copy in possession of the author, and
Annie Oakley, *Powders I Have Used* (Wilmington: Du Pont Powder
Company, 1914). In addition, Annie and Frank compiled invaluable
scrapbooks of newspaper clippings. The originals are held by the
Buffalo Bill Historical Society in Cody, Wyoming, along with documents, ephemera, vertical files, and artifacts. Copies of the scrapbooks
are available at the Western History Collection of the Public Library in
Denver, Colorado.

Several of Oakley's letters as well as Frank Butler, "The Life of
Dave," Bess Lindsey Walcholz, "Annie Oakley," 1909, and Hazel Moses
Robertson, "Moses Memories," 1989, are held by the Annie Oakley
Foundation in Greenville, Ohio (also copies in the author's posses-
sion). Other of Oakley's letters are in the Oakley Collection at the
Nutley Historical Society in Nutley, New Jersey.

Such people as Irene Patterson Black (a niece), Beatrice Blakeley
Hunt (a grandniece), and Lela Border Hollinger (a neighbor) have
shared many useful and interesting memories of Annie. Notes from
interviews, all conducted in January 1993, with these women are held
by the author.

Biographers offer a variety of interpretations of Annie Oakley's life
and career. Clifford Lindsey Alderman, *Annie Oakley and the World of
Her Time* (New York: Macmillan Publishing Co., 1979), analyzes Oakley in the context of her own era. Oakley's first biographer, Courtney
Ryley Cooper, *Annie Oakley: Woman at Arms* (New York: Duffield,
1927), combines facts and legend to present a picture of an achieving,
successful woman. Edmund Collier, *The Story of Annie Oakley* (New
York: Grosset and Dunlap, 1956), gives young readers a fictionalized
account that lionizes Oakley as a child of the frontier. Shannon Garst,
Annie Oakley (New York: Julian Messner, 1958), Jan Gleiter and Kathleen Thompson, *Annie Oakley: Great Tales* (Nashville: Ideals Publishing Corp., 1985), Ellen Wilson, *Annie Oakley: Little Sure Shot* (Indianapolis: Bobbs-Merrill, 1958), and Charles P. Graves, *Annie Oakley:
The Shooting Star* (Champaign, Ill.: Garrard, 1961), after fictionalized
accounts for young readers and characterize Oakley as a young woman

with true grit. More recently, Robert Quackenbush, *Who's That Girl with the Gun? A Story of Annie Oakley* (New York: Prentice-Hall Books for Young Readers, 1988), also ties Oakley to the frontier. Ellen Levine, *Ready, Aim, Fire! The Real Adventures of Annie Oakley* (New York: Scholastic, 1989), interprets Oakley as a courageous, achieving woman, an admirable role model for girls of the late twentieth century. Oakley's niece Annie Fern Campbell Swartwout, *Missie: An Historical Biography of Annie Oakley* (Blanchester, Ohio: Brown Publishing Co., 1947), incorporates many legends into her account and is best when offering her personal recollections of Annie and Frank. Walter Havighurst, *Annie Oakley of the Wild West* (New York: Macmillan, 1954), presents a fictionalized, highly readable account that is generally accurate. Tom Tierney, *Annie Oakley and Buffalo Bill: Paper Dolls in Full Color* (New York: Dover Publications, 1991), reproduces some of the clothing Annie wore.

More thoroughly researched statements are found in Isabelle S. Sayers: *The Rifle Queen: Annie Oakley* (Ostrander, Ohio: N.p., 1973) and *Annie Oakley and Buffalo Bill's Wild West* (New York: Dover Publications, 1981). The most recent biography, and one that makes extensive use of the Oakley scrapbooks, is Shirl Kasper, *Annie Oakley* (Norman: University of Oklahoma Press, 1992).

In addition, a variety of popular articles interpret Oakley in differing ways: Peter P. Carney, "Greatest of Modern Dianas" (n.p., n.d., copy in author's possession); Louise Cheney, "Annie Oakley, Little Miss Sureshot," *Real West* 10 (November 1967): 53–57; special issue on "Annie Oakley and the Wild West," *Cobblestone Magazine*, 12, no. 1 (January 1991); Patricia Croft, "Highlights of Annie Oakley," *Winchester Repeater* 1 (Fall 1984): 37–38; "Annie Oakley" in Stewart H. Holbrook, *Little Annie Oakley and Other Rugged People* (New York: Macmillan Co., 1948); R. Douglas Hurt, "Annie Oakley: An Enduring Western Legend," *True West* 36 (July 1989): 14–19; and Mark Taylor, "Annie Oakley: A Shooting Legend," *American Rifleman* 131 (December 1983): 44–46, 68–69. In addition, Oakley's years in North Carolina are discussed in Claude R. Flory, "Annie Oakley in the South," *North Carolina Historical Review* 43, no. 3 (1966): 333–43; her relationship with Frank is analyzed in Tracy C. Davis, "Annie Oakley and Her Ideal Husband of No Importance," in Janelle G. Reinelt and Joseph R. Roach, eds., *Critical Theory and Performance* (Ann Arbor: University of Michigan Press, 1992), 229–312, and "Shotgun Wedlock: Annie Oakley's Power Politics in the Wild West," in Lawrence Senelick, Ed., *Gender in Performance: The Presentation of Difference in the Performing Arts* (Hanover, N.H.: University Press of New England, 1992), 141–57.

Although seemingly without factual base, a possible underside to Oakley's life is suggested in a novel by Marcie Heidish, *The Secret of*

Annie Oakley (New York: New American Library, 1983). The theme of childhood abuse marks Heidish's novel, as she has remarked that it does her own life and other of her works. Annie's supposed hatred of guns and aversion to hunting is posed in Jim Blair, "The Torment of Annie Oakley," *Elks Magazine*, 1981, 6–8, 29–31, 34.

The dime novel series (eight titles) that appears to be about Annie Oakley is best illustrated by Prentiss Ingraham, *Buffalo Bill's Girl Pard* (New York: Street and Smith, 1980).

Articles comparing Annie Oakley with later women shooters are James Cranbrook, "America's Prettiest Shotgunner," *Guns* 2 (March 1956): 16–18, 39, and K. D. Curtis, "Can Women Outshoot Men?" *Guns* 1 (July 1955): 14–18, 53–54.

An understanding of early Darke County can be gained from *History of Darke County* (Chicago: W. H. Beers and Co., 1880), *A Biographical History of Darke County* (Chicago: Lewis Publishing Co., 1900), and Frazer E. Wilson, *History of Darke County* (Milford, Ohio: Hobart Publishing Co., 1914). The story of Nutley, New Jersey, and Oakley's time there is found in Ann A. Troy, ed., *Nutley: Yesterday, Today* (Nutley: Nutley Historical Society, 1961).

Details of Annie Oakley's lawsuits against William Randolph Hearst's newspaper can be found in *The Federal Reporter* (St. Paul: Westwood Publishing Co., 1906–9).

An overview of mid- and late-nineteenth-century show business and shooting can be found in the following: Jack Burton, *In Memoriam: Oldtime Show Biz* (New York: Vantage Press, 1965); Joseph Durso, *Madison Square Garden: 100 Years of History* (New York: Simon and Schuster, 1979); Douglas Gilbert, *American Vaudeville: Its Life and Times* (New York: Whittlesey House, 1940); John and Alice Durant, *Pictorial History of the American Circus* (New York: A. S. Barnes and Co., 1957); Jaroslav Lugs, *A History of Shooting* (Felthma, Middlesex, England: Spring Books, 1968); and Robert C. Toll, *On with the Show: The First Century of Show Business in America* (New York: Oxford University Press, 1976). Especially useful are the Amon Carter Museum and Don Russell, *The Wild West; or, A History of the Wild West Shows* (Fort Worth: Amon Carter Museum of Western Art, 1970), and the Wild West posters in the Western History Collection, Denver Public Library.

Early rodeos and cowgirls are analyzed in the following: Kathryn Derry, "Corsets and Broncs: The Wild West Show Cowgirl, 1890–1920," *Colorado Heritage* (Summer 1992), 2–16; Kristine Fredriksson, *American Rodeo: From Buffalo Bill to Big Business* (College Station: Texas A&M University Press, 1985); Teresa Jordan, *Cowgirls: Women of the American West* (1982; reprint, Lincoln: University of Nebraska Press, 1991); Mary Lou LeCompte, *Cowgirls of the Rodeo: Pioneer*

Professional Athletes (Urbana: University of Illinois Press, 1992); Joyce Gibson Roach, *The Cowgirls*, 2d ed. (Denton: University of North Texas Press, 1990); Elizabeth Van Steenwyck, *Women in Sports: Rodeo* (New York: Harvey House, 1978); and Sarah Wood-Clark, *Beautiful Daring Western Girls: Women of the Wild West Shows*, 2d ed. (Cody, Wyo.: Buffalo Bill Historical Center, 1991). Also useful is Jack Rennert, *One Hundred Posters of Buffalo Bill's Wild West Show* (New York: Darien House, 1976).

Books and articles on Buffalo Bill Cody and his Wild West abound: Joseph J. Arpad, *Buffalo Bill's Wild West* (Palmer Lake, Colo.: Fetter Press, 1971); M. B. Bailey, ed., *Buffalo Bill's Wild West Route Book* (Buffalo, N.Y.: Courier Co., 1896); Sarah J. Blackstone, *Buckskins, Bullets, and Business: A History of Buffalo Bill's Wild West* (Westport, Conn.: Greenwood Press, 1986), which is especially useful on the idea of performance texts; William E. Deahl, Jr., "A History of Buffalo Bill's Wild West Show, 1883–1913," (Ph.D. diss., Southern Illinois University, 1974) and "Buffalo Bill's Wild West Show, 1885," *Annals of Wyoming* 47 (Fall 1975): 139–51; Louis Pfaller, "Enemies in '76, Friends in '85: Sitting Bull and Buffalo Bill," *Prologue: Journal of the National Archives* 1 (1969): 16–31; Adolph Regli, *The Real Book about Buffalo Bill* (Garden City, N.Y.: Franklin Watts, 1952); Joseph G. Rosa and Robin May, *Buffalo Bill and His Wild West* (Lawrence: University Press of Kansas, 1989); Don Russell, *The Lives and Legends of Buffalo Bill* (Norman: University of Oklahoma Press, 1960) and "Cody, Kings, and Coronets: A Sprightly Account of Buffalo Bill's Wild West Show at Home and Abroad," *American West* 7 (1970): 4–19, 62; Henry Blackman Sell and Victor Weybright, *Buffalo Bill and the Wild West* (New York: Oxford University Press, 1955); Richard J. Walsh, *The Making of Buffalo Bill: A Study in Heroics* (Indianapolis: Bobbs-Merrill Co., 1928); and Nellie Snyder Yost, *Buffalo Bill: His Family, Friends, Fame, Failures, and Fortunes* (Chicago: Swallow Press, 1979). For interpretations of Cody's image, see Wayne M. Sarf, *God Bless You, Buffalo Bill: A Layman's Guide to History and the Western Film* (Rutherford, N.J.: Fairleigh Dickinson University Press, 1983).

Personal insights into the back lot and Cody are found in three works: Tex Cooper, "I Knew Buffalo Bill," *Frontier Times* 33 (Spring 1969): 19–21; Milt Hinkle, "Memoirs of My Rodeo Days," *Real West* 11 (September 1968): 35–37, 65; and M. I. McCreight, "Buffalo As I Knew Him," *True West* 4 (July/August 1957): 25, 41–42. Firsthand accounts that give a view of the Wild West's European tour between 1903 and 1906 are Charles Eldrige Griffin, *Four Years in Europe with Buffalo Bill* (Albia, Iowa: Stage Publishing Co., 1908), and Luther Standing Bear, *My People the Sioux* (Lincoln: University of Nebraska Press, 1975), chapters 24–15.

Also worth perusing are William F. Cody, *Buffalo Bill's Life Story: An Autobiography* (New York: Rinehart and Co., 1920), and Stella Adelyn Foote, ed., *Letters from Buffalo Bill* (El Segundo, Calif.: Upton and Sons, 1990).

The controversy surrounding Native Americans in wild west shows is discussed in L. G. Moses, "Indians on the Midway: Wild West Shows and the Indian Bureau at World's Fairs, 1893–1904," *South Dakota History* 21 (Fall 1991): 205–29, and Chauncey Yellow Robe, "The Menace of the Wild West Show," *Quarterly Journal of the Society of American Indians* 2 (July/September 1914): 224–28.

The story of Gordon "Pawnee Bill" Lillie is found in Glenn Shirley, *Pawnee Bill: A Biography of Major Gordon W. Lillie* (Albuquerque: University of New Mexico Press, 1958), and that of Martha Jane Cannary in Nolie Mumey, *Calamity Jane, 1852–1903: A History of Her Life and Adventure in the West* (Denver: Range Press, 1950).

Index

African Americans: in show business, 50, 59

Alderman, Clifford Lindsey (biographer), 224

Alexandria (princess of Wales), 39–40

Altman, Robert (movie producer), 224

Amateur Trapshooting Association (ATA), 196

American Field (journal), 66, 178

American Sharpshooters Society, 15

American Trapshooting Association (ATA), 214

Ammunition, use of, 53–54, 70–71, 189

Anderson, C. M. (Greenville, Ohio, official), 56

Animal acts, use in Wild West shows, 49, 58

Annie Get Your Gun (film musical), 218–19

Annie Get Your Gun (stage musical), 215–16, 223, 230

Annie Oakley (film), 210–12

Annie Oakley (Garst), 222

Annie Oakley (Kasper), 227

Annie Oakley: A Brief Sketch of Her Career and Notes on Shooting (pamphlet, Butler), 71, 93

"Annie Oakley: An Enduring Western Legend" (Douglas), 225

Annie Oakley: Great Tales (Gleiter/Thompson), 225

Annie Oakley: Little Sure Shot (Wilson), 222

Annie Oakley: The Shooting Star (Graves), 222

Annie Oakley: Woman at Arms (Cooper), 208–209

Annie Oakley and Buffalo Bill: Paper Dolls in Full Color (Tierney), 227

Annie Oakley and Buffalo Bill's Wild West (Sayers), 225

Annie Oakley and Other Rugged People (Holbrook), 207, 216

Annie Oakley and Tagg (TV series), 219–20

Annie Oakley and the World of Her Time (Alderman), 224

Annie Oakley Foundation, 228–29

Annie Oakley in Danger at Diablo (Schroeder), 220–21

Annie Oakley of the Wild West (Havighurst), 217

Annie Oakley Rifle Club, 67

"Annie Oakleys," as term for free passes, 16, 176, 233

"Annie Oakley's Vindication" (article, Butler), 81

Annie Oakley Trapshoot, 222

Anthony, Susan B., 132

"Any Oakley" (burlesque act), 77

Apparel: hunting, 134, 188–89; worn during shooting matches, 114–16, 139, 141–42; worn for bicycling, 54, 139. *See also* Costumes

Arthur, Chester A., 158

Atkins, John (commissioner, Indian Affairs), 147–48

"Attack on the Settler's Cabin, The" (Wild West show enactment), 49, 50

Attorneys, defense, tactics during Oakley libel suits, 79–80

Austin, Mary (author), 234

Auto accident, injuries suffered by Annie Oakley, 191–92

Autobiography, of Annie Oakley, 63, 197, 202, 209, 215, 231

Autry, Gene, 219–20

Babes in Toyland (musical), 170

Back-to-the-home movement, 214, 215, 217

Bailey, James A. (circus manager), 23; as manager of Cody show, 49, 58–59

Baker, Gladys (Johnny Baker's daughter), 121–22, 196

Baker, Johnny (shooter), 31, 35, 54, 91, 112, 183; daughters, 121–22, 196

Baker, Will F. (Greenville, Ohio, official), 56

"Ballad of Annie Oakley," 221–22

Bandle,. Al (shooter), 72

Barnum, P. T., 23, 77

Bates, Gilbert H. (performer), 34

Baughman (shooter), 19

Bayne, George H. (Nutley resident), 126

Beatty, Warren, 223

Beecher, Catharine (reformer), 132

Behavior standards: espoused by Annie Oakley, 130, 231–32; perpetuated by Hollywood of the 1920s, 209

Belasco, David, 59

Benefit shows, participation in, 126–27, 188, 190–91

Benevolence, 232; to relatives, 12, 122, 127, 129; seen as ladylike trait, 126–29, 208. *See also* Orphans, generosity to

Bets, side, as match shooting income, 64

Bicycling, 138–39; apparel for, 54, 139

Biographies, of Annie Oakley, 208–209, 214–15, 222, 224–25, 227

Birds, live: controversy over use as targets, 73–74; use in shooting matches, 45, 57, 66, 72, 88, 89, 113

Birth control methods, before 1900, 120–21

Birth date, discrepancy in Annie Oakley's, 3, 15, 231

Black, Irene Patterson (descendant), 14, 91, 122, 129, 198, 230

Blakeley, Bonnie Patterson (niece), 18, 194

Blakeley, Rush (brother-in-law), 19

Bloomer, Amelia, 234

Bloomer outfits, 115, 139, 141

Blue rock pigeons, as match targets, 66, 88, 89, 113

Boardinghouses, theatrical, 27, 124

Bob Woolf, the Border Ruffian; or, The Girl Deadshot (Wheeler), 172

Bodmer, Karl (artist), 157

Bogardus, Adam H. (shooter), 16, 90; association with Buffalo Bill, 27, 28, 30

Boone, Daniel, 24

Boston Gun Club, 44, 85

Boston Sunday Post (newspaper), 150

Brace, steel, Oakley's use after auto accident, 192, 194, 196

Breakfast, for Annie Oakley, 14, 33

British Blonds (vaudeville act), 22

Brooklyn Citizen (newspaper), 114

Brooklyn Union Standard (newspaper), 76

Brumbaugh, Daniel (stepfather), 8, 186

Brumbaugh, Emily (half sister), 8

Brumbaugh, Martin G. (governor, Pa.), 185

Buffalo Bill. *See* Cody, William F.

Buffalo Bill and the Indians; or, Sitting Bull's History Lesson (film), 224

Buffalo Bill Cody's Wild West exposition. *See* Wild West exposition

"Buffalo Bill" from Prairie to Palace (Burke), 165

Buffalo Bill Historical Center (Cody, Wyo.), 229

Buffalo Bill on Horseback (Remington), 164

Buffalo Bill/Pawnee Bill Wild West, 164

Buffalo Bill's Girl Pard; or, Dauntless Dell's Daring (dime novel), 173–74

Buffaloes, use in Wild West shows, 32–33

Buffalo Girls (McMurtry), 207

"Buffalo Hunt, The" (Wild West show reenactment), 49

Buffalo Ranch Real Wild West, 163

Bullets versus scatter shot, 53–54

Bunner, Henry Cuyler (editor), 127

Buntline, Ned (author), 155

Bureau of Catholic Indian Missions, 147

Burial plots, for Oakley/Butler, 197

Burke, John (publicity agent), 15, 31, 33, 37, 50; and Sitting Bull, 146–48, 149

Burlesque, 22; as strip tease, 175

Butler, Frank (husband), 14, 17–18, 83–84, 126; arena comeback, 61–62; with the Buffalo Bill show, 30–43, 46–47; death of, 203; as devoted protector, 55–56, 74–75, 118–19, 194–95; famed shooting match with Annie: fact and fiction, 15–17, 210–11, 215, 218; hunting escapades, 92–93; during newspaper libel trials, 77–79, 81, 83; personal reputation, 17, 55–56, 84; as poet, 22, 122, 129, 178; relations with UMC, 55, 60, 61, 64, 89–90, 118; retirement years, 176–201; with Sells Brothers Circus, 19, 20, 24–25; as wife's press agent, 62, 71, 93, 117, 118, 146

Butler, Will (Frank's brother), 196

Butler v. Evening Post Publishing Company, 81

Calamity Jane (Martha Jane Cannary), 172–73, 206–207, 219, 230, 234

Cambridge, Md., retirement to, 62, 177, 193

Cantor, Eddie, 175

Cargo ship (WW II), named for Annie Oakley, 213–14

Carnot, Sadi (president, France), 47

Carolina Hotel (Pinehurst, N.C.), wintering at, 181–82, 188

Carter, James S. (show patron), 41

Carver, W. F. (shooter), 16, 28–29, 37

Cary, Mary Ann Shadd (attorney), 137

Catlin, George, 157

Cattle Queen of Montana (film), 218

Character traits, of Annie Oakley, 13–14, 53–54, 231–35

Chariot racing, on Wild West shows, 164

Charity. *See* Benevolence

Charlottenburg Race Track (Berlin, Ger.), 43

Chicago American (newspaper), 76, 78

Chicago Examiner (newspaper), 76, 78

Children
—Annie Oakley: as childless, 120–21, 160; generosity to, 13, 61, 62, 85, 86, 128; love of, 121–23
—books for about Annie Oakley, 221, 222, 225–27

Christie, Julie, 223

Circuses, 23–24, 49, 179; as benefit shows,

126–27, 190; Oakley/Butler with, 19, 20, 24–25, 146; women as running away with, 138

Clark, Edward (English landowner), 91

Clay pigeon shooting, 15, 134, 159, 199

Cleveland, Grover, 148, 152

Cobblestone (magazine), 226–27

Cody, Louisa (Buffalo Bill's wife), 9, 59, 183

Cody, William F. "Buffalo Bill," 25–28, 85, 128, 179
 —death, 182–83
 —in early Edison movie, 171
 —fictionalized accounts of, 165, 173–74, 206, 224; in Oakley/Butler accounts, 211, 227
 —immortalization of the Western frontier, 28, 48–49, 150–51
 —relations with Annie Oakley, 36, 38, 42–43
 —relations with Sitting Bull, 146–47, 151–52
 —views on Native Americans, 153–54
 —*See also* Wild West exposition

Codymania, in England, 41

Cohan, George M., 190

Collier, Edmund (author), 221

Colonel Frederic T. Cummins's Wild West and Indian Congress, 62, 206

Comanche Bill's Wild West show, 45

"Come Across" (poem by Butler), 186

Comes a Horseman (film), 224

Comic books, portrayals of Annie Oakley, 216–17, 220

Comstock Law, on birth control methods, 120–21

Congress of American Cowgirls, 163

Congress of Rough Riders of the World, 50, 152, 163

Cook, Will Marion (composer), 59

Cooks, inability to keep, 14, 125–26

Cooper, Courtney Ryley (author), 208

Cooper, James Fenimore, 156, 171

Cordona, Adelaide (equestrienne), 24

Costumes: in *Annie Get Your Gun*, 215, 218; designing and sewing by Annie Oakley, 21, 123; paper cutouts of, 227; worn during Wild West performances, 32, 54, 57, 114, 162

Coventry, Aubrey (shooter), 27

Cowboy Hall of Fame (Okla.), 229–30

Cowboys, in Wild West shows, 45, 63

Cowgirls: as heroines of dime novels, 172–74; later portrayals of, 207; portrayal in the movies, 212, 217–18; in Wild West shows, 50, 115, 137–38, 158–64

Crawford, Joan, 209, 217–18

Crockett, Davy, 24

Current History (periodical), 208

Curtis, Jamie Lee, 225

Custer, Elizabeth, 150

Custer, George Armstrong, 145

"Custer's Last Fight" (Wild West show re-enactment), 49

Cyclone (hunting dog), 127

Daly, Phil, Jr. (shooter), 66, 72

Dana, Charles, 137

Darke County, Ohio, 3–5

Darke County Children's Home, 62

Darke County Historical Society, 228

Darke County Infirmary (poor farm), 6–7, 123

Dauntless Dell (dime novel series), 173–74

Dave (pet dog), 14, 177, 180, 188, 189, 192

Dave II (pet dog), 195

Davis, Gail (TV actress), 219–20

Day, Doris, 217, 219

Dayton Daily News (newspaper), 197

Deadwood Dick; or, The Sunbeam of the Sierras (melodrama), 46, 166

Deadwood Dick's Eagles; or, The Pards of Flood Bar (Wheeler), 172, 173

Deadwood stagecoach, 28–30, 38, 51, 155

Decker, May (Cody's sister), 183

De Leon, Millie (performer), 170

Dell Publishing Company, "Annie Oakley" comics, 220

Denver Post (newspaper), 183

Desperadoes, female, appearance in print and on stage, 171

Destry Rides Again (film), 212

Dietrich, Marlene, 212

Dime-museum impersonation of Annie Oakley, 74–75

Dime novels, Western themes of, 27, 155, 172–74

Divorce rates, before 1900, 18, 56

Dog(s): Dave as Oakley/Butler pet, 14, 177, 180, 188, 189, 192; Oakley/Butler relations with, 14, 16–17, 56, 127, 195

Domesticity, as Victorian trait, 123–26, 177; concept of woman as civilizing force, 129–31

Drug addiction, Annie Oakley's reaction to reports of, 76–83, 162

Duffy, Georgia (performer), 34

Eakin, Joe (hunter), 92

Edington, Nancy Ann, role in Annie Oakley's childhood, 6–9, 13

Edington, Samuel C., 6

Edison, Thomas Alva, 59, 171

Education. *See* Schooling

Edward (Prince of Wales), 39–41, 65–66

Elephants, ballyhoo about, 23, 24

Embroidery, by Annie Oakley, 124, 130
Endorsements, gun, 69–70
Ethnic diversity, of Wild West performers, 50
Evans, Dale, 217; comic book portrayal of as Annie Oakley, 216–17
Every Evening Printing Company, libel suit against, 81
Exercise, outdoor, promotion of, 139–41
Exhibition shooting, 61, 63, 84–90; expenses, 64, 71

Far East attractions, on Wild West shows, 163–64
Farrel, Della (performer), 34
Farrell, Jeannette (actress), 169
Fastidiousness, Annie Oakley's, 14, 123–24, 178
Father Knows Best (TV series), 217
Feminine Mystique, The (Friedan), 222
Feminism: Annie Oakley's role in, 131–39. See also Women
Field, E. L. (performer), 127
Field and Stream (periodical), 117
Fields, Dorothy and Herbert (musical book authors), 215–16
Films. See Motion pictures
Firearms, prohibition legislation, 198
Flat Iron (performer), 154
Flu (influenza), Spanish, 47
Flying A Productions, 219
Fonda, Jane, 224
Fontenella, Maude (performer), 77
Fort, Samuel, M.D., 177
Foster care, childhood exploitation of Annie Oakley, 7–8
France, tour, 46–47, 65
Fred Stone (horse), 189
Free-love advocacy, 132
Friedan, Betty, 222
"From Circus Fame to Lace and Silver Hair" (article series), 197
Frontier, American. See West, American
Frost, Jack (hotelier), 15, 16

Gaiety Girls, 171
Gardner, Frank (circus leaper), 24
Garst, Shannon (author), 222
Garst Museum (Greenville, Ohio), 228
Geer, Alpheus (performer), 127
Gender discrimination. See Women
George (pet dog), 16–17, 21, 33, 189
Germany, tour, 43, 50
Gibson Girl, the, 137
Gifts: given to relatives, 122, 127, 129, 232; to namesakes, 128; received for exhibition shootings, 85–86, 93
Gillette, William (actor), 59

Gipsy (horse), 52, 167
Girlie shows, 22, 175
Gladstone, William, 39
Glass balls as targets, 16, 24, 155; for Annie Oakley, 32, 52–54, 167, 171, 190
Graham, John (shooter), 19
Graham, William (shooter), 65, 72–73
Grand American Handicap, 67, 73, 89, 115
Grand American Trapshoot, 196
Grapes of Wrath, The (Steinbeck), 210
Graves, Charles P. (author), 222
Great Britain, tours of, 37–43, 156–57, 168
"Greatest of Modern Dianas" (article), 189
Great Train Robbery, The (film), 163
Great White Indian Chief, A (pamphlet), 165
Greenville, Ohio: "Annie Oakley" girl scout patrol, 221; Annie Oakley memorialization, 227–28; support for Annie Oakley, 81, 83; Wild West performance at, 56
Greenwood, Ralph (journalist), 54
Grote, Fred and Hazel (family friends), 202
Gunfire, during Wild West shows, 50, 136
Guns
  —Annie Oakley's, 21, 42, 53–54, 68–70, 72, 136; now in muse ums, 229–30; ornamentation of, 68–70; personal collection, 68, 93, 123, 179, 182
  —as frontier symbol, 51–52, 157
  —legislation on ownership, 198
Guns & Ammo (magazine), 226

Haines, Hulda (Annie's sister), 122, 129, 170, 196, 201, 202
Hairstyles
  —Annie Oakley's, 61, 114, 158, 176; in TV series, 220
  —Buffalo Bill Cody's, 59
Hale, Sarah Josepha (editor), 136, 140, 144
Hall, Elizabeth Butler (Frank's first wife), 196
Hammerstein, Oscar, II, 215
Harding, Warren, 181
Harris, Annie, 45
Hartford Courant (newspaper), 28
Hartigan (Tiffany craftsman), 69
Havighurst, Walter (author), 217
Hayden, Sterling, 218
Hearst, William Randolph, 76, 81, 82
Heart of Maryland (melodrama), 59
Heer, William (shooter), 89
Held, Anna (singer), 59, 66–67
Herbert, Victor, 167, 170
Hickok, Emma Lake (performer), 159
Hickok, Wild Bill, 206
Hinkle, Milt (performer), 183

Hoboken Observer (newspaper), 83
Holbrook, Stewart H. (author), 206–207, 216
Hollinger, Lela Border (hometown neighbor), 123, 135–36, 232
Hollowell, Jack (cartridge company rep.), 60
Hollywood, Calif. *See* Motion pictures
Home, for Oakley and Butler: residences as, 124–26, 177, 195; resort hotels during retirement, 180–82, 188; tents and hotel rooms as, 27, 33, 124, 126, 177
Hon. W. F. Cody and Dr. W. F. Carver's Rocky Mountain and Prairie Exhibition, 28–29
Horses, 52; Cody shooting from, 36, 116, 155; ridden astride, 161, 163, 189; use in stage productions, 167, 170; use of sidesaddle, 54, 116; Virginia Reel performed on, 159; women as show riders, 137–38
Hotels: as home on the road, 27, 124, 126, 177; stays at during retirement, 181–82, 188
Howe, Frank (shooter), 24
Howe, Julia Ward, 132
Hunt, Beatrice Blakeley (descendant), 232
Hunter, Annie Oakley as, 63, 90–93; apparel for, 134, 188–89; during childhood, 6, 11–12, 15
Hunter Arms Company, 69
Hurt, R. Douglas (historian), 225
Hutton, Betty, 218–20

I Love Lucy (TV series), 217
Imposters, contention with, 74–75
Income, 14–15, 118, 176; from matches and exhibitions, 63–64, 85; salary on the Wild West show, 63–64; saving propensity, 13, 19, 21, 63, 127, 231
Indians. *See* Native Americans
Indians (play by Kopit), 224
Influenza (flu), Spanish, 47
Ingraham, Prentiss (author), 27, 155, 173–74
Iron Tail (Sioux chief), 151
Italy, tour, 47, 93
Ithaca Gun Company, 179, 182

Jackson, Helen Hunt (author), 150
Jerry (moose), 37
Johnny Guitar (film), 217–18
Johnson, Miles (shooter), 66
Johnson, Mrs. (amateur shooter), 143
Johnston, Mrs. S. S. (shooter), 67
Jokes, off-color, dislike of, 130
Jolson, Al, 175

Kartzenberger, George and Charles (wild game purveyors), 11–12

Kasper, Shirl (biographer), 10, 61, 227
Keel, Howard, 218
Keen, Jule (show treasurer), 31
Keith, B. F. (theater owner), 167
Kell, Fred (shooter), 64
Kemp Sisters Wild West, 164
Kennedy, Joseph P., 190
Kid, Joe (performer), 42
King, Charles Bird (artist), 157
Kleinman, Abe (shooter), 27
Knowles, Ella L. (attorney), 137
Kopit, Arthur (playwright), 224

Ladyhood, Annie Oakley's concept of, 112–44
Lake, Agnes (circus owner), 159
Lancaster, Charles (gunmaker), 69, 88, 140
Lange, Dorothea (photographer), 210
Last of the Great Scouts (Wetmore), 165
Legends, surrounding Annie Oakley, 12, 39, 64–65, 205, 206–30, 233
Leslie, Amy (journalist), 58, 61, 78, 117, 135
Levine, Ellen, 226
Libel suits, against newspapers, 77–83, 122, 162
Life of Buffalo Bill, The (film), 162
"Life of Dave, As Told by Himself" (Butler), 192–93
Lillie, Gordon W. (Pawnee Bill), 45
Lillie, May Manning, 45, 160
Lind, Jenny (singer), 234
Lindsley, Mrs. M. F. (Wanda) (shooter), 66
Little Bess (horse), 168
Little Sure Shot, the Pony Express Rider (melodrama), 44
Little Tich (performer), 44
London, Eng., 1887 tour, 37–43, 156–57
Longfelder, Mrs. William, 203, 216
Longfelder, William (executor), 202
Luella Forepaugh-Fish's Wild West, 164
Lyons, Roy (butcher), 189

McCabe and Mrs. Miller (film), 223
McCambridge, Mercedes, 218
McCormick, Langdon (playwright), 82, 168
McKinley, William, 59, 142
McLaughlin, James (Indian agent), 147, 149
McMurtry, Larry (author), 207
Mme. Rentz's Female Minstrels, 22
Madison Square Garden (New York, N.Y.), 36, 49, 141
Market hunter: Annie as, 11–12, 15; Bogardus as, 27
Marriage: dates given for Oakley/Butler, 18–19; as ladyhood concept, 118–23

Marsh, Spencer S. (executor), 202
Marshall, Tom (shooter), 89
Martin, Mary, 216
Martinez, Maria (potter), 234
Maxwell, George W. (shooter), 89
May, Karl (German author), 156–57
Medals, Annie Oakley's, 86–87, 93, 114,
    218, 233
Meekin, Jane (shooter), 138
Memorabilia, Annie Oakley, currently in
    museums, 228–30
Merman, Ethel, 215, 220, 223
Mexican Americans, as Wild West per-
    formers, 50
Michael (Grand Duke of Russia), 40, 65
Middlesex Gun Club (N.J.), 134
Midwinter Handicap (Pinehurst, Fla.), 181
Miles, Nelson A. (general, U.S. Army), 151
Military, German, and logistics of Cody
    show, 50
Miller Brothers 101 Ranch Wild West, 163–
    64
Mirror sighting trick, 52, 68, 186
*Missie: An Historical Biography of Annie
    Oakley* (Swartwout), 214–15
Miss Rora (melodrama), Annie Oakley as
    star of, 166–68
Modesty, Annie Oakley's, 113–17
Montgomery, Dave (actor), 84, 177, 179
Morals, showpeople, 130–31
Morgan, Sampson (editor), 136
Moses, C. G. (nephew), 201
Moses, Hazel (grandniece), 195
Moses, Jacob (father), 4–5
Moses, John (brother), 5, 9, 13, 23, 127;
    during Annie Oakley's final days, 196,
    197
Moses, Lee (nephew), 201
Moses, Mary Jane (sister), 5
Moses (Mosey, Mozee), Phoebe Ann. *See*
    Oakley, Annie
Moses, Susan (mother), 4–5, 12, 48, 56, 135,
    180; visits with in later years, 34, 37, 123
Motion pictures: Annie Oakley's desire to
    act in, 179, 182, 191; early days of, 59,
    171–72, 174–75; portrayal of Annie
    Oakley, 209–12, 218–19; portrayal of
    Western women, 212, 217–18, 223–24
Motor Hippodrome and Wild West Show,
    190–91
Mulhall, Lucille (cowgirl), 137
Museums, with Annie Oakley collections,
    228–30
Myths. *See* Legends

National Woman Suffrage Association, 132
Native Americans: Annie Oakley's view of,
    57, 153; Cody's views of, 153–54; Sitting

Bull, 26, 145–52; in Wild West shows, 38,
    45, 50, 147–50, 152–54; women as per-
    formers, 160
Newspapers
—coverage of Annie Oakley, 39–42, 52–
    53, 57, 113, 157–58; clippings saved,
    63, 233; during retirement, 156, 185,
    189, 197; as source for Oakley
    biography, 227
—*Denver Post's* payment for Cody's
    burial, 183
—named in libel actions, 76–83
—reviews of Wild West shows, 28, 30,
    39–40, 150
"New women," 133–34, 208, 233
New York Clipper (performers' newspaper),
    25, 44, 146
New York Ladies Riding Club, 36
New York Morning Journal (newspaper), 156
New York Times (newspaper), 189
New York Tribune (newspaper), 185
Nickelodeons, 171–72
North, Frank (performer), 30
Notting Hill Gun Club (England), 65, 86–
    87
Nutley, N.J.: benefit circus at, 126–27;
    Oakley/Butler residence in, 125–26, 135,
    178; reviews of *Annie Get Your Gun*, 215,
    219
Nutley Historical Society (N.J.), 229
Nutley Rod and Gun Club, 125, 135

Oakley, Annie
—adoption of, by Sitting Bull, 146, 149;
    advice, tendency to give, 87–88, 129,
    231
—birth date controversy, 3, 15, 231
—character traits, 13–14, 53–54, 231–35
—choice of as a name, 20–21
—death, 201–204
—in early Edison movie, 171
—early life, 3–15
—as a feminist. *See* Women
—friendship with Sitting Bull, 26, 145–
    46, 148–52, 170; fictionalized ver-
    sions, 218
—illnesses and injuries, 35, 47, 60, 72,
    191–92
—ladyhood concepts, 113–26, 129–31
—marriage to Frank Butler, 18–20
—meeting with Frank Butler, 15–17; fic-
    tionalized versions, 210–11, 215, 218
—as part of UMC's shooting squad, 89–
    90, 118
—as personification of the West, 55, 57–
    58, 145–75, 199–200
—portrayals of: in comic books and ani-
    mated cartoons, 216–17, 220, 227; in

fiction, 207, 217, 221, 222, 225–27; in films, 210–12, 218–19; in musicals, 215–16, 223; in nonfiction works, 207–209, 214–15, 224–25; in television, 216, 219–20, 225
— professional career: beginning of, 20–26; with the Buffalo Bill show, 30–43, 46–48, 50–60; exhibition shooting, 84–90, 131; with Pawnee Bill shows, 45–46; with Sells Brothers Circus, 24–25, 146; in stage melodramas, 44, 46, 166–71; with Wild West exposition (see Wild West exposition); with Young Buffalo Show, 61–62, 90, 118, 144
— Quaker background, 4, 13, 21–22, 56, 112, 135
— relations with Cody, 36, 38, 42–43; reaction to death, 183–85
— relations with relatives, 122, 127, 180, 196, 201. See also individuals by name
— retirement years, 176–201, 233
— rivalry with Lillian Smith, 34–36, 38, 42, 43
— sewing proficiency, 7, 9–10, 21, 123
— show personality of, 32, 51–53, 57, 80, 130–31
— as victim of false press reports, 75–83
— See also Dog(s); Income; Shooting matches; Schooling; Shooting tricks
Oakleymania, 41
Oatley, Annie (singer), death of, 48
Old Avalanche (Wheeler), 172
Old West. See West, American
One Bear (Native American), 60
One-eye, two-eye shooting debate, 88
Orphans, generosity to, 13, 61, 62, 85, 86, 128
Outerbridge, Mary E. (sportswoman), 133
Outlaw, The (film), 212
Out of the Fold (play, McCormick), 82
Owl, stuffed, 125

Paine, Ira (shooter), 27
Panic of 1893, 59, 152, 167
Parkman, Francis (historian), 157
Parr, Lulu Belle (bronc rider), 137
Passes, free, "Annie Oakleys" as, 16, 176, 233
Pastor, Tony, 22–23, 44, 46
Patterson, Emily Brumbaugh (half-sister), 8, 91, 191, 196
Pawnee Bill (Gordon W. Lillie), 45
Pawnee Bill Historical Wild West Exhibition and Indian Encampment, 45, 163
Peep-show movie machines, 171–72

Peterson, Esther (Women's Bureau), 222
Philadelphia Press (newspaper), 76
Pickford, Mary, 205, 209
Pigeons. See Birds, live
Pinehurst, N.C.: annual Annie Oakley Trapshoot, 222; retirement activities in, 180–82, 185–86, 194
Pinehurst Outlook (weekly newspaper), 180–81, 188
Pistols, 68
Plays, western melodramas, 24, 34; starring Annie Oakley, 44, 46, 166, 168–70, 266–68
Pleasant, Mary Ellen (philanthropist), 234
"Pony Express, The" (Wild West show re-enactment), 49
Poor farm (Darke County Infirmary), 6–7, 123
Porter, Edwin S. (movie producer), 163
Posters, depicting cowgirls, 162–63
Powders I Have Used (pamphlet, Oakley), 178
Prairie Lillie and Nebraska Bill's Wild West, 164
Prairie Waif, The (melodrama), 34
Prince (horse), 52
Prince Ananias (light opera), 167
Principles of Domestic Science (Beecher & Stowe), 132
Programs, souvenir, 164–65
Publicity: of Annie Oakley by Frank Butler, 62, 71, 93, 117, 118, 176; depicting Wild West show girls, 162–63; stunts by Gordon Lillie, 45. See also Newspapers
Purses, as match shooting income, 64

Quackenbush, Robert (author), 226
Quail hunting, 91–92, 180
Quaker background, influence on Annie Oakley, 4, 13, 21–22, 56, 112, 135

Rabbit Ears Productions, animated cartoons of Annie Oakley, 227
Racial diversity, of Wild West performers, 50
Racial stereotypes, in melodramas, 167, 169
Railroads: 1901 train wreck, 60; use by travelling shows, 32, 51
Rain-in-the-Face (chief), 153
Ramona (Jackson), 150
Ready, Aim, Fire! The Real Adventures of Annie Oakley (Levine), 226
Reagan, Ronald, 218
Red Cross fund raisers, 126, 188, 193
Red Mill, The (musical), 179
Red Shirt (performer), 154

Religious beliefs, 135. *See also* Quaker background
Remington, Frederic, 164
Remington Arms Company, 55
"Rescue of the Deadwood Coach" (Wild West show reenactment), 49
Revolution (suffrage journal), 132
Revolver, use by women, 141, 143–44
Richmond, Frank (show announcer), 47
Rifle Queen, The: Annie Oakley (pamphlet), 224
Rifles, 21, 42, 53–54, 68
Robinson, James (bareback rider), 24
Rochester Times, The (newspaper), 76
Rodeos, women in, 58
Rodgers, Richard, 205, 215
Roebuck, hunting of, 91, 92
Rogers, Charles (Tiffany craftsman), 69
Rogers, Will, 190, 198–99, 203
Role model, Annie Oakley as, 54–55, 58, 208, 232
Rolling Stone (Stone), 203
Roosevelt, Alice, 137
Roosevelt, Theodore, 78, 137, 154
Rosie the Riveter (WW II symbol), 212–13
Rothschild (baroness, Austria), 86
Rough Rider (show magazine), 164
Russell, Jane, 212
Ruth, John (shooter), 24

Saddles, adapted for riding astride, 161, 189
St. Louis Star (newspaper), 82
Salary. *See* Income
Salsbury, Nate, 25–29, 85, 128; as Buffalo Bill's partner, 29, 31, 48–49, 58, 152; death of, 61
Salsbury Troubadors, 29
Sayers, Isabelle S. (author), 224, 225
Scalping scenes, in shows, 150
Scatter shot versus bullets, 53–54
Schooling
  —Annie Oakley's: lack of in youth, 3, 7, 9; lessons as adult, 20, 21, 34
  —financial aid to other women, 128–29
Schroeder, Doris (author), 220
Schultze Gunpowder Company, 70–71
Sears, Eleonora (socialite), 133
Seavers, Vernon (Wild West show owner), 61–62, 90
Seavers, Vernon, Jr. (child performer), 61
Secret Service (melodrama), 59
Sells Brothers Circus, 19, 20, 24–25, 146
Senegal, king of, 47
Servants: English attitude toward Frank Butler, 55–56; inability to keep, 14, 125–26, 178
Sewing proficiency, 7, 9–10, 21

Sexual abuse, possibility of during Annie Oakley's youth, 10–11, 121
Shaffer, Annie (bronc rider), 137
Shaw, Joseph (stepfather), 8, 12, 37
Sherman, William Tecumseh, 49, 148
Shooters: acts featured with circuses, 23–24; Annie as symbol to women, 54, 85–86; use of trick devices, 22, 41, 53, 74. *See also* Exhibition shooting; Shooting matches; individuals by name
Shooting and Fishing (periodical), 54, 55, 69
Shooting lessons, for women, 140–41, 181, 188, 198
Shooting matches
  —Annie Oakley's initial encounter with Frank Butler, 15–16, 65, 94, 119; as fictionalized, 210–11, 215, 218
  —following retirement from Cody show, 61, 63–74, 133–34, 199
Shooting tricks, performed by Annie Oakley, 52, 56, 68, 181, 186
Shotguns, 21, 42, 53–54, 68–70, 72, 229; 20-bore shotgun controversy, 89
Sidesaddle riding, 54, 116
Sideshows, as part of Wild West shows, 49, 58
Sitting Bull (Sioux chief), 26, 145–52; as fictionalized, 218
Sitting Bull Combination (tour group), 147
Smith, Charles (performer), 127
Smith, Lillian Frances (shooter), 37, 46, 200; during London tour, 40–41; rivalry with Annie Oakley, 34–36, 38, 42, 43, 66, 67
Social life, of the Butlers, 120; on the road, 27, 33, 124, 126, 177
Southwell, Charles M. (impresario), 45
Spain, tour, 47, 128
Spanish-American War, 59, 142, 186
Spectacles, use by Annie Oakley, 190
Sports, women's participation, 133, 136
Sportsman's Review (journal), 178
Sportsmen's Club (Cincinnati, Ohio), 15
Stagecoach, Deadwood, 28–30, 38, 51, 155
Stage performances, starring Annie Oakley, 44, 46, 166–71
Standing Bear, Luther (chief), 154
Stands, one-and-two-day, 58–59
Stanton, Elizabeth Cady, 132
Stanwyck, Barbara, 210–12, 217–18
State of Nebraska (steamship), 38
Statue, of Annie Oakley, 228
Status, women's. *See* Women
Stein, Joe (brother-in-law), 15
Stein, Lydia Moses (sister), 15, 188
Steinbeck, John, 210
Stephan, Joseph A. (clergyman), 147

Stirrat, Al (Nutley, N.J., friend), 127
Stirrat, Joseph (Nutley, N.J., friend), 126
Stone, Allene Crater (actress), 84
Stone, Dorothy, 204, 232
Stone, Eaton (performer), 125
Stone, Fred (performer), 84, 179–80, 190, 202
Stone, Lucy, 132
Story of Annie Oakley, The (Collier), 221
Story of the Wild West and Camp-Fire Chats (Cody), 43, 165
Stout, Ernest (reporter), 76, 83
Stowe, Harriet Beecher, 132
Suffrage, women's, 113, 131–32, 135, 137, 208
Suitors, would-be, 119–20
Sumpter, Mrs. J. J., Jr., 128
Swartwout, Anna Fern Campbell (niece), 14, 21, 119, 126, 130, 135; on aunt's fastidiousness, 123–24; biography of Annie Oakley, 214–15; as companion during libel trials, 80, 82, 122; on Oakley/Butler's retirement years, 177, 182, 200; view of aunt as Westerner, 160
Swing Shift Maisie (film), 213

Tagg (fictional TV brother), 219–20
Taking Aim (newsletter), 228
Tall Tales and Legends (TV series), 225
Taylor, Buck (performer), 31, 155
Teller, Henry M. (sec., U.S. Dept. of the Interior), 147–48
Tent, as home on the road, 33, 124, 126, 177
Thompson, Kathleen (author), 225
Thompson, Lydia (performer), 22
Thompson, Minnie (co-owner, Wild West show), 160
Tierney, Tom (author), 227
Tiffany and Company (jewelers), 69
Tiger Bill's Wild West, 163
Tilley, Vesta (impersonator), 167
Tippett, J. D. (performer), 161–62
Tompkins Real Wild West and Frontier Exhibition, 163
Travel, constant, as performers, 32, 51, 64, 130
Trick devices, shooting: Annie Oakley's refusal to use, 22, 53; Lillian Smith accused of, 41; use by English music-hall performers, 74
Troupe members, Annie Oakley's relations with, 56–57, 130
True West (magazine), 225
Twain, Mark, 150

Uncle Tom's Cabin (film), 175
Union Metallic Cartridge Co. (UMC), 71, 92–93; Butler as representative of, 55, 60, 61, 64, 71; sponsorship of matches, 83–84; sponsorship of shooting team, 89–90, 118

Values: espoused by Oakley/Butler, 51, 56, 235; ladyhood concepts, 112–44. *See also* Quaker background
Variety shows, 22–23
Vaudeville, 22–23, 44, 59
Victoria (princess, Great Brit.), 65
Victoria (queen, Great Brit.), 37, 41, 43, 228
Victorian lady, as Annie Oakley's aspiration, 54, 112, 116, 131
Violence, implied in use of weapons, 57
Virginian, The (Wister), 163
Virginia reel, on horseback, 159

Wah-Ki-Kaw (chieftain), 45
Walcholz, Bess Lindsey (grandniece), 127–29, 192, 196, 232
Walsh, J. J. (editor), 113
Ward, Lillian (performer), 160
Weather: effect on outdoor shows, 30, 34; as factor in matches, 72–73
Wells, Lucy (ranch owner), 159
"We're the Janes Who Make the Planes" (song), 213
Wessel, Christian C. (clergyman), 201–202
West, American: Annie Oakley's identification with, 55, 57–58, 145–75, 199–200; Hollywood versions, 212, 217–18, 223–24; immortalization of through show themes, 28, 36, 48–49, 150–51; as popular theme, 28, 38, 207; view of in the 1930s, 209–10; women of, 158–59
Western Girl, The (melodrama), 168–70
Wetmore, Helen Cody (author), 165
"What a Little Bird Said" (poem, Butler), 22
Wheeler, Edward L. (author), 172–73
White Boy Chief; or, The Terror of the North Platte (Wheeler), 173
Who's That Girl with the Gun? A Story of Annie Oakley (Quackenbush), 226
Widows, George (suitor), 119, 178
Wig, use by Annie Oakley, 61, 158
Wild West exposition (Buffalo Bill's), 15, 25–27, 171; early seasons, 29–37; 1887 London season, 37–43, 156–57; 1889 European tour, 46–47; 1893 season, 50–51; 1901 season, 59–60; route schedules of, 155–56. *See also* Cody, William F.; Native Americans
Wild West shows, 179; cowgirl performers, 50, 115, 137–38. *See also* individual shows
Wilhelm (crown prince/kaiser, Ger.), 43, 186, 188, 229

Will and testament, last, of Oakley/Butler,
    196
Wilson, Ellen (author), 222
Wilson, Woodrow, 186
Winchester Repeater (periodical), 93
Winchester Repeating Arms Company, 70
Winnemucca, Sarah (Paiute), 150, 234
Winona. *See* Smith, Lillian
Wister, Owen (author), 163
"Without Shooting Herself, Taught by
    Annie Oakley" (article series), 141
Wizard of Oz, The (musical), 84
"Wolves," foster parents viewed as, 7–8
Woman's Journal (suffragist periodical),
    132
Women
    —Annie Oakley: encouragement of
        shooters, 66–67, 85–86, 131, 139–42,
        185, 197; encouragement of wage
        earners, 135–36, 213; as example to,
        54–55, 58, 232; influence of self-re-
        liant models on, 13, 136; shooting
        lessons by, 140–41, 181, 188, 198;
        wartime offers of sharpshooters,
        142, 187; Wild West show appeal
        due to, 50, 136

—athletic ability, 133, 136, 209
—attendance at exhibitions and
    matches, 67–68, 86
—attendance at Wild West shows, 50, 158
—changing roles of: during World War
    II, 212–13; in the 1930s, 209–11; in
    the 1950s, 217–18; in the 1960s, 222–
    23; in the 1970s, 223–24
—as owners of Wild West shows, 160,
    164
—suffrage movements, 132–33, 137, 208
—as Westerners, 158–59; in dime novels,
    172–74; film portrayal, 212, 217–18
—*See also* Cowgirls
Woodhull, Victoria (activist), 132
World's Fair (1893, Chicago), 56, 152, 229
World War I, Oakley/Butler contributions,
    186–87
World War II, role of women, 212–13

Yellow Robe, Chauncy (performer), 154
Young Buffalo Show (Vernon Seavers's),
    165; Oakley/Butler's arena comeback
    with, 61–62, 90, 118, 144, 176

Ziegfeld, Florenz, 59, 66